Law and Bioethics

W0234676

George P. Smith, II is a leading figure in the world of medical law and ethics. During his long career he has addressed some of the most important issues in bioethics and has contributed much original thought to debates in the field. This book celebrates his contribution to scholarship in this area and brings together his key writings in bioethics. The chapters include previously published material which has been substantially updated to reflect more recent developments. The book covers topics such as: human rights and medical law; the allocation of resources and distributive justice; ethical relativism; science and religion; and public health emergencies. Taken as a whole, this book examines the extent to which law, medicine, economics, and bioethics interact as synergistic vectors of force in shaping and setting both personal and public responses to the complexities of biotechnology, or what has been referred to as, "The New Biology." All too often, past considerations of this topic have neglected to recognize the synergistic influences of law as a catalyst for codifying contemporary values into normative standards. Professor Smith reaches the conclusion that if traditional bioethical principles are to be seen as pertinent constructs for policy making, they must be broadened through the law of public health and human rights. *Law and Bioethics: Intersections along the Mortal Coil* casts law as the pivotal force in bringing stability to the ongoing debates on how to maintain bioethical relevance in decision-making and in doing so, it offers an excellent overview of the current bioethical issues in medical law considered in light of recent and ongoing technological developments in medicine.

This book will be of particular interest to academics and students of Law, Political Science, Philosophy, Economics and Human Rights.

George P. Smith, II has been seen as a pioneer in the field of Bioethics since 1967 and for the past 36 years has taught law at The Catholic University of America School of Law and lectured internationally. Professor Smith has been acknowledged by U.S. Judge Richard A. Posner as "one of the world's leading experts on the legal and ethical issues raised by modern medicine."

Law and Bioethics

Intersections along the Mortal Coil

George P. Smith, II

Routledge
Taylor & Francis Group

LONDON AND NEW YORK

First published 2012
by Routledge
2 Park Square, Milton Park, Abingdon, Oxon OX14 4RN

Simultaneously published in the USA and Canada
by Routledge
711 Third Avenue, New York, NY 10017

Routledge is an imprint of the Taylor & Francis Group, an informa business
First issued in paperback 2013

© 2012 George P. Smith, II

The right of George P. Smith, II to be identified as the author of this work has
been asserted by him in accordance with sections 77 and 78 of the Copyright,
Designs and Patents Act 1988.

All rights reserved. No part of this book may be reprinted or reproduced or utilised
in any form or by any electronic, mechanical, or other means, now known or
hereafter invented, including photocopying and recording, or in any information
storage or retrieval system, without permission in writing from the publishers.

Trademark notice: Product or corporate names may be trademarks or registered
trademarks, and are used only for identification and explanation without intent to
infringe.

British Library Cataloguing in Publication Data
A catalogue record for this book is available from the British Library

Library of Congress Cataloging in Publication Data
Smith, George Patrick, 1939-
Law and bioethics : intersections along the mortal coil / George P. Smith, II.
p. cm.
ISBN 978-0-415-78335-4 (hardback) -- ISBN 978-0-203-12251-8 (e-book)
1. Medical care--Law and legislation--United States. 2. Bioethics.
I. Title.
KF3821.S638 2012
344.7304′1--dc23
2011041277

ISBN 978-0-415-78335-4 (hbk)
ISBN 978-0-415-74143-9 (pbk)
ISBN 978-0-203-12251-8 (ebk)

Typeset in Garamond
by Taylor & Francis Books

"For in that sleep of death what dream may,
When we have shuffled off this mortal coil,
Must give us pause: there's the respect
That makes calamity of so long life. ... "

William Shakespeare
Hamlet, Prince of Denmark
Act III, Scene 1

To
George J. Annas, Belinda J. Bennett, Rosalind Croucher,
Tal S. Grinblat, Jonathan Herring, Allan E. and Linda
Kaulbach, Douglas W. and Carol Kmiec, Roger S.
Magnusson, Nell Jessup Newton, Colleen K. Pauwels,
Lauren K. Robel, Clint A. Rosso, Ivan A. Shearer,
Loane Skene and Cameron Stewart whose enduring
friendship, continuing support and faith in me has
enriched my journey beyond all measure

Contents

Other related books by the author

Distributive Justice and the New Medicine (2008).
The Christian Religion and Biotechnology: A Search for Principled Decisionmaking (2005).
Human Rights and Biomedicine (2000).
Family Values and the New Society: Dilemmas of the 21st Century (1998).
Legal and Healthcare Ethics for the Elderly (1996).
Bioethics and the Law: Medical, Socio-legal and Philosophical Directions for a Brave New World (1993).
The New Biology: Law, Ethics and Biotechnology (1989).
Final Choices: Autonomy in Health Care Decisions (1989).
Medical-Legal Aspects of Cryonics: Prospects for Immortality (1983).
Ethical, Legal and Social Challenges to a Brave New World (1982).
Genetics, Ethics and the Law (1981).

Preface

For a career in legal education which began upon my graduation from the Indiana University School of Law-Bloomington in 1964, and has extended over some 47 years, the challenge and the opportunity to teach in the fields of Law, Science, and Medicine (today, often termed Bioethics) and Health Law and—as a scholar—to study, to research, and write in these fields has been an exciting adventure. To be enabled to contribute original ideas—in the marketplace of ideas—to the ongoing dialogue, and often debate, on the points of intersection and interaction in establishing socio-legal and medical directions for maintaining normative conduct in contemporary society—has been both a challenge and a welcomed professional opportunity. Exploring, and then beginning to chart points of equilibrium which seek to establish policy and suggest law-making within the vectors of force which comprise the frontiers of The New Biology has—over the years, at times—been as much a daunting undertaking as an exciting adventure. But, working in the teaching laboratory—and experiencing the pleasure which has been derived from a privileged association with dynamic young students, has made all the difference for me as both a teacher and as a scholar. There is, simply, no substitute for the realism of the classroom.

Over the span of my 36-year career here at The Catholic University of America School of Law, four Deans have been especially supportive of my scholarship and I must recognize: Dean John L. Garvey, Dean Steven P. Frankino, Dean Douglas W. Kmiec, and Dean Veryl V. Miles. Without their stalwart support and encouragement, I would have never been able to meet my scholarly agenda over the years.

My trusted and valued administrative assistant of some 15 years, A. Laurie Fraser, has shown exceptional forbearance, depth of understanding, high level of professionalism and a consistent measure of good cheer as this manuscript—and others over the years—has been prepared. To Laurie, I acknowledge my life-time debt of appreciation.

During my affiliation in June, 2010, with the University of Glasgow's Institute for Law and Ethics in Medicine at The School of Law, I completed the final manuscript for this book. I owe a large debt of gratitude to Professor Sheila A. M. McLean, the Director of the Institute, her colleague, Sarah

Elliston, and associate Grace McGuire, for not only their high level of professional support, but for their gracious Gaelic hospitality during my stay.

The provenance of this book derives from—in substantially revised and re-ordered form—portions of several law reviews as well as papers and lectures that I have presented. Excerpts from the following sources appear with the kind permission of the respective copyright holders. Chapter 2 is drawn in part from *Judicial Decisionmaking in the Age of Biotechnology*, 13 NOTRE DAME JOURNAL OF LAW, ETHICS AND PUBLIC POLICY 93–120 (1999) and *Biomedicine and Biomedical Ethics: De Lege Lata, De Lege Ferenda*, 9 JOURNAL OF CONTEMPORARY HEALTH LAW AND POLICY 233–58 (1993). Chapter 3 utilizes *Law, Medicine, and Religion: Towards a Dialogue and a Partnership in Biomedical Technology and Decisionmaking*, 21 JOURNAL OF CONTEMPORARY HEALTH LAW AND POLICY 169–203 (2005), a paper entitled, "God, Caesar, and Darwin: Re-defining the Boundaries of The Town Square through Law, Religion and Biotechnology," presented at McGill University, Canada, in September 2007 and the Justice Michael D. Kirby Lecture entitled, "Of Panjandrums, Pooh-Bahs, Parvenus, and Prophets: Law, Religion, and Medical Science," Macquarie University, Sydney, Australia, in July 2005. Chapter 4 relies on *Human Rights and Bioethics: Formulating a Universal Right to Health, Health Care, or Health Protection?* 38 VANDERBILT JOURNAL OF TRANSNATIONAL LAW 1295–1321 (2005). Chapter 5 draws from *Social Justice and Health Care Management: An Elusive Quest*, 9 HOUSTON JOURNAL OF HEALTH LAW AND POLICY 1–38 (2009) and *Setting Limits: Medical Technology and The Law*, 23 SYDNEY LAW REVIEW 283–96 (2001). Chapter 6 relies upon *Re-shaping the Common Good in Times of Public Health Emergencies: Validating Medical Triage*, 17 ANNALS OF HEALTH LAW 1–34 (2009). Chapter 7 derives from *The Vagaries of Informed Consent*, 1 INDIANA HEALTH LAW REVIEW 111–29 (2003) and a paper entitled, "Pain Management, Palliative Care and Self-Determination," presented at the Thirtieth Congress of the International Academy of Law and Mental Health, in Padova, Italy, June 2007. Chapter 8 is taken in part from *Terminal Sedation as Palliative Care: Revalidating a Right to a Good Death*, 7 CAMBRIDGE QUARTERLY OF HEALTH ETHICS 382–87 (1998) © Cambridge University Press, *Utility and The Principle of Medical Futility: Safeguarding Autonomy and The Prohibition against Cruel and Unusual Punishment*, 12 JOURNAL OF CONTEMPORARY HEALTH LAW AND POLICY 1 (1996) as well as a University Lecture given at St. Andrews University, Scotland, entitled, "The Quality of Mercy and Common Dignity: Safeguarding The Last Right," in March 2007.

I have included an Appendix to this book which presents a complete bibliography of my scholarship in the fields of study which shape the forces of what is known as Bioethics.

1 Introduction and overview

Sir Isaac Newton's Third Law of Physics applies as much to scientific advancement as it does to other aspects of life itself. Accordingly, for each and every action there is an equal and opposite re-action.[1] For every new and daring biotechnological advancement, a new medico-legal challenge is presented; a challenge rooted in complex social, religious, moral, and ethical vectors of force.

The reality of Newton's law is seen dramatically within the science of Synthetic Biology.[2] No doubt, the very *zeitgeist* animating this, the New Age of Biotechnology, is to be found among those members of the scientific community who are exploring ways to design and then develop new life forms in much the same way as either a bridge or a car is assembled.[3] Predicated on the fact that organisms can, largely, be broken down into a "set of parts," and spurred on by the previous and ongoing success of making DNA, synthetic biologists are pursuing efforts to discover a "basic" cell into which everything else can be "slotted."[4] One particularly tantalizing success in this field of research was reported on May 20, 2010; for, on this date, a synthetic cell was created which was controlled entirely by a bacterial genome.[5] Dr. J. Craig Venter, the lead scientist working on this discovery, described the converted cell as "the first self-replicating species we've had on the planet whose parent is a computer."[6]

Presently, genetic manipulation normally involves a process, termed cloning, whereby a gene from one cell is harvested and put into a transfer vehicle—often a sub-cellular structure or plasmid—which is then inserted into a different cell which activates the gene. This process then leads to the production of a useful protein for scientific or commercial purposes.[7] The new synthetic process of transplanting a genome into bacterium holds great promise for a future where microbes could be manufactured with novel functions, for example, as an absorbent for pollutants or as a means for biofuel production.[8] There is a fear among some ethicists that this new process could lead to the production of biological weapons as well as dangerous life forms.[9] The consensus, however, is that this new scientific advancement creates no new hazards beyond those present ones encountered when tweaking genes; neither is this process seen as a new threat to biosecurity.[10]

Bioethical intersections

Historically, bioethics can be seen as having no defined essence which sets it apart as a distinct study or discipline. Rather, its individuation derives from a *de facto* set of issues interrelated by what might be termed "family resemblance." While a common thread joining all of the issues is exceedingly difficult to find, the central core comprising the list of these issues—without question—is a felt concern over the technology of control of one's body, mind, and quality of life.

In a very real sense, bioethics encompasses a whole political movement which seeks to harness political forces to deal with a plethora of ethical problems relating to health care delivery, both at the *micro* and the *macro* level of economic distribution.[11] Consequently, many of the concerns of bioethics are concerns of public policy—or with legislation, and policy guidelines at state, local and federal levels—that need to be enacted and enforced with respect to all of the issues comprising the *de facto* set. It has been suggested that bioethical concerns are but those prohibitions all rational people urge everyone to follow in an effort to avoid evils on which common agreement exists.

Outside the individual context of determining how one treats another, at the broader societal level of moral acceptability, a democratic consensus must be reached acknowledging that a certain good must be promoted even though its promotion causes some degree or other of harm. It is within this setting where much of what is recognized as "bioethics" is focused. While individual morality operates primarily within a system of restraints, policies affecting society as a whole operate on a level where promotion of good is a moral option. The pivotal question thus becomes, what goods ought to be restrained (*e.g.*, scientific research)? Of necessity, priorities, values, and goods must be weighed, balanced, and compared. Whenever the benefits and the risks of a particular course of action are weighed, it is well to remember that those very elements in the balancing test are based upon judgments about values, with the ultimate goal being the formulation and validation of a final action which—consistent with art utilitarianism—minimizes human suffering and maximizes the social good.[12] If the pace of scientific advancement is not measured and approached rationally, a principle of precaution may well become a principle of paralysis.[13]

Expanding the outreach

As a discipline or field of research and study, bioethics emerged in the United States in the 1960s and 1970s as an effort to assess, critically, "the significance of medicine in terms of its conceptual and value assumptions"[14] and as a response to medical paternalism.[15] Today, bioethics is commonly understood as focusing on ethical and legal controversies arising from the delivery of healthcare, the practice of medicine, and biomedical research.[16]

What originally were acknowledged as the three fundamental principles undergirding the field of bioethics—Autonomy, Beneficence, and Justice[17]—have, for some, been expanded to include one or more of the following:

non-malfeasance, which holds to the premise that one held to a duty of care which forbids the infliction of evil, harm, or risk of harm on others; confidentiality, which imposes a standard of non-disclosure of information received by one person to another with the promise—implicit or explicit—of its secrecy; distributive justice (refined from the earlier designation as justice) to include a mandate that benefits and burdens of any medical resource allocation should not only be distributed equitably but that scarce resources be distributed fairly and—furthermore—no one person or group receive a disproportionate share of either benefits or burdens; and truth telling, a principle which demands honesty and integrity in the disclosure of all information about an individual to that individual, himself.[18]

Moving from principlism to utilitarian and Kantian theories and Natural Law teachings, today, new interactions or approaches to understanding and applying bioethical theory have been posited and include: narrative bioethics; virtue bioethics; ethics of caring; religious bioethics; casuistry; pragmatism; law and economic theory; critical race theory and feminist bioethics.[19] There is an obvious overlap among all of these approaches. Indeed, most bioethical decision-making is based either on the foundational principles of this discipline or a combination of these approaches.[20]

As bioethical principles and analytical approaches to understanding and applying bioethics to decision-making and policy have expanded over the years, so—too—has the scope of it as a discipline. One such ranking of contemporary bioethics includes within it the study of: end of life care (which includes aging and dementia); genetics; research ethics; global international health issues; cloning and stem cells; organ transplants; ethics of public health; feminism (*i.e.*, commodification of female reproduction); technology; disability; and ecogenetics.[21] In another such ranking, seven other activities were listed as inclusive of contemporary bioethics: patient centered care; evidence-based medicine and pay for performance; community dialogue; cross-cultural concerns; race and health disparities; and new technologies.[22] Interestingly, religion and sociobiology are both absent from these listings.[23]

In not only normative theory but in professional regulation, bioethics and medical ethics are being challenged today by a new extended emphasis and a growing popular transnational approach to international human rights.[24] Norms which heretofore were considered as within the sole province of bioethics and medical ethics, have been re-processed and codified in not only the 2005 Universal Declaration on Bioethics and Human Rights[25]—known popularly as the Universal Bioethics Declaration—but through the 2003 adoption of the International Declaration on Human Genetic Data[26] and, in 1998, the Universal Declaration on the Human Genome and Human Rights.[27] Indeed, international human rights law may be seen as a calibrating or synergistic force in health law and policy.[28] As well, the law of human rights is having a profound effect in re-interpreting and reconciling traditional bioethical principles—thereby giving them a new outreach, application, and relevance through its incorporation into human rights theory and practice.[29]

Without this reconciliation, bioethics—as a rather sterile philosophical and theoretical discourse—is at risk of becoming an irrelevant normative discourse.[30] The great and ongoing public health debates are enriched by bioethical theory—especially notions of social responsibility and social justice. But, make no mistake: human rights is the foundation upon which both public health and bioethics have contemporary credibility.[31]

Deliberative democracy

Central to the bioethical issues presented at the six points of intersection in this book must be a realization that as ethical, socio-legal, economic, and medical conflicts persist in modern society, unabated controversies will continue to proliferate. Foundational issues such as the role of religion in tempering or actually impeding the pace of scientific advancement and its potential for extending the limits of artificial reproduction and genetic advancement,[32] claims of a human right to health, the equitable allocation of health care resources nationally, globally, and during times of public health emergencies, together with the extent to which rights of autonomy and self-determination during the end-of-life cycle, all guarantee a vigorous bioethical discourse over succeeding years.[33] Central to the success or the failure of this dialogue is the question of what the proper foundation upon which informed, bioethical debates can be undertaken. Deliberative democracy has come into vogue, recently, and has been advanced as the foundation upon which this dialogue can commence.[34]

With the central purpose of deliberative democracy being to promote the legitimacy of collective decisions,[35] this concept seeks to expand both the number and use of deliberative forums where citizens may enter into discourse over the contentious issues of the new Age of Biotechnology. Through moral disagreement comes—ideally—a "manifest mutual respect" for opposing views, or in other words, mutually respectful decision-making.[36]

Deliberative democracy, viewed as but a complement to the legislative process, is an attractive idea. The principal drawback to its effective implementation is that the average, ordinary, reasonable American is not informed—sufficiently—to enter into meaningful discourse on the ramifications of the new Age of Biotechnology. Logic is all too often put on "hold" while emotional feelings control and often resolve the debate.[37] Similarly, hard economic realities are ignored or postponed—repeatedly—until the time their ultimate and forced implementation causes more discord and havoc than would have occurred if they had been considered as a first-order priority.[38]

Stated otherwise, perhaps the greatest single reason why—even with an ethic of openness within a deliberative democracy—little "intelligent conversation," let alone constructive debate can occur at the community level, is the inability of the public to understand the language of the scientists; or in other words, the language of statistics.[39] To be sure, the foundations of humanity—"our sentiments, loves, attributes, more and character, as well as the familial, socially religious and political institutions that nourish and are nourished by them"[40]—are not anchored in scientific rationality. Yet, conduct and decision-making must be, in a participatory democracy, informed and guided by a level of understanding which allows for reasonable courses of action.[41] Given an unsophisticated citizenry as is seen today concerning issues of medical science, biotechnology, and finely nuanced bioethical issues, and subsequent paralytic legislative's miasmas which often occur, it remains for the judiciary to recognize its ultimate responsibility to act to safeguard and promote the common utilitarian good.[42]

Law's purpose

There is general agreement that the principal purpose of law is not to only define and protect individual rights and ensure public order, but to resolve disputes and redistribute wealth and thereby optimize economic efficiency.[43] Additionally, laws should dispense justice, provide a structure for preventing or compensating injury, and be "a lever for moving human behavior."[44] Accordingly, all legal systems may be viewed correctly as existing "to effect some change in human behavior."[45] By seeking to alter socio-cultural influences, law can truly shape and re-shape behavior.[46]

As seen, law is the language of social regulation.[47] It thus obeys systemic imperatives often irrelevant and in conflict with efforts to achieve a genuine understanding and wise resolution of moral issues.[48] Although it would be incorrect to hold that every moral obligation "involves a legal duty," it would, however, be proper to recognize that "every legal duty is founded on a moral obligation."[49] It remains for the state—through the promulgation of laws—to determine which particular review or ideal of morality should guide.[50] Ideally, and of necessity, that moral standard which best recognizes autonomy and thereby "maximizes freedom" without harming others, must be embraced.[51] As a language, law competes with other languages of religion and morality, of love and friendship, of custom and compromise, of pragmatism and social accommodation. Interestingly, these other languages are spoken more comfortably, fluently, and with more conviction in daily life than the language of law.[52]

Chapter 2 establishes the predicate for analysis of various bioethical challenges presented to contemporary social ordering. As observed, these galvanic challenges conduce—essentially—to one controlling concern: specifically, how to both harness and then govern the uses of biomedical technology both nationally and globally and, secondly, how to allocate its benefits in order to make individual lives better.[53] The extent to which bioethical theory can be a dominant force in meeting this challenge has yet to be established.[54]

Science and religion

The two great systems of human thought are science and religion. The predominant influence over the conduct of most individuals may be said to be religion. When science intrudes into daily life it does not make its presence felt intellectually, but rather through technology.[55] Although there is a religious perspective present in the lives of most, religion's stylized, institutionalized role has declined sharply over the years. While traditional Christian doctrines are being displaced from personal consciousness, they are not replaced—however—by rational scientific thought; for science is just as elusive and inaccessible to the public as organized religions.[56]

Because contemporary existence has been altered dramatically by scientific achievement through technological applications, lives are changed radically—with the corresponding conclusion reached that traditional religions often appear to be lacking in modern relevance in resolving both personal and social problems.[57] The deep questions of existence are approached differently by science and religion. While science is based on careful observation and experimentation which in turn allows for theories to be constructed connecting different experience, religion asserts unalterable truths, which cannot be modified to accommodate changing ideas. Accordingly, the true believer stands by his faith regardless of whatever evidence may be deduced against its efficacy.[58] Yet, for the scientist, if scientific irregularities prove a theory to be fallacious, it will be abandoned and a new approach adopted.[59]

The reality of social behavior is that science and technology are the great engines of modern times; and these engines drive and force constant change. Far from becoming simpler, the very real promise of science and technology is that they will become more difficult and, indeed, unyielding. Finding definitive solutions to both the tendentious problems and the opportunities they present is especially difficult since no "solution" can ever be taken as final—this, because "with changing technology come changing dimensions of the problems."[60] Ultimately, the restraint of medical science should be limited only to those actions seen as unreasonable or, in other words, when the long- and short-term costs of its effect outweigh the enduring benefits to the common good that would derive from its study and implementation.

Religion and its denominational theologies and specific teachings structure normative standards for ethical conduct but also serve as constructs for determining social policies and facilitating decision-making.[61] Some have argued that these norms and constructs not only interpret, but reconcile and stabilize law as well as medical science.[62] Moral and ethical theories and principles have, indisputably, derived from religion. It is law—not religion—however, which must assume the primary role of both directing and stabilizing all courses of human affairs.[63] Yet, as observed, law is shaped by social experience[64] and religion is certainly a major part of that historical and contemporary experience in America.

Spirituality, as a personal phenomenon, is invariably—to one degree or other—rooted in a religious experience involving a quest for meaning and purpose in life. As spiritual health encompasses values and attributes of love, charity, meditation, self-actualization, and hope, so also is hope integral to the whole healing process; for, once hope is abandoned, the very will to both become and remain healthy is eroded.[65]

The Darwinian theory of evolution—its acceptance or rejection—"creation science," its teaching and restrictive use in the curricula of public schools, forms of faith recognition by municipalities and states, together with limitations on scientific investigatory freedoms (*e.g.,* IVF experimentation, embryonic abortions), all arise from concerns raised by various religions that the sacredness of personhood is not only threatened but compromised by these various levels of conduct. Concerns of this nature are grounded, obviously, in moral ethics which are derived from spiritual values and tenets of religious faiths. Chapter 3 studies broadly the *yin-yang*—positive and negative—relationships between science and religion and concludes that there is a synergistic energy which allows both to work, independently, in order to advance the common good, spiritually, and through medical science.[66]

In modern society, no definitive points of separation are to be found among health law, bioethics, and human rights in public health practice.[67] The language of medical ethics, as seen, is one grounded in principles of self-determination and beneficence which, in turn, facilitates—ideally—an ongoing dialogue which seeks to determine what, for any autonomous patient exercising informed consent regarding medical treatment, is in his or her best interests.[68]

This language and its use is severely restricted in its application in countries where there is a scarcity of not only physicians but of medical resources.[69] As will be seen within the global context, this restriction applies actually to all members of the transnational community; for, there are no boundaries of containment for these two scarce resources. While public health deals with the prevention of disease within populations, bioethics focuses on the individual clinical applications of autonomy, beneficence, non-malfeasance, and social or distributive justice within specific cases or *micro* groupings.

The inter-relationships between Bioethics and Human Rights—nationally and internationally—are examined in Chapter 4. More specifically, the extent to which Bioethics serves as a framework, if perhaps not a foundation, for advancing a claim that there is a human right to health care[70] is studied using the recent work by UNESCO with the passage by the United Nations of the Universal Declaration on Bioethics and Human Rights of 2005.[71] This chapter, in turn, serves as a bridge to Chapter 5 where the systemic failures of the U.S. health care delivery system for allocating scarce medical resources are investigated and proposals offered for improving the system.

Distributive justice

In tackling the issue of distributive and social justice in health care reform, caution must be taken to separate the term "medical and health care."[72] Conflation of the two often leads to confusion in that while health care is within the "purview of a responsible polity," it is a much broader conception which must remain second in priority of concern and action to medical care.[73] Accordingly, first-order efforts must be directed toward assuring treatment for those in present need of it rather than shaping a national public policy designed to cultivate an overall improved health status which has a goal of preventing future illness.[74] "Relief of suffering precedes cultivation of health, important as it surely is."[75]

The goal of medical care, then, must be to enhance the well-being of the patient.[76] The most vexing issue in achieving this goal is to both develop and to administer an equitable system of access to care which balances patient autonomy with quality of life—this, particularly, when age and disease are more progressively toward incapacitating the individual.[77] Invariably, the ethics of medical care and of health care are tied, inextricably, to applying *micro* economic policy at the point of patient entry into the health care delivery system and *macro* economics in determining the rational parameters of health care policy.[78] Inasmuch as health care resources are finite, they must be rationed[79]—with the consequence being that there can be no recognized or absolute duty to provide full medical treatment for all people at all times.

The scarcity of, and competition among, diseases for financial support was recently brought into dramatic focus when Dr. Francis Collins, Director of the National Institutes of Health (NIH), told the U.S. Senate in hearings on appropriations for medical research that restrictive federal funding was threatening continued study of the etiologies and effects of Alzheimer's disease—this, because of the competition with research allocations for continuing studies of heart disease, cancer, and diabetes.[80] Much of the Nation's leading biomedical research is paid for by the NIH. With a budget of nearly $31 billion, and calls by the House of Representatives to curtail overall governmental spending, the NIH now faces critical choices regarding the allocation of monies for funding of medical research.[81]

Presently, some 5.4 million Americans are victims of Alzheimer's disease.[82] Their care in nursing homes alone is said to be costing more than $170 billion a year—much of which is paid by Medicare and Medicaid.[83] It is projected that by 2050, some 13 million Americans will be diagnosed with this disease and cost the economy $1 trillion a year.[84]

The extent to which medical resource allocations are provided is under ongoing review and assessment. Indeed, the standards for "codifying" the elements of distributive justice is an issue of great national concern and the focus of Chapter 5.[85] Finding an acceptable unit or metric for measurement of disease burden is exceedingly problematic and lacking in uniformity. One construct growing in popularity for making the determination is found in the Quality-Adjusted Life Year calculation—a measurement by which the quality of life lived is computed, statistically in order to determine whether there is a sustainable value for a particular medical intervention.[86] Cost-effectiveness, thus, is of central importance in this measurement. Another tool for evaluating the use of a medical resource is found in a growing reliance on the practice of evidence-based medicine which is a systematic process of reviewing, appraising, and using clinical research findings to aid in the delivery of optimum clinical patient care.[87]

Public health emergencies trigger multiple issues of health care resource allocation, the extent to which autonomy and the primacy of personhood can be honored or, alternatively, must be compromised in the name of the common good or public welfare, the character of beneficence as well as the normative social standards which direct its use under emergency situations.[88] Co-ordinating the primary state responses to events of this nature—within a federal public health emergency system—is fraught with sensitive political, legal, ethical, and health delivery issues.[89] Chapter 6 continues to explore the manner in which medical resources are allocated in public health or national emergencies[90] and evaluates the principle of *triage*—demonstrating as such, its efficacy as an ethical principle and as a medical construct for clinical decision-making.

Chapter 7 examines the concept, ideal, or principle of autonomy—grounded, as such, within various ethical and philosophical traditions[91]—exercised here through the doctrine of informed consent in health care decision-making. As will be seen, there is no coherency to the concept of autonomy[92]; and this often leads to theory often being inconsistent with actual practice.[93] All too frequently, autonomy is conflated with consent—thus leading to further tensions and inconsistencies.[94]

The legal catalyst for triggering autonomy within health care decision-making is to be found in the standard of competency or decisional capacity.[95] Thus, if one is adjudged to be legally competent, this legal status should lead to the assumption that they are capable of understanding information presented to them.[96] Yet, in reality, this legal status fails to provide a guarantee "that the competent person will, or can, always make an autonomous decision."[97] There must be, additionally, communication skills by the physician, an ability of the patient to understand what is communicated and a level of mutual trust before an autonomous decision can be verified.[98] This chapter suggests ways to re-conceptualize autonomy and thereby strengthen its clinical use and implementation through informed consent in medical decision-making.

The extent to which free and competent choice is allowed by the state in end-of-life decision-making is considered in Chapter 8. Today, managing death has become a complicated and meddlesome process—this, because of the "medicalisation of death" which has led, in turn, "to an over-emphasis in law or the ethics and the expertise of the doctor, and a subsequent under-representation of other value systems."[99] A physician's knowledge and medical beliefs have, accordingly, a profound influence on both judicial agendas "and the bases on which they reach conclusions."[100]

Rather than impose cumbersome and unduly restrictive regulations which impede a merciful and as dignified as possible death, the state should facilitate assistance at death for those incapable—because of their futile medical conditions—from exercising their liberty of self-determination. For the state to fail to act in this way would simply be a condonation of cruel and unusual punishment for the terminally ill.[101]

What connects the chapters within this book are analyses of the foundational notions of social and distributive justice, religion, humanism, scarce health care resource allocations and gatekeeping, the implementation of beneficence and humaneness in the assessment and delivery of health care services, the advancement and pursuit of scientific knowledge and its perceived limits, and the dignity of personhood at the beginning and end-points of existence.

Explaining and alleviating human suffering is the goal of medicine. Indeed, both clinical medicine and experimental medical science are directed to this task. Similarly, the theologies of the religions of the world and the tenets of humanistic thought suggest approaches and responses to pain and existential suffering. The primacy or integrity of the person is essential, then, to both medicine and to religion; and this is the unifying vector of force throughout these studies of the bioethical and socio-legal intersections which are encountered in life. The central question presented in this book is, thus: how do bioethics, public health, and human rights law unite to provide a framework for rational decision-making at the legislative, judicial, executive, administrative, and clinical points of health care service and—thus—thereby seek to validate and safeguard the claim that all citizens are to be respected as autonomous individuals, be treated with beneficence and without non-malfeasance or undue risk or with harm, and have a fair opportunity to receive the benefits of medical resource allocations?

The extent to which bioethics shapes policy and prompts responses to the animating issues of existence within not only the clinical or *micro* setting, but the institutional or *macro* environment, remains—as observed—an open and ongoing point of debate. What is apparent from the analyses in this book is that the national debates on health care reform are grounded inextricably in the bioethical principles recognized previously and, therefore, must yield policies which seek to maximize, fairly, the delivery of health care resources.

These debates must seek, as well, to identify and then distinguish basic from non-basic health and proceed to shape equitable criteria and rational, common-sense strategies for the distribution of these scarce medical resources.[102] From these ongoing conversations will come an assessment of the extent to which there is a human right to health protection or health care and the ethical constructs under which they may be offered and delivered. If ethics were then to be accepted as an integral component of quality in medical programs—much as in the same way that a linkage is seen between clinical and organizational ethics—a bold step toward quality assurance could be achieved in the delivery of health care resources.[103]

Decision-making at the various intersections of life discussed in this book should, in the final analysis, be guided, as seen, by a spirit of rational, humanistic, thinking and basic common sense, by humaneness and compassion, ethical values, and by an unwavering respect for free and competent choice regardless of what "negative" moral consequences may be seen by others to result from decisions of this nature. To the extent possible, a nuanced accommodation or a point of balance should be sought in bioethical decision-making; one which assesses the gravity of the harm of a questioned activity and weighs it against the utility of the good which would redraw to the benefit of the common good.

The fulcrum of this balancing test is pivotal—for, it influences or guides the whole analytical process. For some, the fulcrum will be moral ethics or religious principles; others will see economics or the common good as the point of balance. Still others will consider love or compassion as the guiding force in all bioethical and health care conflicts experiences over life's journey. This book studies all of these perspectives. Ideally, from this examination will come not only an appreciation of and sensitivity to the complexity of the whole process of informed decision-making, as well as a framework for reaching principled yet practical, rational judgments and for determining health policies.[104]

Notes

1 ALVIN HUDSON & REX NELSON, UNIVERSITY PHYSICS at 98–100 (2nd ed. 1990). *See* VAN NOSTRAND'S SCIENTIFIC ENCYCLOPEDIA at 1972 (Douglas M. Considine, ed., 7th ed. 1989).

2 Steven A. Benner & A. Michael Sismour, *Synthetic Biology*, 6 NAT. REV. GENETICS 535 (2005).

3 Olivia Judson, *Baby Steps to New Life Forms*, N.Y. TIMES, May 28, 2010, at A19. *See* Drew Endy, *Foundations of Engineering Biology*, 438 NATURE 449 (2005).

4 Judson, *ibid. See* W. Wayt Gibbs, *Synthetic Life*, 290 SCIENTIFIC AMERICAN 74 (2004).

5 Nicholas Wade, *Synthetic Bacterial Genome Takes Over a Cell, Researchers Report*, N.Y. TIMES, May 21, 2010, at A17; David Brown, *Creating a Cell from Scratch*, WASH. POST, May 21, 2010, at A3.

6 Wade, *ibid.*

7 *Ibid. See generally* Julian Savulescu, *Genetic Interventions and The Ethics of Enhancement of Human Beings* in THE OXFORD HANDBOOK OF BIOETHICS at 516 (Bonnie Steinbock, ed. 2007).

8 Wade, *supra* note 5. *See* Diamond v. Chakrabarty, 447 U.S. 303 (1980) (allowing for patent protection of a micro-organism to digest oil spilled in water).

9 Brown, *supra* note 5.

10 *Ibid. See generally* Loane Skene, *Recent Developments in Stem Cell Research: Social, Ethical, and Legal Issues for the Future*, 17 IND. J. GLOBAL STUD. 211 (2010).

President Obama's Commission for the Study of Bioethical Issues—the successor to President George W. Bush's Council on Bioethics—issued its first report dealing with synthetic biology on December 16, 2010. Seeking to offer practical policy guidance, the Commission submitted some 18 recommendations designed to offer guidance for the development of this new science and—at the same time—provide for steps for ongoing government oversight. While not calling for a moratorium on research of this nature, the Commission suggested a number of environmental safeguards designed to minimize risks that laboratory-made microbes do not cause unexpected catastrophes. Rob Stein, *Concerns in 'Synthetic Biology.'* WASH. POST, Dec. 16, 2010, at A4.

11 Carl E. Schneider, *Bioethics in the Language of The Law*, 24 HASTINGS CENTER RPT. 16 (1994). *See also* ROGER W. DWORKIN, LIMITS: THE ROLE OF LAW IN BIOETHICAL DECISION MAKING 5–7, 11 (1997).

12 *See generally* GEORGE P. SMITH, II, BIOETHICS AND THE LAW: MEDICAL, SOCIO-LEGAL AND PHILOSOPHICAL DIRECTIONS FOR A BRAVE NEW

WORLD (1993) and George P. Smith, II, *Biomedicine and Bioethics: De Lege Lata, De Lege Ferenda*, 9 J. CONTEMP. HEALTH L. & POL'Y 233, 237 (1993); Norman Daniels *et al., Is Justice Enough? Ends and Means in Bioethics*, 26 HASTINGS CENTER RPT. 9 (1996).

13 *See e.g.,* Rob Stein & Spencer S. Hsu, *Judge Blocks Stem Cell Rules*, WASH. POST, Aug. 24, 2010, at A1. *See generally* JOHN C. POLKINGHORNE, EXPLORING REALITY: THE INTERTWINING OF SCIENCE AND RELIGION (2005).

14 H. TRISTRAM ENGELHARDT, Jr., BIOETHICS AND SECULAR HUMANISM: THE SEARCH FOR A COMMON MORALITY 10 (1991).

George J. Annas argues the catalyst for the development of American Bioethics was the Nuremberg Doctors' Trials after World War II and the Nuremberg Code. AMERICAN BIOETHICS AFTER NUREMBERG: PRAGMATISM, POLITICS AND HUMAN RIGHTS 5 (2005).

15 *See generally* THE STORY OF BIOETHICS (Jennifer K. Walter *et al.,* eds. 2003).

16 RONALD A. LINDSAY, FUTURE BIOETHICS: OVERCOMING TABOOS, MYTHS & DOGMAS 19 (2008).

17 ALBERT R. JONSEN, THE BIRTH OF BIOETHICS (1992).

18 BARRY R. FURROW, *ET AL.,* BIOETHICS: HEALTH CARE LAW AND ETHICS 4 (6th ed. 2008). *See generally* TOM W. BEAUCHAMP & JAMES F. CHILDRESS, PRINCIPLES OF BIOMEDICAL ETHICS (6th ed. 2009); ETHICS AND LAW FOR THE HEALTH PROFESSIONS chs. 1, 2, 5 (Ian Kerridge, *et al.,* eds., 3rd ed. 2009).

19 FURROW, *et al., ibid.* at 11–14.

20 *Ibid.* at 114.

21 THE OXFORD HANDBOOK OF BIOETHICS 7 (Bonnie Steinbock, ed. 2007).

22 *Ibid.*

23 *Ibid.*

24 THOMAS A. FAUNCE, *Will Human Rights Subsume Medical Ethics?* Intersections in the UNESCO Universal Bioethics Declaration, 31 J. MEDICAL ETHICS 173 (2004).

25 *See   http://portal.unesco.org/en/ev.php-URL_ID=31058&url_do=DO_TOPIC&URLSECT   See generally* THE UNESCO UNIVERSAL DECLARATION ON BIOETHICS AND HUMAN RIGHTS: BACKGROUND, PRINCIPLES AND APPLICATIONS (Henk A. M. J. ten Have & Michelle S. Jean, eds. 2009).

26 UNESCO 32/C. Res. 22 (October 16, 2003).

27 UNESCO, Final Report, BIO-97CONF. 201/9 (July 22–25, 1997).

28 THOMAS A. FAUNCE, WHO OWNS OUR HEALTH (2007).

29 ARTHUR B. LaFRANCE, BIOETHICS: HEALTH CARE HUMAN RIGHTS AND THE LAW (1999).

30 Michael D. Kirby, *Human Rights and Bioethics: The Universal Declaration of Human Rights and the UNESCO Universal Declaration of Bioethics and Human Rights*, 25 J. CONTEMP. HEALTH L. & POL'Y 390, 325 (2010).

31 Jonathan Mann, *Health and Human Rights: Protecting Human Rights is Essential for Promoting Health*, 312 BR. MED. J. 924 (1996).

32 *See* SHEILA A. M. McLEAN, MODERN DILEMMAS: CHOOSING CHILDREN, ch. 1 (2006); JOHN FLETCHER, THE ETHICS OF GENETIC CONTROL (1974). *See also* Tim Townsend, *Bishops Not Indulgent on Infertility*, WASH. POST, Feb. 20, 2010, at B12 (reporting on a meeting of the U.S. Catholic Bishops where a document was approved with certain reproductive technologies, *e.g.,* artificial insemination, were condemned as not morally legitimate ways to combat infertility).

33 *See generally* J. KENYON MASON & GRAEME T. LAURIE, LAW AND MEDICAL ETHICS, 7th ed. (2006); SHEILA A. M. McLEAN, OLD LAW, NEW MEDICINE (1998).

Ethics may be seen as but "reasoned public discourse in search of the common good." Edmund D. Pellegrino & David C. Thomasma, *The Conflict between Anatomy and Beneficence in Medical Ethics: Proposal for Resolution*, 3 J. CONTEMP. HEALTH L. & POL'Y 23, 34 (1987).

34 Amy Gutmann & Dennis Thompson, *Deliberating About Bioethics*, 27 HASTINGS CENTER RPT. 38 (1997).

35 *Ibid.* at 39.

36 *Ibid.* at 40.

37 *See* Daniel Callahan & Sherwin B. Nuland, *The Quagmire: How American Medicine is Destroying Itself*, THE NEW REPUBLIC 16 (Jun. 9, 2011). *See generally* SUSAN JACOBY, THE AGE OF AMERICAN UNREASON (2008).

38 *See* Stephen F. Williams, *Limits to Economics As a Norm for Judicial Decision*, 21 HARV. J.L. & PUB. POL'Y 39 (1998).

39 Robert Schwartz, *Genetic Knowledge: Some Legal and Ethical Questions* in BIRTH TO DEATH: SCIENCE AND BIOETHICS at 25 (David C. Thomasma & Thomasine Kushner, eds. 1996); Roger B. Dworkin, *Bioethics? The Law and Biomedical Advance*, 14 HEALTH MATRIX 43 (2004).

40 LEON R. KASS, LIFE, LIBERTY AND THE DEFENSE OF DIGNITY: THE CHALLENGE OF BIOETHICS 281 (2002).

41 *Ibid.*

42 *Supra* note 39.

43 Owen D. Jones, *Law and Biology: Toward an Integrated Model of Human Behavior*, 8 J. CONTEMP. LEGAL ISSUES 167 (1997).

44 *Ibid.* at 167.

45 *Ibid.*

46 *Ibid.*

47 *Ibid.* at 168.

48 Schneider, *supra* note 11 at 16, 22.

49 R v. Instan (1893), 1 QB at 453 (per Lord Chief Justice Coleridge).

50 SHEILA A. M. McLEAN, ASSISTED DYING: REFLECTIONS ON THE NEED FOR LAW REFORM 202 (2009).

51 *Ibid.*

52 Schneider, *supra* note 11 at 21.

53 Lisa S. Cahill, *Bioethics and Justice: Catches Up with the Real World Order*, 33 HASTINGS CENTER RPT. 34, 39–42 (Sep.–Oct. 2003).

54 PETER SINGER, WRITINGS ON AN ETHICAL LIFE 8–15, 115 (2001).

55 *See* PAUL DAVIES, GOD AND THE NEW PHYSICS 1 (1983).

56 *Ibid.*

57 *Ibid.* at 2.

58 *Ibid.* at 6.

59 *Ibid. See generally* George P. Smith, II, *Pathways to Immortality in the New Millennium: Human Responsibility, Theological Direction or Legal Mandate*, 15 ST. LOUIS U. PUB. L. REV. 557 (1996).

60 Michael D. Kirby, *Health Law and Ethics*, 5 J. L. & MED. 31, 34–35 (1997); Callahan & Nuland, *supra* note 37.

61 GEORGE P. SMITH, II, THE CHRISTIAN RELIGION AND BIOTECHNOLOGY: A SEARCH FOR PRINCIPLED DECISIONMAKING 48 (2005).

62 *Ibid.* at 48.

63 *Ibid.*

64 *See* Oliver Wendell Holmes, Jr., *The Path of The Law*, 10 HARV. L. REV. 457, 467 (1897).

65 SMITH, *supra* note 61 at 34.

66 *See generally* SMITH, *supra* note 61.

67 KENNETH R. WING, *ET AL.*, PUBLIC HEALTH LAW 793 (2007).

68 *Ibid.* at 777.

69 *Ibid.*

70 *See* GEORGE P. SMITH, II, HUMAN RIGHTS AND BIOMEDICINE (2000); ten Have & Jean, *supra* note 25.

71 Professor Edmund D. Pellegrino, M.D., Georgetown University Medical Center, former Chairman of the President's Council on Bioethics, email communication to Professor George P. Smith, II, Washington, D.C., Sep. 9, 2009.

72 *Ibid. See generally* M. Gregg Bloche, *The Emergent Logic of Health Law*, 82 S. CAL. L. REV. 389, 455–60 (2009) (suggesting the best way to address the fragmentation an incoherence of Health Law is—instead of proliferating new administrative mechanisms to resolve the disarray—to establish, instead, self-organizing networks of decision-makers who follow evidence-based guidelines in the practice of medicine). *See also* THOMAS H. LEE & JAMES J. MORGAN, CHAOS AND ORGANIZATION (2009).

73 Pellegrino, *supra* note 71.

74 *Ibid.*

75 DAVID C. THOMASMA, HUMAN LIFE IN THE BALANCE 184 (1996).

76 *Ibid.* at 183.

77 *See* George P. Smith, II, *Social Justice and Health Care Management: An Elusive Quest*, 9 HOUSTON J. HEALTH L. & POL'Y 1 (2009).

78 Peter Singer, *Why We Must Ration Health Care*, N.Y. TIMES MAG., Jul. 19, 2009, at MM38.

79 JONATHAN HERRING, OLDER PEOPLE IN LAW AND SOCIETY 293 (2009). *See generally* RICHARD A. POSNER, AGING AND OLD AGE (1995).

80 Lauran Neergaard, *How to Square Budget Cuts, Need for Alzheimer's Studies*, WASH. EXAMINER, May 18, 2011, at 25.

81 *Ibid.*

82 *Ibid.*

83 *Ibid.*

84 *Ibid.*

85 *See generally* GEORGE P. SMITH, II, DISTRIBUTIVE JUSTICE AND THE NEW MEDICINE (2008).

86 *Ibid.*

87 *See* SHARON E. STRAUS, *ET AL.*, EVIDENCE-BASED MEDICINE: HOW TO PRACTICE AND TEACH EBM (2003).

88 *See* George P. Smith, II, *Re-shaping the Common Good in Times of Public Health Emergencies: Validating Medical Triage*, 17 ANNALS HEALTH L. 1 (2009), *Refractory Pain, Existential Suffering, and Palliative Care: Releasing an Unbearable Lightness of Being*, 20 CORNELL J. L. & PUB. POL'Y 469, 507, 518 (2011).

89 Benjamin E. Berkman *et al.*, *Assessing the Impact of Federal Law on Public Health Preparedness*, 4 ST. LOUIS U. J. HEALTH L. & POL'Y 155 (2010).

90 *See* GEORGE J. ANNAS, WORST CASE BIOETHICS: DEATH, DISASTER AND PUBLIC HEALTH (2010).

91 SHEILA A. M. McLEAN, AUTONOMY, CONSENT AND THE LAW 14 *passim* (2009).

92 *Ibid.* at 28.

93 *Ibid.* at 228.

94 *Ibid.* at 216.

95 *Ibid.* at 48.

96 *Ibid.*

97 *Ibid.*

98 McLEAN, *supra* note 33. *See generally* PENNY LEWIS, ASSISTED DYING AND LEGAL CHANGE (2007).

99 McLEAN, *supra* note 33. *See generally* Edmund D. Pellegrino, *The Human Person, the Physician and The Physician's Ethics*, 62 LINACRE Q. 74 (1995).

100 *See generally* McLEAN, *supra* note 50; M. GREGG BLOCHE, THE HIPPOCRATIC MYTH (2011) (discussing his concerns that the practice of medicine is—because of continuing conflicts over the nature and extent of patient beneficence—no longer "a caring endeavor").

101 *See generally* IAN DOW BIGGIN, A MERCIFUL END: THE EUTHANASIA MOVEMENT IN MODERN AMERICA (2003).

102 ROBERT A. PEARLMAN, *Introduction to the Practice of Bioethics* in BIOETHICS: AN INTRODUCTION TO THE HISTORY, METHODS AND POLICIES at 309, 319 (Nancy S. Jenker, *et al.,* 2nd ed. 2007).

103 *Ibid.* at 317–18.
     By comparing health care practices with performance measures, ethics quality is sought to be accessed. *Ibid.*

104 *See* Smith, *supra* notes 12, 77.

2   Bioethical challenges

Setting parameters?

On November 20, 2007, independent teams of researchers in Wisconsin and Japan announced the achievement of a scientific advancement which, over time, may well force a conclusion of the longstanding debate on whether embryonic stem cell research is "appropriate" morally.[1] Specifically, these scientists created human embryonic stem cells from human skin cells, without destroying any human embryos.[2] The hope is that, in due course, these new cells could yield eventually the very same medical promise as embryonic stem cells being developed, as such, to treat heart disease, diabetes, Parkinson's disease, and also create heart and nerve tissue.[3]

When this technique was presented for discussion at a meeting sponsored by the Vatican, a spokesman stated that there was "no moral problem with it at all."[4] The chief domestic policy adviser to then President George W. Bush observed that this new scientific achievement held the promise of allowing medical progress without compromising moral standards. Indeed, this new laboratory success shows "science has overtaken politics" and that real progress can be achieved without having "a culture war."[5]

Others in the scientific community are quick to remind that this level of medical research, while indeed promising, could take many years before it could be used clinically and applied to humans. Accordingly, they urge a continuation of research and experimentation in all other "traditional" areas of stem cell research. And this continuation means that the ethical and moral issues surrounding the legal status of embryos remains in play.[6]

Earlier in November 2007, another new stem cell research achievement was recorded when a group of Oregon scientists announced that they have not only created, but harvested, stem cells from fully formed monkey embryos.[7] As such, this success becomes a worldwide "first." Created from a skin cell from a single monkey, this research validates what has heretofore been subject to wide speculation: namely, whether primates are capable of being clones biologically.[8] The scientists undertaking this research did not transfer the embryos which were created to the wombs of female monkeys with the purpose of growing them into full-blown clones as has been done with other species (*e.g.*, mice). Rather, the Oregon experiment merely retrieved, successfully, embryonic stem cells from the embryos.[9]

Although this research was limited, specifically, to the development of stem cells, concerns have been raised that this cloning technique could be applied to humans.[10] Indeed, this scientific achievement could well re-ignite the ongoing congressional debate over the extent to which restrictions on the cloning of human embryos should be either loosened further or tightened. While no legal restrictions have been imposed for private work here, federally funded scientists are prohibited from engaging in research of this nature.[11]

This scientific achievement in Oregon must be added to other equally path-breaking ones which seek to perfect human cloning,[12] create designer pathogens,[13] develop more fully *in vitro* fertilization and other forms of assisted reproduction,[14] perfect organ transplantation,[15] and face[16] and womb transplants,[17] cryogenic preservation *pre or post mortem*,[18] genetic enhancement through eugenic experimentation,[19] and genetically modified genes and foods designed, as such, to enrich and prolong a life resistant to disease.[20] Additionally, a new dimension was added to what has become known as the "New Medicine"[21] when, in September 2007, the British Human Fertilization and Embryo Authority ruled that it was proper for part-human-part-animal embryos, termed chimeras, to be developed and used in medical experimentation.[22] This particular scientific option is a source of considerable concern for some because it is feared that some hybrid embryos could be transferred, illegitimately, to wombs of women where they might well develop.[23] Present British regulations required all "human" embryos used in research to be destroyed within 14 days after their creation.[24]

On September 19, 2008, the United States Food and Drug Administration released its much anticipated guidelines governing the genetic engineering of animals for food, drugs, or medical devices.[25] The new guidelines regulate, tightly, the process by which companies seek to create an engineered animal. Presently under development are genetically engineered cows, goats, pigs, and salmon. Once created, the animals will serve one of two uses: as food or, alternatively, as sources of production for medically useful substances—such as hormones or antibodies—in either their organs or body fluids.[26]

Biopolitics

A significant part of contemporary bioethics, under which the complex ethical, philosophical, socio-legal, and medical issues of the New Medicine are presented,[27] has been seen as being "biopolitic" in that it has become "embryocentric"[28]—this, because of limitations on federal funding for human embryonic stem cell research.[29] Rather than develop policy which is viewed as part of a nation "political agenda" designed to limit embryonic research to pre-existing stem cell lines, it is argued that policies should be developed and pursued which seek to advance liberal care for the present millions of uninsured Americans and one which thereby works to achieve respect and dignity for all people—not just embryos.[30]

Bush v. Obama

President George W. Bush shaped the development of public bioethics largely by his decisions to limit federal funding of stem cell research.[31] The policy shaping this decision was one which acknowledged that biomedical research must respect "the fundamental quality of all human beings, regardless of their developmental stage, conditions of dependence, quality of life, circumstances, or the extent to which they are esteemed or valued by others."[32]

In December 2009, President Barack Obama chose a new and dramatic policy supporting the advancement of scientific research by approving new lines of human embryonic stem cells for research and experimentation—with 76 stem cell lines being vetted presently and at least 254 more planned for subsequent approval.[33] The National Institutes of Health had, previously, authorized 31 research grants totaling approximately $21 million for human embryonic stem cell research—all contingent, as such, on new lines being approved. Particular interest was expressed within the grant projects for developing cells which could be used to treat particular disease affecting the heart and nervous systems.[34]

Previous to this December announcement, the government sought to assure the vocal opponents who continue to argue that it is immoral to fund embryonic research which requires destruction of embryos, by imposing strict ethical requirement before new stem cell lines could be experimented upon.[35] Specifically, before federal funding will be approved for the development of new lines, the embryo destroyed to create a line must be proved to have been discarded after a failed *in vitro* fertilization procedure, that the donors have been informed that the discarded embryo would be destroyed for research purposes and—further—made cognizant of the full consequences of their choices. No inducements of any financial nature or otherwise will be allowed to be made to the donors.[36]

In March 2010, it was reported that the noble efforts of the Obama Administration to advance stem cell research were encountering considerable difficulties in their implementation. Indeed, some scientists have complained that the new policy is more burdensome than advantageous for their research.[37] The issue of concern focuses on the ethical efficacy of the original 21 stem cell lines authorized by President George W. Bush for which millions of dollars have been expended over the course of nearly a decade.[38] Thus, the question is whether the stem cell lines derived at a period of time when ethical standards were less detailed are now within those set by President Obama.[39]

Of the new 43 lines approved by the NIH, only one of the 21 "Bush lines" has met the new ethical requirements. And only two more of these original lines are being presently evaluated among 115 lines under review.[40] While scientists with present federal grants are allowed to continue their research on the old line regardless of their approval under the Obama policies, research involving new grants is only permitted on stem cell lines approved and consistent with these new policies.

The result of this confusion is a dilemma for the scientists: they can delay their research in hopes that the stem cell lines that they have been using will be approved by NIH or, they can discard their past research and start anew on lines which meet the Obama policies.[41] It has been suggested that a fair and equitable resolution to this quandary would be to simply revise the NIH guidelines and thereby allow researchers to continue their work on the existing "Bush lines" for a two-year grace period until new formal approval can be obtained for them.[42] What was hoped to be a new level of scientific momentum in embryonic research has now resulted in nothing less than a tragic miasma.[43]

On August 23, 2010, U.S. District Court Judge Royce C. Lamberth in Washington, D.C., enjoined the Obama Administration from continuing to fund human embryonic stem cell research through the National Institutes of Health.[44] Finding 1996 legislation enacted by Congress prohibits the federal government from funding "research in which a human embryo or embryos are destroyed, discarded, or knowingly subjected to risk of injury or death greater than that allowed for research on fetuses in utero," Judge Lamberth concluded that the language of the controlling legislation was unambiguous in prohibiting "all research in which an embryo is destroyed not just the piece of research in which the embryo is destroyed."[45] Efforts to draw a distinction between funding embryonic research for experiments involving cells from the procurement of embryos from which the cells are a part were not accepted by the Court.[46]

The day following the ruling by Judge Lamberth, the National Institutes of Health announced that new funding of human embryonic stem cell research had not only been suspended, but that all presently funded experiments would be terminated when they are subject to renewal.[47] The Lamberth ruling does not preclude private foundations and benefactors or state governments from continuing to fund embryonic research.[48] In addition, experimentation may continue on stem cells from adults or induced pluripotent stem cells which are derived from adult cells—this, even though there is a strong division of thought in the scientific community regarding whether embryonic cells are superior to all other cellular sources.[49] Interestingly, on April 29, 2011, a three-judge panel of the U.S. Court of Appeals lifted the Lamberth injunction thereby allowing the restoration of previously restricted funding of human embryonic stem cell research proposed by the Obama Administration.[50]

Regrettably, scientific issues become—inevitably—political issues because of one principal fact: they put in focus the extent to which the government can restrict private medical research undertakings—either in the name of generational safety, morality, or the public good.[51] The multiple and varied concerns of applying the New Medicine, derived as such from the New Biology, conduce—essentially—to a suspicion "continued reductionism in the biological analysis of humans will erode the notions of autonomy, dignity and personal integrity that have traditionally justified the constitutional protection of civil liberties."[52]

The American ideal

There is a strong, lingering sense if indeed nothing less than a magnificent obsession, that the new powers of medical technology may narrow if not blunt the very meaning of the American ideal which promotes the right to live in a free society and to pursue happiness.[53] The fundamental concern, then, becomes to what degree of usefulness is there in pursuing goals beyond therapy towards genetic enhancement.[54] Are there, in other words, limits to the right of scientific investigation?[55] And, if there are, what are they?[56] Finally, is there a standard of "genetic responsibility"[57] which should be either self-imposed or set by society upon those working in the field—this, even though such a responsibility may very well be viewed as an unnecessary burden on the freedom of scientific inquiry?[58]

Medical technology is so uniquely powerful that its impact is felt not only in daily life but in the way life is viewed. For example, the technology of mechanical ventilators, combined with heart transplantation, brought a societal re-examination of how death should be defined and led to the conclusion that the death of the entire brain is equivalent to, for all purposes, death of the whole person. This new definition, in turn, allowed the "harvesting" of hearts and other vital organs from individuals who—although dead under a brain death criteria—continued to have both circulation and respiration maintained artificially by medical ventilation.[59]

While Americans might decide to limit "halfway" or exotic, science-fiction inspired technologies, such as artificial hearts or brain transfers into robot bodies, it would appear unlikely they would ever approve limitations on medical research whose focus is to discover technologies, drugs, and scientific techniques which not only maintain qualitative existence but extend life.[60] The reason for this position is simple and direct: "there is no coherent argument for arbitrarily ending a life that could be prolonged with reasonable quality at a reasonable price."[61]

Since the end of this century, the public has been almost overwhelmed with scientific information regarding the genome, the complexities of gene therapy and stem cell research.[62] Yet to come will be efforts to grow certain tissues for grafting—including skin, bladder, and cartilage. Reportedly, cultured cells have been used successfully in an experimental setting to treat stroke victims; and in 2006 it was reported that seven children and teenagers had new implanted bladders grown from their own muscle and bladder cells.[63]

It is expected that the use of similar cells can be used to treat other disabling brain diseases. Genomics-derived drugs hold the potential to expand greatly the range of treatments achievable with human cells—this, because of their ability to control the cells as they grow and specialize.[64] Even more opportunities for regenerative medicine will be charted when the insights from the clonal experiment with Dolly the sheep are realized first with a re-set of the genetic clock inside a cell and, subsequently, without the need for egg cells.[65]

Essentially, all efforts to achieve justice in the distribution of health care resources of the New Medicine are utilitarian in character and definition.[66] Since these resources are not infinite, they cannot be offered to or used by everyone. This, of necessity, then forces choices between those individuals and among groups seeking their use. Allowing improper distribution of these scarce resources is not only inefficient, it is wasteful.[67]

For utilitarians, the general good is seen as superior to personal goal satisfaction.[68] Because of the difficulty in calculating the net good deriving from a utilitarian approach to decision-making,[69] some have argued that this approach to health care decision-making is not only unjust—but unfair.[70] Not only is utilitarianism viewed as cold and calculating, it is seen as denying the individual of what is his due.[71] The needs of those who are worse off are either ignored or neglected.[72]

Autonomy, beneficence, and justice

As seen, there are three foundational principles—alternatively referred to as duties, rights, and values—within bioethics: autonomy or self-determination, beneficence, and justice.[73] There is continuing debate over the dependence or independence of these three principles and the role they play in bioethical decisions.[74] Rather than perceive conflict and disharmony, however, what should be recognized here is the complementary focus and blending of all three principles in the ultimate goal of minimizing human suffering and maximizing the social good. Thus, autonomy, beneficence, and justice are all balanced against one another in an effort to maximize the social utility and personal good of an individual in controversy. Their relationship is inextricable. The state exists to better life for its citizens and, indeed, each citizen seeks to better himself by the conferral of positive benefits that, in turn, promote the good life for him. Autonomous, reasonable people act accordingly in undertaking those courses of action designed to advance well-being. Justice, thus, becomes an aspirational codification of the common good.

Autonomy

Autonomy, or self-determination, finds its essence and current expression in the rich and evolving tradition of human rights which in turn has had a significant impact on Western social and political thought over the last four centuries.[75] This newly refined and activated right of self-determination has fast become the benchmark of the new patients' rights movement. It is integral, as well, to issues of informed consent in clinical and research settings, abortion (where the right of control of one's body is asserted under the rubric of "free choice"), euthanasia[76] (where the right to die with dignity is asserted), and within a wide range of other health care delivery issues ranging from allocation of limited resources and regulation of health care to responsibility for dependent persons.[77]

Put directly, "the claim for autonomy is a claim for self-ownership and self-governance that each person has for his own body or person and the labor it generates."[78] Some would seek to distinguish between the ideal or principle of autonomy and the principles of respect for personal autonomy—the latter of which obligates a respect for the autonomous choice and the actions of others.[79] It is important for the maintenance of moral life that individuals be competent, informed, and act voluntarily in their decisions.[80] Personal choices may be exercised, however, that delegates this inherent first-order decisional power or that responsibility to make decisions regarding the rightness and wrongness of particular patterns of conduct. Accordingly, an individual may wish to yield to his physician when a particular medical procedure is proposed, or to deter to his religious institution of affiliation in matters of sexual ethics.[81]

In accepting the principles of respect for autonomy, not only must a determination be made regarding whether a patient is autonomous, but—additionally—a determination must be made as to what has in fact been chosen, with the patient's present consents and dissents being placed within a broad temporal context that encompasses both the past and the future, because obviously different preferences are expressed at different times.[82] All too often, analysis and application of the principle of respect for autonomy focuses on the present; for example, has informed consent or refusal been given at this time?[83] A central question raised as a consequence of this position asks when there is justification in overriding a patient's present autonomous choices or actions in light of his past or (anticipated) future choices and actions. Under proper conditions, the principle of respect for autonomy can be overridden or infringed upon. Thus, non-autonomous persons—traditionally children and the insane—would be likely candidates. Even when this occurs, an explanation and justification of the action should be made to those whose autonomy has been infringed or to their surrogate agents.[84]

Beneficence

The prevention of harm and the production of good are the two distinct but related foci of the principle of beneficence; with medical ethics emphasizing the first under the normative command: "Do no harm." Accordingly, for the health care professional, in context, this principle means that he or she must take care in his or her actions not to compound an ill patient's condition by causing or complicating further illness.[85] This principle is expanded and applied by bioethicists to their research by adherence to a standard of concern for the protection of human subjects. It is coupled with an advance assessment of the possible negative social consequences that might come from new bio-medical technologies in order to protect large groups of individuals from potential harm.[86] Because biomedical advances carry significant social costs, it has been argued that society should be willing to adopt a less permissive and more critical stance toward new technologies in this field.[87]

Even though no sharp breaks can be found on the continuum between "preventing harm" and "producing good," beneficence—as a positive principle—is regarded as being more directive because it requires conferring benefits rather than avoiding harm. In the sense that it allows the risk of at least some harm in the ultimate course of attempting to produce great benefits, the positive principle may thus be less stringent than the negative. Indeed, it is because of the promise of advances in scientific or medical knowledge that biomedical research is often justified. In the fields of gene experimentation and therapy and *in vitro* fertilization, advocates of new biomedical and behavioral technologies contend that the long-term societal benefits accruing from this technology far outweigh their micro, negative side effects.[88]

Justice

Any use of biotechnology brings with it the ever-present problem of how to distribute its benefits justly and fairly among various social groups.[89] Presently, the vast majority of distributional problems are decided on a local *ad hoc* basis. Because demand will normally exceed supply, the threshold question becomes, for example: who should receive a kidney transplant, an artificial heart, or become a candidate for gene therapy? What is the fairest principle for distribution—first come, first served or medical compatibility? Should equal access to health care be recognized as an important social goal? To what extent is there an inequitable distribution of biomedical research risks to the institutionalized? Finally, is it unjust to distribute health care as a free market commodity or consider the social utility of persons in distributing scarce medical services? No definitive answers can be postulated.[90] Indeed, as Richard A. McCormick, S.J., has cautioned, the operative watchwords should be: "beware of ethicists bearing solutions!"[91] Anyone claiming to have explicable rules that cut through the philosophical agonies of ambiguity and uncertainty in our present pluralistic society is guilty of deception.[92] "All too often the question of how to distribute justly often is reduced to who shall decide how to distribute."[93]

Although wide social consensus will never be achieved on developing a framework for resolving difficult medical issues of the New Biology (simply because the criterion of final selection will vary with the nature of the medical dilemma or particular biomedical technology used), policies that aid decision-making can and must be advanced. Such a set of policies must be formulated not only to provide protection for the vulnerable, while respecting familial and personal autonomy and privacy, but also to recognize inherent common values and not so much the centrality of technical expertise. Such values foster humility as well as tolerance and grace.[94]

Ethical relativism?

In order to guide scientific study and advancement, a standard of ethical relativism is suggested; one which recognizes moral values are in no way absolute but rather determined by certain variables "usually of social phenomena"[95] and a standard which nevertheless incorporates the value of ethical responsibility.

Others have suggested that ethics is neither relative nor subjective.[96] Rather, it is asserted, ethical conduct is universal and forces the individual— in this present context of analysis, the medical scientist—to choose a course of action that has the "best consequences," on balance, for all affected.[97] In a very real way, then, this approach advocates a form of utilitarianism. Yet, it is different from classical utilitarianism in that "best consequences" is defined as what, "on balance, furthers the interest of those affected rather than merely what increases pleasure and reduces pain."[98]

Rather than be straight-jacketed by an *a priori* ethic which would have the practical effect of ceasing the development of scientific knowledge in many areas, what is needed is an ethic shaped by the particular situation of present investigation.[99] Such an ethic recognizes the needs of the medical and bio-technological sciences to provide humane and technologically appropriate (*e.g.*, reasonable) care for the sick and minimize human suffering, prizes the value of genetic improvement and the corresponding elimination of inheritable disease,[100] as well as embraces an understanding of a need for economic fairness in the distribution of the benefits of science.[101] The situation ethic is grounded in an ungirding or inherent force which directs ultimate actions be undertaken with love, kindness, and humaneness which, in turn, advance and preserve human dignity.

Participatory democracy

Noble though the sentiment may be that "active liberty refers to a sharing of a nation's sovereign authority among its people,"[102] and is tied—of necessity— to connecting frameworks grounded in responsibility, participation and capacity,[103] the hard reality is that ordinary individuals have little interest in considering complex policy issues and—indeed—have little aptitude for evaluating complex intellectual matters[104]—and especially those involving medical science.[105] Consequently, it is unrealistic to expect either sound and thoughtful ideas or sensible and understandable policies to be shaped in public discourses under present conditions of "intellectual disorder."[106] Because of this state, the scientific community is reluctant—understandably—to accept public oversight and direct participation in regulating the parameters of the new biotechnology and its offspring, the new medicine.[107] It is well to remember that even though science promises an unpredictable future, futures are inevitably unpredictable.[108] Accordingly, it is well to understand that "doing nothing has just as many consequences as doing something."[109]

Such a state of affairs means that there can be no direct way to move from any level of moral assessment to a clear public policy. Instead, all that can be expected is that a level of information will be provided. Quite often, then, owing to a failure to develop adequately the moral dimensions of formulating public policy in a liberal pluralistic society, presumptions in favor of reproductive autonomy and scientific freedom, for example, are indulged and, indeed, advanced.[110]

Driven by "painful technologies and sciences," the new medicine runs the risk of being seen as no longer "patient based."[111] The ideal of philosophical reasoning and meanings for such ethical terms as responsibility, rights, duties, interests, beneficence, and justice is mired often in confusion and conjecture.[112] Indeed, many of the new ethical questions raised from the development and practice of the new medicine are set within a "blurred outline."[113] Perhaps all that can be hoped for is that the Cartesian aspiration of reaching a "clear and distinct idea" be pursued with objectivity.[114] And, from this may well come acceptance of a societal obligation not to achieve all the good that can be achieved, but—rather—to effect all the good that can be done within the limits morality imposes upon the development and use of the technologies of the new medicine.[115]

Although, traditionally, the ethics of medicine has focused on the obligations of physicians to their individual patients, there is—as well—a need to appreciate broader ethical issues arising from a recognition that medicine "is always practiced within a social context."[116] "Social medicine" or, alternatively, "the medicine of society," becomes crucial to shaping the parameters of application and use in the Age of The New Medicine.[117]

Distinct from clinical medicine, which is directed toward healing and relieving human suffering among individual patients, the medicine of society is concerned with the use of medical knowledge to advance the health of society.[118] Yet, while these two fields of medicine have differing ends, they enjoy a symbiotic relationship—this, because "the end of each is essential for human well-being."[119] Advancing and pursuing health care, then, is an obligation that "a good society owes its citizens in justice."[120] A balanced moral relationship between the goals of the individual patient and the common good must always be sought.[121] So long as this ethic and point of equilibrium guides the development and use of the new medicine, the moral compass is set correctly and humanely. Applying this ethic is always problematic, however, because "fiscal scarcity" drives the new medical economics and forces a "general tightening of health care ethics as government and business attempt to gain control over their skyrocketing expenditures."[122]

Conclusion

The core issues which encompass the discipline of Bioethics will continue to evolve. They will defy permanent resolution. Rather, such issues about abortion, the uses of assisted reproductive technologies, and the beginnings of life together with the right to die, will continue to change. New scientific developments and new administrative findings, together with legislative initiatives and judicial determinations will destabilize momentary moments of equilibrium. The political and social environment of the Nation, together with the ebb and flow of biotechnology, will also test deeply held moral beliefs and, thus, elude efforts to achieve any real consensus.[123] Determining what are reasonable courses of action for resolving these problematic issues will be challenging and complex—this, simply because what is reasonable is, indeed, fact sensitive.[124] If unsound philosophical standards of reasonableness are not applied in decision-making, inevitably policies will be shaped according to wants and desires,[125] and in turn surely falter if—indeed—not stagnate scientific advancement.[126]

Much of the ethical theory surrounding biomedicine attempts to harmonize individual desires with the greater social welfare.[127] Moral dilemmas in biomedicine may be thought of as arising from real or apparent conflicts between perceived obligations to distant generations and to the present generation.[128] In determining whether continued investigations into genetic engineering will jeopardize future life, the central inquiry should be whether an act with uncertain consequences will be harmful to one's own children.[129] Humankind should not inflict on future generations that which can be disastrous to a present generation.[130]

One scholar has suggested a bioethical creed for individuals. The creed states that "the future survival and development of mankind, both culturally and biologically, is strongly conditioned by man's present activities and plans."[131] The creed encompasses a corresponding commitment to live life and to influence the lives of others to promote the evolution of a better world for future generations by avoiding actions that would detrimentally impact the future.[132]

The major challenge of contemporary bioethics is "to express complex arguments in a way comprehensible to a broad public."[133] In order to meet this challenge, it remains for bioethics, then, to find not only a public voice, but one that is also "popular."[134] Before this becomes a practical—as opposed to aspirational—goal, bioethics must develop explicit doctrines which demonstrate how ethical arguments fit into not only political discourse but the ultimate public policies which emerge from this discourse.[135] Bioethics should assist in structuring practical decisions.[136]

There is disagreement within the field of bioethics whether "a more activist sense of mission" is required for this discipline to have prominence in a deliberative democracy such as in America, or whether a more direct "engagement" is sufficient to assure its role in both the political arena and in the shaping of public policy.[137] Not only does uncertainty exist in defining clearly the distinctions between these two analytical approaches, but a more central argument emerges: namely, whether bioethical reasoning is being followed properly in evaluating socio-medico issues of great moments in today's society.[138]

The traditional scholastic view is to present the chief challenge of bioethics as "reasoning correctly from given facts to desired moral conclusions."[139] A contrary view stresses the need for a greater understanding that much of unethical conduct arises not necessarily from poor reasoning but from a perceptual issue or, in other words, "moral blindness." Fine tuning moral perceptions, then, becomes the central focus of this position.[140]

Moral perceptivity is deepened when a wider level of life experiences is factored into analytical constructs for bioethical decision-making.[141] An expanded range of these experiences is to be found, for example, by considering not only feminist insights regarding disparities in economic and social power[142] but, as well, the issue of "white privilege" in contemporary society.[143] This is a highly volatile and emotional issue and presents a continuing challenge for the field of bioethics and its practitioners to understand and, when appropriate, integrate into their decision-making policies.

In an effort to counter the lack of "a common moral understanding" held by "moral strangers,"[144] in contemporary America, secular humanism has arisen as a tool for resolving moral controversies when individuals share neither a moral tradition nor a commitment to a specific moral conduct. Thus, the goal of secular humanists is to mediate those controversies where the participants in the controversies are separated by faith, culture, or moral traditions.[145] Similarly, the goal of secular policy-making is to facilitate a process whereby "what rational men and women should hold to be the case regarding issues such as abortion, euthanasia and justice in health care"[146] is made manifest.

In the contest of the distribution of health services, result-balancing forces an evaluation of competing individual interests or social values.[147] Accordingly, the value and cost to society of expending scarce health care resources, for example, to maintain individuals who have a futile medical prognosis, is balanced against the economic utility of providing care to those whose health care can be restored or rehabilitated.[148] Age, as well, should not be seen as the determinative factor in the health care services balancing test. Rather, a patient's medical condition, informed or negotiated consent to treatment, together with his primary physician's professional judgment as to the need for the commencement or cessation of medical services, should be controlling.[149] What is the most efficacious and humane treatment and in a patient's best interests—while varying from situation to situation—is, nonetheless, a medical judgment.[150] When that judgment may be called into question by a patient's family—for example—the preferred avenue for resolving disagreement should always be to resort to a hospital ethics committee.[151] Judicial intervention should only be sought when all else fails.

Restraining scientific inquiry should be limited only to action seen as unreasonable. Accordingly, an undertaking would be regarded as unreasonable when the long- and short-term cost of its effects would outweigh the enduring benefits that would derive from its study and implementation. Viewed as being not only an aid to the tragedy of infertility in family planning, but as a tool for improving the health of a nation's citizens, vital scientific research must continue in the new reproductive technologies and in efforts to engineer man's genetic weaknesses out of the line of inheritance. Healthier and genetically sound individuals have a much better opportunity for pursuing and achieving the "good life"—and, in turn, they make a significant contribution to society's greater well-being.

"If democracy is to be more than a myth and a shibboleth in the age of mature science and technology,"[152] a new thoughtful and questioning attitude must be developed—one that while not viewing scientific discovery with deference and uncertainty, nonetheless refuses to allow scientific and technological directions to be set without participation and question.[153] If moral ordering is to be of significance and value in medical-legal decision-making in the twenty-first century, a practical situation ethic—with universality, or worldwide acceptance, as a underpinning—must be observed. This ethic must accept genetic enhancement as valid a goal as the reasonable and efficient delivery of humane and technologically appropriate care for the sick.[154]

Hopefully, in the final analysis, the law will be seen as a new "culture" capable of setting and translating standards of normative conduct for this new Age of Biotechnology which are both practical *and* understandable by the citizenry. Ultimately, "[i]t is for our society to decide whether there is an alternative or whether the dilemmas posed by modern science and technology ... are just too painful, technical, complicated, sensitive and controversial for our institutions of government."[155]

Notes

1 Rick Weiss, *Advance May End Stem Cell Debate: Labs Create a Stand-In Without Eggs, Embryo*, WASH. POST, Nov. 21, 2007, at A1.

2 *Ibid. See* Rob Stein, *Cell Technique Works without Embryos*, WASH. POST, Oct. 1, 2010, at A2 (reporting on the work of researchers in synthetic biology at Harvard University who have induced pluripotent stem cells to re-program ordinary skin cells into entities that appear virtually identical to embryonic stem cells which can then turn those cells into ones that would be used for transplants).

3 *See* Gautman Naik, *Advance in Stem-Cell Work Avoids Destroying Embryos*, WALL ST. JOURNAL, Nov. 21, 2007, at A1.

4 *Ibid.* at A4 (quoting Richard Doerflinger of the U.S. Conference of Catholic Bishops).

5 Michael Abramowitz & Rick Weiss, *A Scientific Advance, a Political Question Mark?* WASH. POST, Nov. 21, 2007, at A4.

6 *Ibid.* (quoting Robert Lanza). *See generally* Symposium, *Human Primordial Stem Cells*, 29 HASTINGS CENTER RPT. 30 (1999).

7 Rick Weiss, *Monkey Embryos Cloned from Stem Cells*, WASH. POST, Nov. 15, 2007, at A1.

8 *Ibid.*

9 *Ibid.*

10 *Ibid.* at A16 (reporting on the concern of Rev. Thomas Berg, Executive Director, The Westchester Institute).

11 *Ibid.* at A16. *See generally* Paul C. Giannelli, *Daubert and Forensic Science: The Pitfalls of Law Enforcement Control of Scientific Research*, 2011 U. ILL. L. REV. 53 (2011).

12 KERRY L. MACINTOSH, ILLEGAL BEINGS: HUMAN CLONES AND THE LAW (2006).

13 *See* Nan Moss & Sue Jamieson, *50m pound Research to Create Revolutionary Personalized Drugs*, THE DAILY TELEGRAPH, Apr. 4, 2006, at 5. *See generally* REPROGENETICS: LAW, POLICY AND ETHICAL ISSUES (Lori P. Knowles & Gregory E. Kaebnick eds. 2007); THE FOUNTAIN OF YOUTH: CULTURAL, SCIENTIFIC, AND ETHICAL

PERSPECTIVES ON A BIOMEDICAL GOAL (Stephen G. Post & Robert H. Binstock eds. 2004).

14 DEBORAH L. SPAR, THE BABY BUSINESS: HOW MONEY, SCIENCE, AND POLITICS DRIVE THE COMMERCE OF CONCEPTION (2006). *See generally Symposium on Assisted Reproduction Technology* (ART), 39 FAM. L. Q. 573 (2005).

15 Rosamond Rhodes, *Justice in Transplant Organ Allocation* in MEDICINE AND SOCIAL JUSTICE at 350 (Rosamond Rhodes, Margaret R. Battin, & Anita Silvers eds. 2002).

16 Gay Hartman, *Face Value: Challenges of Transplant Technology*, 31 AM. J. L. & MED. 7 (2005); Angela Doland, *Face Transplant Recipient Meets Cameras, Questions*, WASH. POST, Feb. 7, 2006, at A17.

17 Rob Stein, *U.S. Uterus Transplant Planned*, WASH. POST, Jan. 15, 2007, at A1.

18 GEORGE P. SMITH, II, MEDICAL LEGAL ASPECTS OF CRYONICS: PROSPECTS FOR IMMORTALITY (1983); George P. Smith, II, *Pathways to Immortality in The New Millennium: Theological Direction or Legal Mandate*, 15 ST. LOUIS U. PUB. L. REV. 447 (1996).

19 EDWIN BLACK, WAR AGAINST THE WEAK: EUGENICS AND AMERICA'S CAMPAIGN TO CREATE A MASTER RACE (2003); George P. Smith, II, *Eugenics and The Family: Exploring The Yin and The Yang*, 8 U. TASMANIA L. REV. 4 (1984).

20 FINN BOWRING, SCIENCE, SEEDS AND CYBORGS (2003).

21 ALBERT R. JONSEN, THE NEW MEDICINE AND THE OLD ETHICS (1990).

22 Rick Weiss, *Britain to Allow Creation of Hybrid Embryos*, WASH. POST, Sept. 6, 2007, at A11. See Mark Henderson & Francis Elliott, *Human and Animal Worlds Collide as MPs Allow Creation of Mixed Embryos*, THE TIMES (LONDON), May 20, 2008, at 4 (reporting how Parliament—keen to promote research into the causes of Alzheimer's, Parkinson's, motor neuron diseases, and to develop therapies to combat these diseases as well as to combat infertility—amended Human Fertilization and Embryology legislation to allow research and experimentation on "admixed" embryos, as opposed to "true hybrids." These admixed embryos are termed "cytoplasmic" or cybrids and are made by moving a human nucleus into an empty animal egg; they are genetically 99.9 percent human).

23 *Ibid.*

24 *Ibid.*

25 73 FR 54407–01, 2008 WL 4264799 (F.R.).

26 David Brown, *Rules on Bioengineered Animals*, WASH. POST, Sept. 18, 2008, at A2.

27 *See generally* GEORGE P. SMITH, II, BIOETHICS AND THE LAW: MEDICAL, SOCIO-LEGAL AND PHILOSOPHICAL DIRECTIONS FOR A BRAVE NEW WORLD (1993).

28 *Ibid. See generally* Judith F. Daar, *Embryonic Genetics*, 2 ST. LOUIS U. J. HEALTH L. & POL'Y 81 (2008).

29 George J. Annas, Monograph, AMERICAN BIOETHICS AFTER NUREMBERG: PRAGMATISM, POLITICS AND HUMAN RIGHTS 13 (2005). *See generally Stem Cell Symposium*, 9 YALE J. HEALTH POL'Y L. & ETHICS 483–622 (2009); George P. Smith, II, *Biomedicine and Biomedical Ethics: De Lege Lata, De Lege Ferenda*, 9 J. CONTEMP. HEALTH L. & POL'Y 233 (1993).

30 George J. Annas & Sherman Elias, *Politics, Morals and Embryos*, 431 NATURE 19 (Sept. 2, 2004).

31 O. Carter Snead, *Public Bioethics and The Bush Presidency*, 32 HARV. J. L. & PUB. POL'Y 867, 908 (2009).

32 *Ibid.* at 907.

33 Rob Stein, *U.S. Set to Fund More Stem Cell Study*, WASH. POST, Dec. 3, 2009, at A3.

34 *Ibid.* at 4.

35 Shankar Vedantam, *Rules on Stem Cell Research are Easy*, WASH. POST, Jul. 7, 2009, at A1.

36 *Ibid.*

37 Rob Stein, *Stem Cell Research Waiting on 'Lines'*, WASH. POST, Mar. 15, 2010, at A13.

38 *Ibid.*

39 *Ibid.*

40 *Ibid.*

41 *Ibid.*

42 *Ibid.*

43 *See generally* Loane Skene, *Recent Developments in Stem Cell Research: Social, Ethical, and Legal Issues for the Future,* 17 IND. J. GLOBAL STUD. 211 (2010); *Symposium, Biomedical Research and the Law—Embryonic Stem Cells, Clones, and Genes: Science, Law, Politics, and Values,* 37 HOFSTRA L. REV. 313–515 (2009).

44 Rob Stein & Spencer S. Hsu, *Judge Blocks Stem Cell Rules,* WASH. POST, Aug. 24, 2010, at A1 (referencing the case of Sherley v. Sebeluis, 704 F. Supp. 2d 63 (D. D.C., 2010)).

   The original challenge in this case in 2009 was to the authority of the Secretary of Health and Human Services for implementing and applying human embryonic stem cell research guidelines; and Judge Lamberth held stem cell researchers, among other patients, bringing the suit had no standing. 686 F. Supp. 2d 1 (D. D.C., 2009). An appeal resulted in a remand to Judge Lamberth's court for reconsideration, 610 F. 3d 69 (D. D. Cir. 2010), which—in return—led to the issuance in August of a preliminary injunction restricting the funding of embryonic stem cell research. 704 F. Supp. 2d 63 (D. D. C., 2010). Judge Lamberth's injunction was vacated, however, by a three-judge panel of the U.S Court of Appeals on April 29, 2011. Del Quentin Wilber, *Ban on Human Stem Cell Funding is Lifted,* WASH. POST, Apr. 30, 2011, at A3. *Infra* note 50.

45 The Dickey–Wicker Amendment referenced in Judge Lamberth's ruling as dispositive is the name given an appropriation rider passed by Congress in 1996 prohibiting the Department of Health and Human Services from using federal funds for the creation of human embryos for research purposes or for research in which human embryos are destroyed. 704 F. Supp. 2d 63. See CFR 46.208(a)(2) and Section 498b(b) of the Public Health Service Act, 42 U.S.C. § 289g(b).

46 *Supra* note 44; 704 F. Supp. 2d 63.

47 Rob Stein, *NIH Cuts Off Stem Cell Funding after Court Order,* WASH. POST, Aug. 25, 2010, at A2.

48 *Ibid.*

49 *Ibid.*

50 2011 WL 1599685 (C.A.D.C.). *See* Wilber, *supra* note 44.

   Finally, and dispositively, on Jul. 27, 2011, Judge Lamberth ruled on his preliminary injunction that the NIH guidelines on stem cell research did not violate the Dickey-Wicker law and thereby dismissed the original challenge made in 2010. Sherley v. Sebelius, WL3111925. James Vicini, *Judge Upholds Stem Cell Research Funding,* WASH. POST, Jul. 28, 2011, at A2.

51 *See generally* George P. Smith, II, *Distributive Justice and Health Care,* 18 J. CONTEMP. HEALTH L. & POL'Y 421 (2002).

52 Sheila Jasanoff, *Biology and The Bill of Rights: Can Science Reframe The Constitution?* 13 AM. J. L. & MED. 249 (1990). *See Symposium, The Constitutional Law and Politics of Reproductive Rights,* 118 YALE L. J. 1312–1432 (2009).

53 President's Council on Bioethics, BEYOND THERAPY: BIOTECHNOLOGY AND THE PURSUIT OF HAPPINESS xviii (2003).

54 *Ibid.* at 277. It has been suggested that genetic enhancement should not be viewed as part of basic health care entitlements and, thus, should be excluded from the domain of distributive justice. ALLEN BUCHANAN, *ET AL.,* FROM CHANCE TO CHOICE, 17, 129 (2000). *See* Leon Kass, *The Pursuit of Biohappiness,* WASH. POST, Oct. 16, 2003, at A25. *See also* George P. Smith, II & Thaddeus J. Burns, *Genetic Determinism or Genetic Discrimination,* 11 J. CONTEMP. HEALTH L. & POL'Y 23 (1994).

55 *See* George P. Smith, II, *Setting Limits: Medical Technology and The Law,* 23 SYDNEY L. REV. 283 (2001).

56 *Ibid.* See also George P. Smith, II, *The Province and Function of Law, Science, and Medicine: Leeways of Choice and Patterns of Discourse,* 10 U. NEW SO. WALES L. J. 103 (1987). But *see* AP, *Rules Are Clarified to Spur Medical Advances,* N.Y. TIMES, Jan. 31, 2003, at A23 (reporting on how the Food and Drug Administration—responding to a sharp decline in the development of novel treatments and medical devices to spur medical innovation—has clarified, and some claim relaxed, its requirements for approval of research on new products).

57 PHILIP KITCHER, THE LIVES TO COME: THE GENETIC REVOLUTION AND HUMAN POSSIBILITIES 204 (1996).

58 George P. Smith, II, *Toward an International Standard of Scientific Inquiry,* 2 HEALTH MATRIX 167 (1992).

59 GEORGE J. ANNAS, STANDARD OF CARE: THE LAW OF AMERICAN BIOETHICS 253 (1993). *See* Rob Stein, *FDA Approves Artificial Heart for Those Awaiting Transplant,* WASH. POST, Oct. 19, 2004, at A3. *See generally,* GEORGE P. SMITH, II, THE NEW BIOLOGY: LAW, ETHICS AND BIOTECHNOLOGY (1989).

60 *See* George P. Smith, II, *The Frankenstein Myth and Contemporary Experimentation: Spectre, Legacy, Curse or Imperative,* 2 BIOLAW §463 (1990). *But see* Chris Mooney, *Nothing Wrong with a Little Frankenstein,* WASH. POST, Dec. 1, 2002, at B1. The science of creating cyborgs—"individuals" with electronically powered legs, arms, hands, and eyes—is progressing rapidly. Roger Highfield & Colin Joyce, *We Can Rebuild Him. We Have the Technology. Almost,* THE DAILY TELEGRAPH, Apr. 4, 2006 at 5; David Brown, *For 1st Woman with Bionic Arm, a New Life is within Reach,* WASH. POST, Sep. 14, 2006, at A1.

61 ANNAS, *supra* note 59 at 216. See ALBERT R. JONSEN, BIOETHICS BEYOND THE HEADLINES: WHO LIVES? WHO DIES? WHO DECIDES? (2005). *See generally,* George P. Smith, II, *Utility and The Principle of Medical Futility: Safeguarding Autonomy and The Prohibition against Cruel and Unusual Punishment,* 12 J. CONTEMP. HEALTH L. & POL'Y 1 (1996).

62 *See* ARTHUR R. CAPLAN, AM I MY BROTHER'S KEEPER? ch. 17 (1997). See also Michael D. Kirby, *The Human Genome* in THROUGH THE WORLD'S EYE at ch. 4 (2000); George P. Smith, II, *Harnessing The Human Genome through Legislative Constraint,* 5 EUROP. J. HEALTH L. 53 (1998); Geoffrey Carr, *Survey: The Human Genome,* THE ECONOMIST at 54 (Jul. 1, 2000).

63 Anthony Atala, *et al., Tissue-engineered Autologous Bladders for Patients Needing Cystoplasty,* 361 THE LANCET 1241 (Apr. 15–21, 2006). *See generally* George P. Smith, II, *Genetic Enhancement Technologies and the New Society,* 4 MEDICAL LAW INT'L 85 (2000).

64 William Haseltine, *Genomics: The Path Ahead for Science, Medicine and Society,* BROOKINGS REV. 21 (Winter, 2001). *See also* Arthur L. Caplan & David Magnus, *New Life Forms: New Threats, New Possibilities,* 33 HASTINGS CENTER RPT. 7 (2003); Barry Commoner, *Unraveling the DNA Myth,* HARPERS, Feb. 2002 at 39, 47 (cautioning that the potential consequences of transferring a DNA gene between species before the consequences of its release are fully understood is problematic).

65 *Ibid. See* CHET FLEMING, IF WE CAN KEEP A SEVERED HEAD ALIVE ... : DECORPORATION AND U.S. PATENT 4, 666 (1988); George P. Smith, II, *Intimations of Immortality: Clones, Cryons and The Law,* 6 UNIV. NEW SO. WALES L. J. 119 (1983); Robert Bahr, *A New Ethical Question: Head Transplants?* SCIENCE DIG., May 1977, at 76.

66 Matti Häyry, *Utilitarian Approaches to Justice in Health Care,* ch. 4 in MEDICINE AND SOCIAL JUSTICE (Rosamond Rhodes, *et al.,* eds. 2002).

67 *Ibid.*

68 *Ibid.* at 62.

69 *Ibid.* at 54.

70 *Ibid.*

71 *Ibid.*

72 *Ibid.* Utilitarian logic does not discount the life of the individual. Rather, it balances the interest of one individual against the interests of other individuals. GERALD R. WINSLOW, TRIAGE AND JUSTICE 83 (1982) (relying on the ideas of Joseph Fletcher).

It has been argued that explicit quantifiable utilitarian principles, together with decision analysis, should be applied by bioethicists in reaching ethical judgments. *See* JONATHAN BARRON, AGAINST BIOETHICS (2006).

73 BARRY R. FURROW, *ET AL.*, BIOETHICS: HEALTH CARE LAW AND ETHICS, ch. 1 (6th ed. 2008). Non-malfeasance is, among other values, commonly added by some. *Ibid.* at 4. *See* THOMAS L. BEAUCHAMP & JAMES F. CHILDRESS, PRINCIPLES OF BIOMEDICAL ETHICS (6th ed. 2009); Leroy Walters, *Bioethics as Field of Ethics*, in CONTEMPORARY ISSUES IN BIOETHICS, 49, 50–51 (Tom L. Beauchamp & Leroy Walters eds. 1978).

74 *See* James Gustafson, *Basic Ethical Issues in the Bio-Medical Fields*, 53 SOUNDINGS 151 (1970).

75 Walters, *supra* note 73 at 51.

76 *See* GEORGE P. SMITH, II, FINAL CHOICES: AUTONOMY IN HEALTH CARE DECISIONS 89–118 (1989); George P. Smith, II, *Re-Thinking Euthanasia and Death with Dignity: A Transnational Challenge*, 12 ADELAIDE L. REV. 480 (1990).

77 Walters, *supra* note 73 at 50.

78 Richard A. Epstein, *The Utilitarian Foundations of Natural Law*, 12 HARV. J. L. & PUB. POL'Y 713, 727 (1989).

79 James F. Childress, *The Place of Autonomy in Bioethics*, 16 HASTINGS CENTER RPT., 12 at 13 (Jan.–Feb. 1990).

80 *Ibid.* at 13.

81 *Ibid. See* Edmund D. Pellegrino & David C. Thomasma, *The Conflict between Autonomy and Beneficence in Medical Ethics: Proposal for a Resolution*, 3 J. CONTEMP. HEALTH L. & POL'Y 23 1 (1987).

82 *See* Childress, *supra* note 79 at 13.

83 *Ibid.*

84 *Ibid.* at 15, 16. *See also* JAMES F. CHILDRESS, WHO SHOULD DECIDE? PATERN-ALISM IN HEALTH CARE (1982).

85 Walters, *supra* note 73 at 50; *see also* Tom L. Beauchamp, *The Promise of the Beneficence Model for Medical Ethics*, 6 J. CONTEMP. HEALTH L. & POL'Y 145 (1990). *See generally* EDMUND D. PELLIGRINO & DAVID C. THOMASMA, FOR THE PATIENT'S GOOD: THE RESTORATION OF BENEFICENCE IN HEALTH CARE (1988).

86 Walters, *supra* note 73 at 50.

87 Leon R. Kass, *The New Biology: What Price Relieving Man's Estate?* in CONTEMPORARY ISSUES IN BIOETHICS 60, 71 (Tom L. Beauchamp & LeRoy Walters, eds. 1978). *See* Michael Kirby, *Bioethical Decisions and Opportunity Costs*, 2 J. CONTEMP. HEALTH L. & POL'Y 7 (1986).

88 Walters, *supra* note 73, at 50–51.

89 *See generally* JOHN RAWLS, A THEORY ON JUSTICE (1971).

90 Kass, *supra* note 87, at 65; Walters, *supra* note 73.

91 RICHARD A. McCORMICK, THE CRITICAL CALLING 358 (1988).

92 *Ibid.*

93 Kass, *supra* note 87, at 65.

94 Alexander M. Capron, *Autonomy and Community*, FRONTLINES, Dec. 1988, at 7, 10.

95 JULIUS STONE, HUMAN LAW AND HUMAN JUSTICE, Ch. 8 (1968).

96 PETER SINGER, WRITINGS ON AN ETHICAL LIFE 9, 10 (2000).

97 *Ibid.*

98 *Ibid.* at 22.

99 *See generally* JOSEPH FLETCHER, MORAL RESPONSIBILITY: SITUATION ETHICS AT WORK (1967).

100 George P. Smith, II, *Genetic Enhancement Technologies and The New Society*, 4 MED. LAW INT'L 85 (2000).

101 GEORGE P. SMITH, II, GENETIC, ETHICS, AND THE LAW 2 (1981). *See generally* George P. Smith, II, *Manipulating The Genetic Code: Jurisprudential Conundrums*, 64 GEO. L. J. 697 (1976).

102 STEPHEN BREYER, ACTIVE LIBERTY at 15 (2005).

103 *Ibid.* at 16.

104 *See* RICHARD A. POSNER, LAW, PRAGMATISM AND DEMOCRACY 106–7 (2003). *See generally* SUSAN JACOBY, THE AGE OF AMERICAN UNREASON (2008).

105 *See* William J. Broad & James Glanz, *Does Science Matter?* N.Y. TIMES, Nov. 11, 2003, at F1 (commenting on the inability of most Americans to endorse scientific rationality).

106 POSNER, *supra* note 104 at 107. This situation is more understandable when it is realized that half of the U.S. population has an IQ below 100. *Ibid. See also* RICHARD J. HERRNSTEIN & CHARLES MURRAY, THE BELL CURVE: INTELLIGENCE AND CLASS STRUCTURE IN AMERICAN LIFE chs. 1–4, 13–16 (1994).

107 Maureen L. Condic & Samuel Condic, *The Appropriate Limits of Science in the Formation of Public Policy*, 17 J. L. ETHICS & PUB. POL'Y 157, 167 (2003).

108 Owen D. Jones & Timothy H. Goldsmith, *Law and Behavioral Biology*, 105 COLUM. L. REV. 405, 499 (2005).

109 Michael D. Kirby, *Seven Ages of a Lawyer*, 26 MONASH U. L. REV. 1, 10 (2000).

110 *See* George P. Smith, II, *Judicial Decisionmaking in The Age of Biotechnology*, 13 NOTRE DAME J. ETHICS & PUB. POL'Y 34 (1999).

111 ALBERT R. JONSEN, THE NEW MEDICINE AND THE OLD ETHICS at 158 (1990). *See generally* William M. Sage, *The Lawyerization of Medicine*, 26 J. HEALTH POLITICS, POL'Y & L. 1179 (2001).

112 *Ibid. See also* RUSSELL C. COILE, Jr., THE NEW MEDICINE: RESHAPING MEDICAL PRACTICE AND HEALTH CARE MANAGEMENT (1990).

113 JONSEN, *supra* note 111. *See generally* George P. Smith, II, *Uncertainties on the Spiral Staircase: Metaethics and The New Biology*, 41 THE PHAROS MED. J. 10 (1978); George P. Smith, II, *Manipulating The Genetic Code: Jurisprudential Conundrums*, 64 GEO. L. J. 697 (1976).

114 JONSEN, *supra* note 111 at 1.

115 Gilbert Meilaender, *Case Studies: The Anencephalic Newborn as Donor*, 16 HASTINGS CENTER RPT: 23 (1986).

116 Edmund D. Pellegrino & David Thomasma, *The Good of Patients and The Good of Society: Striking a Moral Balance* in PUBLIC HEALTH POLICY AND ETHICS at 17 (M. Boylan, ed. 2004). *See Symposium, Public Health Ethics: Mapping the Terrain*, 30 J. LAW MED. & ETHICS 170 (2004).

117 Pellegrino & Thomasma, *ibid.* at 18.

118 *Ibid.*

119 *Ibid.* at 21. *See generally* GEORGE J. ANNAS, JUDGING MEDICINE (1988).

120 Pellegrino & Thomasma, *supra* note 116 at 27. See ALAN CRIBB, HEALTH AND THE GOOD SOCIETY (2005); George P. Smith, II, *Human Rights and Bioethics: Formulating a Universal Right to Health, Health Care, or Health Protection*, 39 VANDERBILT J. TRANS-NAT'L. L. 1295 (2005).

121 Pellegrino & Thomasma, *supra* note 116 at 34. See RUSSEL HARDIN, TRUST AND TRUSTWORTHINESS (2001); Barr, *Reinventing in the Doctor-Patient Relationship in The Coming Age of Scarcity*, 6 AM. J. BIOETHICS 33 (2006).

122 E. HAAVI MORREIM, BALANCING ACT: THE NEW MEDICAL ETHICS OF MEDICINE'S NEW ECONOMICS 50, 51 (1991). *See* JONATHAN HERRING,

MEDICAL LAW AND ETHICS ch. 9 (2006); Shana Alexander & Andrew Latos, *The Doctor-Patient Relationship in The Post-Managed Care Era*, 6 AM. J. BIOETHICS 29 (2006).

123 BARRY R. SCHALLER, UNDERSTANDING BIOETHICS AND THE LAW 197 (2008).

124 LEON R. KASS, LIFE, LIBERTY AND THE DEFENSE OF DIGNITY: THE CHALLENGE OF BIOETHICS 263 (2002).

125 *Ibid.*

126 Smith, *supra* note 56.

127 *See generally* ALASTAIR V. CAMPBELL, MORAL DILEMMAS IN MEDICINE 1, 13 (1972).

128 Daniel Callahan, *What Obligations Do We Have to Future Generations?* 164 AM. ECCLE-SIASTICAL REV. 265, 275 (1971).

129 *Ibid.* at 279.

130 *Ibid.* at 279–80. *See* Sherry F. Colb, *To Whom Do We Refer When We Speak of Obligations to "Future Generations"? Reproductive Rights And The Intergenerational Community*, 77 GEO. WASH. L. REV. 1582–1619 (2009).

131 VAN R. POTTER, BIOETHICS: BRIDGE TO THE FUTURE 196 (1971).

132 *Ibid.*

133 Albert R. Jonsen, *History and Future of Bioethics* in BIOETHICS IN CULTURAL CON-TEXTS ch. 1 at 19 (Christopher Rehmann-Sutter *et al.*, eds. 2006).

134 *Ibid.*

135 *Ibid.*

136 Daniel Callahan, *The Emergence of Bioethics as a Discipline and Discourse* in BIOETHICS: AN INTRODUCTION TO THE HISTORY, METHODS AND PRACTICE at 21 (2nd ed. 2007).

137 HOWARD BRODY, THE FUTURE OF BIOETHICS 217–25 (2009).

138 *Ibid.* at 105.

139 *Ibid.*

140 *Ibid.*

141 *Ibid.*

142 *Ibid.* at 107.

143 *Ibid.* at 109.

144 H. TRISTRAM ENGELHARDT, Jr., BIOETHICS AND SECULAR HUMANISM: THE SEARCH FOR A COMMON MORALITY 15 (1991).

145 *Ibid.* at 17.

146 *Ibid.*

147 Patrick M. McFadden, *The Balancing Test*, 29 B.C.L. REV. 585, 601 (1988). *See generally* Jared A. Goldstein, *Equitable Balancing in The Age of Statutes*, 96 VA. L. REV. 485 (2010).

148 *See* George P. Smith, II, *Utility and The Principles of Medical Futility: Safeguarding Autonomy and The Prohibition Against Cruel and Unusual Punishment*, 12 J. CONTEMP. HEALTH L. & POL'Y 1 (1996). *See also* Michael D. Kirby, *Bioethical Decisions and Opportunity Costs*, 2 J. CONTEMP. HEALTH L. & POL'Y 7 (1986).

149 Negotiated consent supports "shared decision making"—although not full equality—among patient, family, surrogate health care decision-maker and physician. GEORGE P. SMITH, II, LEGAL AND HEALTHCARE ETHICS FOR THE ELDERLY at 48 (1996). *See also* Harry R. Moody, *From Informed Consent to Negotiated Consent*, 28 THE GERONTOLOGIST 64 (Supp. 1988).

150 SMITH, *supra* note 149 at 75.

151 George P. Smith, II, *The Ethics of Ethics Committees*, 6 J. CONTEMP. HEALTH L. & POL'Y 157 (1990).

152 MICHAEL D. KIRBY, REFORM THE LAW: ESSAYS ON THE RENEWAL OF THE AUSTRALIAN LEGAL SYSTEM 238 (1983).

153 *See ibid.*; Skene, *supra* note 43. *See generally* LEON R. KASS, TOWARD A MORE NATURAL SCIENCE: BIOLOGY AND HUMAN AFFAIRS (1985).
154 *See generally*, George P. Smith, II, Monograph, GENETIC ENHANCEMENT OR EUGENIC IMPROVEMENT: CONTROLLING THE BRAVE NEW WORLD (1999).
155 KIRBY, *supra* note 152 at 238–39. *See also* JANE GREGORY & STEVE MILLER, SCIENCE IN PUBLIC COMMUNICATION, CULTURE AND CREDIBILITY ch. 3 (1998).

3   Law, religion, and medical science

Introduction and overview

Faith, religion, spirituality, and prayer have a current focused outreach and easy parlance in the market places and public squares of the nation.[1] News stories[2] and court cases abound of dramatic challenges to the placement of monuments to the Ten Commandments in public buildings and grounds,[3] the use of God's name in school pledges of allegiance,[4] the teaching of Darwinian or evolutionary science in public education,[5] the role of faith and religion in health care healing,[6] the value of affirmations of religious faith on the political hustings,[7] and—internationally—the efforts of then President Jacques Chirac of France, to ban "overt religious symbols" in public schools in France in an effort to maintain secularism throughout the educational system.[8]

On December 4, 2008, the European Court of Human Rights ruled that France:

> could limit the freedom to manifest a religion, for example by wearing an Islamic head scarf, if the exercise of that freedom clashes with the aim of protecting the rights and freedom of others, public order and public safety; [and especially because] secularism ... presupposes denominational neutrality.[9]

More recently, in January 2009, President Nicolas Sarkozy—in addressing the French Assembly—stated that the burka—the garb some Muslim women wear to cloak their bodies and faces—was "an unacceptable symbol of enslavement" and should be forbidden through appropriate legislation.[10]

The impact that these occurrences have on the fiber of contemporary society is significant, and—at the same time—truly incalculable. It is made more problematic because of a failure of the system to agree, in the first instance, on a unified definition of religion.[11] This situation parallels that state which also exists in international law.[12] Because of this present vacuum, it has been suggested that in lieu of defining religion, it would be more practicable to consider it as a belief, identity, or way of life.[13] Regrettably, the law—from a national context or perspective—has not risen to the challenge and structured an unerring definition. Rather, the United States Supreme Court has chosen to define religion in United States v. Seeger by stating that:

> [T]he test of belief "in a relation to a Supreme Being" ... is whether a given belief that is sincere and meaningful occupies a place in the life of its possessor parallel to that filled by the orthodox belief in God. ...[14]

In August 2001, the then Chief Justice of the Supreme Court of Alabama, Roy Moore, installed a two and a half ton monument to the Ten Commandments as the centerpiece of the rotunda in the Alabama State Building—intending, as such, to remind the citizens of the state of his personal belief in the sovereignty of the Judeo-Christian God over both the state and the church. The Federal District Court ordered, subsequently, the removal of the monument finding its placement to be in violation of the Establishment Clause of the 1st Amendment to the Constitution.[15] On appeal, the Eleventh Circuit affirmed[16] and the United States Supreme Court refused to review the case.[17] While the judicial disposition of this case is now settled,[18] the issues of the extent to which the acknowledgment and expression of religious faith, within the ambit of state action, and is consistent with the Establishment Clause of the Constitution, remains a highly vexatious matter.[19]

An interesting parallel case concerning the placement in 1961 by the Fraternal Order of Eagles of a six-foot high granite monument etched with the Ten Commandments on the Texas state capitol grounds was held to be a proper display and not violation of the constitutional separation of church and state. In November 2003, the U.S. Court of Appeals for the Fifth Circuit ruled that the Texas state legislature—in accepting the monument—sought to honor the Eagles' significant efforts at successfully reducing juvenile delinquency.[20] In addition to the display, textually, of the commandments, the monument depicts two tablets with Hebrew text, an American flag being grasped by an eagle, two diminutive Stars of David, an eye inside a pyramid and a symbol representing Christ. Displayed prominently, as well, is an inscription acknowledging that the monument was donated by the Eagles. It is placed on land on the state capitol grounds designated a National Historic Landmark together with 16 other monuments honoring other Texans and historical events.

Both the Federal District Court[21] and the Federal Court of Appeals,[22] ruled that the monument is not to be seen as a personal code of conduct for youths nor construed as promotive of a sectarian religious code and, thus neither a promotion nor endorsement by the State of any religion in contravention of the First Amendment's establishment clause. Indeed, its primary effect is but to commemorate "people, ideals and events that compose Texan identity."[23] The Appeals Court acknowledged, further, that had the monument been installed more recently, it might well have raised a stronger inference of religious purpose.[24] But, since it has been installed initially in 1961, this "adds force to the contention that the legislature had a secular purpose" when approving its placement.[25]

Defining the appropriate role of religion in town square and the nation's public buildings has, of late, however, focused on the extent to which religious monuments may be placed appropriately on public land.[26] This has become a new, energized national issue because of the pervasive concern that distinctive American moral values that underpinned the founding of the Nation are eroding and, further, that society is becoming Godless.[27] In addition to the Alabama[28] and Texas[29] cases, it has been reported that some two dozen disputes over the placement of monuments to the Ten Commandments or similar displays have—since 2000—been taken to the courts for settlement.[30]

Early in 1980, the United States Supreme Court recognized the Ten Commandments as a "sacred text in Jewish and Christian faiths" for which "no legislative recitation of a supposed secular purpose can blind us to that fact."[31] It did not hold, however, that not all government uses of the Commandments are taken as impermissible.[32] Subsequently, in 1988, the Court—while acknowledging the subtle ways in which the values of the Establishment Clause were "not susceptible to a single verbal formulation"[33]—reaffirmed its decision in Everson v. Board of Education in 1947[34] which structures the framework for analyzing issues under the Establishment Clause:

> The 'establishment of religion' clause of the First Amendment means at least this: Neither a state nor the Federal Government can set up a church. Neither can pass laws which aid one religion, aid all religions, or prefer one religion over another. Neither can force nor influence a person to go to or remain away from church against his will or force him to profess a belief or disbelief in any religion. No person can be punished for entertaining or professing religious beliefs or disbeliefs, for church attendance or non-attendance. No tax in any amount, large or small, can be levied to support any religious activities or institutions, whatever they may be called, or whatever form they may adopt to teach or practice religion. Neither a state nor the Federal Government can, openly or secretly, participate in the affairs of any religious organizations or groups and vice versa.[35]

Religious liberty and equality are, thus, guaranteed to "the infidel, the atheist, or the adherent of a non-Christian faith such as Islam or Judaism."[36]

On February 25, 2009, the U.S. Supreme Court held—in unanimous opinion—that a public park in Pleasant Grove City, Utah, which contained 15 permanent displays, including a monument honoring the September 11th terrorist attack in New York City as well as a Ten Commandments monument (donated by the Fraternal Order of Eagles), was not required to display a stone monument of the Summum Church which would have entailed "the Seven Aphorisms of Summum" similar in size (and nature) to the Ten Commandments Monument.[37] The Court reasoned that city's original decision not to accept this monument was not subject to the Free Speech Clause of the Constitution—this, because the decision of the municipality to accept certain privately donated monuments—while rejecting the Summum Church's monument—was best viewed as a form of government speech. Further, since the Pleasant Grove park was a traditional public forum for speeches and other transitory expressive acts, displays of permanent monuments in a public park were not to be considered forms of expression but rather a form of "government speech" which entitled the government to say what it wished.[38]

The purpose of this Chapter is to explore the conjunctive and disjunctive influences that religion has in one specific field of current socio-political debate: namely, biomedical technology and ethical decision-making.[39] More specifically, the role of religion as an equal—or, as the case may prove to be— limited partner with law and medical science in assessing the dimensions and patterns of application of the new startling biotechnologies will be evaluated. Central to this inquiry will be a consideration of the legitimacy of, in the first instance, evolutionary science and its acceptance in public education[40]—for, it is this science from which the whole study of genetics and eugenics arise and which in turn direct and validate the very framework for the new biomedicine.[41]

From this analysis it will be seen that far from being antagonistic to law and medicine, religion and religious principles stabilize the field of biomedicine and serve, additionally, as vectors of force in shaping both ethical and moral constructs for decision-making.[42] In turn, each of these three disciplines complements and strengthens what should be the ultimate goal of the state, namely: to secure the happiness, spiritual tranquility, and well-being of its citizens. This purpose is, in turn, advanced—and thus enhanced—by safe-guarding the genetic well-being and general health of its citizens.[43] Working toward this goal and meeting it eventually will have the effect of minimizing human suffering and maximizing the social good that derives from rational and humane actions taken to displace man's genetic weaknesses from the line of inheritance.[44]

Shaping a constructive dialogue

A primary goal for many religious thinkers has been to develop a process for determining how to lead science and technology toward a level of awareness and appreciation of human and environmental values.[45] Given the growing trend of placing and then testing scientific development within a framework of moral understanding and normative values, the choice is "having theologians and religious ethicists contribute a theological perspective or having scientists attempt to be moral philosophers."[46]

The foundational texts of most religious communities, as well as scripture itself, do not address the complex issues of biotechnology and molecular biology. While the religious texts do establish broad ethical norms for purposeful living, the task becomes one of adapting a mechanism for them to apply to the biomedical issues of contemporary society; in other words, how to re-shape and, thus, modernize them into a constructive dialogue with science—one which escapes the confines of abstract applications and offers specific guidance and modern ethical norms for resolving concrete biomedical conflicts.[47]

Whether it is practical to pursue the development of a common framework for morality and ethical analysis within the context of the New Biology is problematic.[48] Advocates of post-modernism argue that a "Christian rather than denominational approach to bioethics" is to be preferred. Whatever course is followed, the challenge remains the same: namely, how to show—and thereby attempt to restate—the relevance of these religious principles to a skeptical secular society.[49]

In an effort to address the basic theological and ethical issues associated with the new medico-science technologies and, thus, engage the issue, much study has been undertaken over the years by various ecumenical and denominational bodies beginning in 1973 with the efforts of The World Council of Churches to study the ethical significance of science and technology.[50] Through the succeeding years, various other studies were commissioned by various organizations such as the World Conference on Faith and Science and The Future. Interestingly, their findings were never granted any official standing but merely accepted as the views of each study panel.[51] The Roman Catholic Church did—however—in 1987, begin to both clarify and shape the official dialogue for its members through the issuance of its "Instruction on Respect for Human Life in Its Origin and on the Dignity of Life."[52]

All too often, a recitation of traditional beliefs is set forth without an interpretation of their implications for scientific applications.[53] While of marginal universal significance, these faith-based denominational efforts nonetheless provide a rich opportunity for education and interaction as well as for the development of a broader-based perspective on the religious, moral, and ethical ramifications of the New Biology.[54] Only time will tell whether these "seedlings" will take root from these critical engagements and provide normative values for biomedical decision-making.

As the astonishing positive successes of genetic research and engineering and of genetic medicine continue to be charted with clarity, the role of moral theology—grounded in various faith traditions—should be used to frame guidelines for determining if and when various specific applications of these technologies, within an appropriate ethical context, may be utilized. Richard McCormick suggested the controlling consideration should be, "Will this or that intervention (or omission, exception, policy, law) promote or undermine" the integrity of the human person.[55]

The central concern of Fr. Richard A. McCormick is the integrity of personhood. For him, personhood begins at conception and, accordingly, would be violated by human stem cell experimentation, cloning, and generally, *in vitro* fertilization.[56] In this regard, McCormick is micro—as opposed to macro—in his viewpoint. Long-range or societal benefits from scientific advances of this nature and other genetic research are of secondary concern.

Drawing upon a contemporary interpretation of *tikkun olam*—or the mandate to participate in an active partnership in the repair and perfection of the world—the Jewish community supports scientific discoveries and human applications of genetic research.[57] And, interestingly for Presbyterians, "prophetic inquiry" directs that they endeavor to utilize modern technology and science in affirming the dynamic character of the creation through the teachings and interpretations of the biblical tradition.[58]

Law and policy-making as well as administrative and judicial decision-making should not—indeed, cannot—favor one denominational theology over another. Rather, balanced decisions must be made incorporating, when appropriate, moral, ethical (*e.g.*, religious) values with scientific objectives for individual growth and societal advancement. When cases or issues for consideration arise, they are just that: individual and fact sensitive. Yet, nevertheless, their evaluation can be undertaken by a template shaped by a balancing of costs versus benefit: use or non-use—all designed to achieve a positive, just good.

No substantive resolutions are needed. The role for the various church theologies should be, rather, "interrogative."[59] For any dialogue between science and religion to be effective, "fallibilism" must then be an acknowledged given. In other words, both parties need to accept the proposition that they may not only be incorrect in their understandings of each other, but "in their inferences about the implications of their positions, in their development of their own arguments and even in some basic claims they have never questioned."[60]

Humanism

Secular humanism—or, the attempt to shape culture and public policy in terms of what non-religious values and attitudes humans share among themselves—is underlying modern approaches to bioethics and health care decision-making.[61] While not appearing as an "enemy to the mildly religious," secular humanism seeks a rational, as opposed to spiritual, approach to analysis and ultimate decision.[62] Rationally justified viewpoints, not grounded in or tied to intuitions, religious premises, or moral assumptions is the ideal.[63] A culture that is secularized and based on secular humanism, then, is not so much promotive of atheism or agnosticism as it is one where "people ideologically uncommitted or religious issues ... become almost entirely alienated from the modes of thought and definitions of reality which have made religiosity explicable and relevant in the past."[64]

No doubt, one of the greatest challenges that organized religions face today is to sustain a relevance or vitality to the all-pervasive growth of humanism. In order to meet this challenge, then, religions must seek to demonstrate that the tenets of their creeds and specific programs of social action are complementary—rather than antithetical—to the foundational values of a contemporary and humanistic society. Just as the larger community champions social justice and love of neighbor—humanistic values to be sure—so too do religions. Indeed, a persuasive argument could be made that there is an inextricable link between the advancement of humanistic "people centered" values and the acceptance of the principles of love and justice which shape and direct codes of morality, ethical standards, and religious creeds. Rather than preach a gospel of inflexibility, religion must show that the human propensity for morality—and, by extension, truth and love—is conferred by God (or, as the case may be, is God).[65] Humanism and religion should not be viewed as estranged but as complementary forces which assist man's earthly pilgrimage for justice, truth, and agape.

Love and justice

While there are differences between a legal order, system of morality, and set of religious beliefs, it does not follow that contemporary legal order does not contain elements of moral religious beliefs.[66] All laws are norms set within a hierarchy whose foundation is to be found in love; for it is within the primary form of love that justice is found.[67] Indeed, Augustine saw the ethics of love as the essence of justice.[68] For him, without the ethics of love, there could be no true orderliness—this, because nature would be disturbed by man's willfulness.[69] "Without love there could be no justice for there would be lacking a cogent motive, and pattern, for men to render to other men their due. ... without love as a gift of God's grace man could not love the proper things properly."[70] In addition to including rules and concepts, law is—at its most basic level—but a set of relationships among people.[71] Despite the obvious tensions or discontinuities between law and religion, one cannot truly flourish without the other. Without religion, law degenerates into little more than a mechanical legalism; and religion without law loses its social effectiveness.[72]

There are four elements shared by law and religion: ritual, tradition, authority, and universality.[73] Within every religion is found two legal elements— one which relates to the social processes of the particular community sharing a faith and the other "to the social processes of the larger community of which the religious community is a part."[74] Indeed, it has been suggested that the two major dimensions of man's social life may be seen as law and religion even though, as such, they are dialectically interdependent vectors of force.[75]

In the final analysis, perhaps it is best to see law as a way in which both justice and love are translated into complex social situations within various communities.[76] Since love is situational, it has been argued persuasively that it—rather than binding rules and a priori principles—should direct moral responses (micro and macro) at all levels of decision-making in issues of the New Biology.[77] Accordingly, the standard of humane treatment in end-of-life cases should be shaped and guided by love just as scientific decisions regarding the suitability of investigation. In one case, the construct is personal and in the other it is communitarian.[78]

America's emerging constitutional philosophy

Ever since America was founded, the national symbol has been an eagle supported in its flights and its destiny by two powerful wings: plain reason or common sense and humble faith.[79] The founding generation drew its common sense from not only the traditional wisdom of ancient philosophers and moralists, but from the scriptures[80]; for, it was evidence to them that a faith in the God of Abraham, Isaac, and Jacob was an ideal magnification of human reason.[81] Indeed, for the founders, of all philosophies and religions, Judaism and Christianity served as the best unified foundation for republican institutions because they encouraged virtue and sharpened a zest for liberty.[82]

From the very beginning of the Nation, the "dominant metaphor for church-state relations was that public officials must act as 'nursing fathers' to the religious and moral habits of the people ... "[83] Put simply, as a religious people, the majority of early Americans believed wholeheartedly that they owed their liberty to their creator.[84]

In the United States Constitution, the action to separate church from state was driven significantly by the same recognition that religion concerns itself with differing senses or levels of reality than those of the political world.[85] Accordingly, two clauses in the First Amendment enunciate with clarity the boundaries of church and state—the Establishment Clause forbids the government from making any "law respecting the establishment of religion," and the Free Exercise of Religion Clause prohibits the government from restricting religious belief or practice.[86] While these two clauses, especially the second one, are taken in contemporary society as affirming rights of individual conscience together with the appropriateness of religious pluralism, there is strong historical evidence suggesting however that the framers were more interested in recognizing the establishment of religious duties free from state interference.[87]

One of two driving and very practical forces behind the crafting of the religion clauses in the First Amendment was an evangelical conviction that religion—and not just individual conscience—was to control a limited government that in turn must be subordinate to a sovereign God. A second fundamental conviction undergirding the separation of church and state was that the state should, quite simply, be secular and not religious. It was this unyielding view that was in direct opposition to the Republican belief that the state should support religion in order to promote public morality. It was mainly on the arguments that, for the sake of religious integrity, religion should be insulated from state support, that the secular view of the state triumphed in the Establishment Clause.[88]

Religion's role

The role of religion in a constitutional democracy is, surely, at the apex of current legal and social debate.[89] Since questions about religion involve moral issues, they are presented regularly both to the courts and to the legislatures. And, furthermore, since these two bodies are not "philosophically reflective enough to deal with moral issues which are integral to debates on religious issues,"[90] difficulties in meaning, interpretation, and application are a given. Under these circumstances, it could be viewed as improper to demand of the state that it be subject always to "the higher law of God."[91] Nevertheless, it has been suggested that since the "bedrock of moral order is religion," politics and morality can only be viewed as inseparable.[92] Interestingly, today political activists now include religious believers who seek not only to shape public policy but often to seize state power.[93]

If the proposition is advanced that only religion provides morality with a foundation,[94] then it follows that religion may be taken as an "independent moral force" in American society.[95] Yet, the extent of its independence remains a complex and volatile issue. While some religions advance civic responsibility as a noble virtue and set high levels of moral performance in daily life, others stress a form of political withdrawal and personal passivity and, still others, are obsessive and fanatical.[96]

Historically, however, religion is seen as an associative force that serves to strengthen moral solidarity as well as political attachment.[97] This is seen dramatically in the work of various communities of faith where strong welfare organizations are developed which, in turn, draw upon high levels of popular participation in promoting multiple forms of everyday assistance.[98]

Political underpinnings

Religions, and the moral theologies attendant to them, have a decidedly political character.[99] Indeed, Judaism, Christianity, and Islam are regarded, in the main, as political. While being prophetic, they have sought nevertheless, and continue to seek, to challenge the socio-political status quo and attack the economic inequalities of society as well as endeavor to protect the sick and unhealthy and be a voice for the abused and other marginalized interest groups.[100]

When ecumenical political dialogue is engaged, it is a significant and positive undertaking because it provides a forum where citizens and members of faith communities can seek consensus or more often to merely diminish dissension or simply clarify issues of common disagreement, "but always to cultivate the bonds of political community, by reaffirming their ties to one another, in particular their shared commitment to certain authoritative politico-moral premises."[101]

Often defined as a Christian nation, America still advocates a discursive type of religious pluralism.[102] Allowing, indeed tolerating, an open debate on religion itself becomes the short run or immediate goal. When, however, religion does not inform the debate, but rather undergirds it, the central concern is the extent to which "belief or nonbelief in a God makes the difference in one's normative stance."[103]

A distinct feature of modernity is the notion that law is totally secular, without a founding God and, thus, independent of any divine command other than the force of human reason[104] which is, of necessity, directed toward the establishment of intelligible order.[105] A contrary view suggests, "everyone must invoke some God or other because ... everyone has to speak normatively"—for participation in any public activity calls for an acknowledgment of the need for law.[106]

No doubt, the central question to be posited today is: in a constitutional democracy defining itself as a secular polity, can religion ever be represented as the basis of the rule of law?[107] Can the law's secular legitimacy be derived from religious principles, values, moral teachings or practices apart from validating a specific historical religion?[108] Finally, does moral adherence to a body of law require belief in a God or not?[109] Throughout most of recorded human history, there has always been a connection between God and the law.[110] For example, the all inclusive name the Bible uses for "God" is elohim which means "authority"—first, divine and second, human.[111]

Whatever the template for contemporary analysis is tied to—a convenantal theology of the Bible, Platonic natural law, Hobbesian natural law or a philosophically informed morality seen in the English Common Law—in America, "the majority of the citizens believe themselves obligated by a prior, divine morality, despite the fact that most of them are unable to argue for it theoretically."[112] It is for the philosophers and moral theologians to make these arguments.[113]

Evolution and Christian thought

While Charles Darwin's Origin of Species first appeared in 1859 and advanced a theory of organic evolution, arguing—as such—current living species evolved from pre-existing species, more than a century earlier a French naturalist, Chevalier de Lamarck, advanced a theory of progressive evolutionary development derived from "vital forces within living things and the inheritance of acquired characteristics."[114] Rather than accept Lamarck's theory that the process of natural selection was driven by a benign process of individual adaption, Darwin postulated a "survival of the fittest" process in evolutionary development. Indeed, the central feature of Darwinism became the concept of natural selection.[115]

For the Christian world at that time, the ultimate challenge of Darwinism to it was stated thusly: "Beneficial variation was random and natural selection cruel. If nature reflected the character of its creator, then the God of a Darwinian world acted randomly and cruelly."[116] The Darwinian theory of a mindless process of natural selection suggests a universe not only blind to life and humanity but totally indifferent to its operation.[117] Yet, within this theory was found the elements of what is termed "evolution theodicy." This, in turn, gave rise to a movement that advocated the acceptance of God's aloofness or separation from natural evil and thus stood outside a strictly scientific framework of analysis but instead was wed to metaphysical presuppositions about the nature of God.[118]

Interestingly, while philosophy and science have always been influenced by theology—and especially so with evolutionary theory—evolutionists deny steadfastly the influence.[119] Yet, as observed, a central metaphysical presupposition infuses the whole of the technical ordering of evolutionary science: namely, that evolution's success is tied to a doctrine of God. In other words,

"It is a theological view that preceded evolution historically and became the metaphysical landscape on which the theory was constructed."[120] Today, one of the leading authorities in the field has suggested that the process of evolution should be seen within a historical context which, in turn, serves as an enhanced guide to understanding nature.[121]

It is thought that evolutionary information comes from two central sources: the science of genetics and from contemporary culture.[122] From this comes the view that religion is to be seen "as an information system within culture that is part of the effort of nature to understand itself and conduct itself in freedom."[123]

The interrelatedness of all creation is shown time and again by scientific work in genetics. Indeed, the new DNA discoveries restate with convincing clarity the shared evolutionary heritage of all living things[124] and the constant lifetime interaction between genes and the environment.[125] Interacting with the biological sciences as a co-efficient, or at least a vector of force, in influencing the total development of the individual is the environment—both the cultural and the physical. Because of the fact that, as cultural beings, individuals shape the contexts in which social interactions occur, they exhibit an inherent capacity for ethical behavior and spiritual development.[126] Indeed, the mystery of the human spirit and the capacity for self-transcendence will never be eliminated by the New Biology.[127]

While human nature is illuminated by genetic science, it is not explained totally. The complexity, transcendence, and mystery of the human person remains and thus serves as a reference point of intersection between culture and theology as well as the natural sciences.[128] A positive force in contemporary society is to be seen in the new and ongoing dialogue between genetics, molecular biology, and the theology of human nature which seeks to build upon these very points.[129] When a distinctly religious voice in, for example, medical ethics becomes passive or is lost, this in turn encourages a form of moral philosophy for the market place and thus places law as the dominant source of morality.[130] It can only be hoped that from this intercultural discourse will come new frameworks for principled decision-making which, in turn, promote reasoned and balanced ethical responses to personal and societal challenges of this age of the New Biology.[131]

Papal clarifications and caveats

On October 23, 1996, in an address by John Paul II to the Pontifical Academy of Science, the Holy Father suggested science and religion are compatible. "Science can purify religion from error and superstition, religion can purify science from idolatry and false absolutes. Each can draw the other into a wider world, a world in which both can flourish."[132] As to the specific issue of the theory of evolution, the Pope acknowledged that it is "more than just a hypothesis."[133] While not mentioning Charles Darwin by name, the statement is seen nonetheless as advancing the idea that religious faith and the teaching of evolution can co-exist easily.[134] Indeed, while observing that there are a number of different theories of evolution, the Holy Father went on to observe that, "It is possible to accept evolution as a theory while affirming that the spiritual and philosophical elements must remain outside the competence of science."[135] At least for Roman Catholic theology, what had been—up to this time—the most significant point of argument and division between the genetic revolution and theology as a body of thought,[136] is no longer an issue.

Today, a consensus has been reached not only among scientists—and biblical scholars, but mainstream religions and educators as well, that the theory of evolution is a verifiable account of the origins of life.[137] With the Pope's acceptance of evolution as a theory, comes the realization that, as such, "Science is not a threat to faith."[138] Accordingly, what John Paul II has done, hence, is to chart a middle position between the creationists and evolutionists which, in turn, fosters not only dialogue but an openness to truth.[139]

Benedict XVI, John Paul's successor, has—however—expressed his unhappiness with evolutionary science which seeks, he observes, to discount "creative reason ... that has created everything without a form of supernatural guidance."[140] While both Benedict and the present 14th Dalai Lama believe that a religious text—whether the Bible or the Diamond Sutra—should not be given a strictly literal reading, they share with evangelicals an aversion to the notion that life merged blindly without supernatural guidance.[141]

Some have been quick to suggest intelligent design complements and fortifies Benedict's attack—for, the hand of intelligent design sounds suspiciously as though it is a euphemism for God.[142] Others note that there has been no ringing endorsement by His Holiness—rather, it is but a papal position that science should not be used to banish God.[143] Indeed, "many church experts believe Pope Benedict has fewer problems with the science of evolution than with its use to wipe God more clearly from a secular world!"[144] In an outdoor Mass celebrated in Munich, Germany, September 2006, the Pope urged science and reason should not make us "deaf" to God.[145]

Both in previous writings as the then-Cardinal Ratzinger and subsequent remarks as the Holy Father, Pope Benedict has sought to fortify his attack on scientism or, in other words, the failure of science to acknowledge that it does not have the answer to everything in life.[146] In 2004, in his voice as Cardinal, Pope Benedict endorsed the scientific view that the earth is roughly 4 billion years old and that species changed through evolution.[147] And, in August 2006, Cardinal Christopher Schonborn, Archbishop of Vienna, observed that "the possibility that the creator used evolution as a tool is completely acceptable for the Catholic faith."[148] Yet, in 2005, Cardinal Schonborn expressed his doubts that Darwinism and Catholicism were compatible.[149]

Again, in 2003, in Truth and Tolerance, Joseph Cardinal Ratzinger observed that when claims are made that the doctrine of evolution is the sole indicator of systematic knowledge of rationality, both sides in the debate need to demonstrate a "willingness to listen" and approach this claim "objectively."[150]

"The dream of the absolute autonomy of reason and of its self-sufficiency" is exactly that, said Cardinal Ratzinger: nothing but a dream. To be informed and enlightened, "human reason needs a hint from the great tradition of mankind."[151]

The positions on evolution taken by His Holiness Pope John Paul II and His Holiness Pope Benedict XVI can be seen as having their genesis in Pope Pius XII's encyclical, *Humani Generis*, issued in 1950.[152] For, in this encyclical, His Holiness affirmed the need of theologians and those working on the exegesis of the Scriptures, to be well informed regarding the results of the latest scientific research.[153] The Pope affirmed, further, that there is no conflict between evolution or "evolutionism" and the doctrine of faith regarding man and his vocation; and that, as such, "evolutionism" was a serious hypothesis which should be investigated and studied together with the opposite hypothesis.[154]

While care must be taken not to stifle the spirit of scientific investigation, the goal for the Christian and for religions in general remains the same: to work toward the minimization of suffering and to advance the collective good thereby assuring that the search for the infinite will be undertaken within a framework of enlightened reason which maintains the dignity of man, human values, and compassion. It is well to remember that even though science promises an unpredictable future, futures are inevitably unpredictable.[155]

Writing as Joseph Cardinal Ratzinger, His Holiness Pope Benedict XVI has cautioned wisely that in itself, "change is not good." The degree to which "it is good or bad depends on its particular content and how it relates to other things."[156] To think "that the main task in the struggle for freedom" is to change the world is but "a myth."[157] The then-Cardinal concludes by cautioning that the central task confronting society is "to struggle for the relatively best possible framework of human coexistence in our present day and, in doing so, to preserve anything good that has already been achieved, to overcome anything bad that exists at the time, and to guard against the outbreak of destructive forces."[158]

Karl Rahner observes that the Christian must rejoice "if the Church, within the framework of divine law, changes its human law and adapts to a new situation."[159] He rejoices further when he sees the Church re-thinking the Gospels and not simply repeating monotonously the old, though true and valid formulas, set out in them.[160] Indeed, Rahner urges the Christian to "strive to feel the impact of new questions and to understand the mentality of the human beings who raise these questions out of the distress of their own personal lives. He is not entitled to think everything is perfectly clear already or something is false by the very fact it is new."[161]

Darwinism and intelligent design

In 1991, Phillip E. Johnson constructed the philosophical underpinnings of a contemporary intelligent-design movement which, in essence, asserts the theory of Darwinian evolution is based on inaccurate assumptions and weak evidence.[162] More specifically, the small and vocal number of biologists, chemists, philosophers, and mathematicians who constitute the membership of the movement, argue that because of the refusal of mainstream science to consider anything but natural explanations for things, it is therefore biased subjectively against proofs of supernatural intervention in the evolutionary process. Thus, the efficacy of the evidence for evolution through natural processes is called in question.[163]

Proponents of the theory of intelligent design believe, simply, that an intelligent agent (but not necessarily using the word, God) has guided the history of the earth.[164] Criticized as not being a science, the president of The National Academy of Science has termed intelligent design as nothing more than a "way of restating creationism in a different formulation."[165]

For the vast majority of the scientific community, evolution began billions of years ago and was both unsupervised and impersonal. Yet, others find significant gaps in the scientific record that leave evolution more a theory than a documented fact. Accordingly, they put forth the notion that the evolution of the species took place over time by the grand design of a transcendent personal creator. These Creationists also contend that the true age of the earth should, as inferred from the Bible, be computed in thousands of years—not billions.[166]

With the publication in 1965 of The Genesis Flood, the term, "creation science," was introduced into the American vocabulary.[167] Soon thereafter, a whole movement took shape.[168] Followers of the creation science movement, termed creationists, adopt the Biblical narrative of the book of Genesis as their theory of origin,[169] accepting as such the creation of the world by a personal God.[170] For the creationists, only two possible constructs can be employed to resolve the question of the origin of life and of the universe: theistic and atheistic. In other words, God is acknowledged as the creator of history or life and seen as a evolutionary dynamic.[171]

The book of Genesis has not been accepted in the public school classrooms of the Nation as a teaching source nor has creation science succeeded in re-shaping mainstream science. Indeed, led by the National Academy of Science, mainstream scientific organizations have rejected totally the creationist approach.[172]

Central to the claims of the legitimacy of creationism is an apparent conundrum: normally, if creationists accept the Bible as true and infallible, why is it regarded as important to link science with it? The answer given is that since creationism does not qualify as a science in that it does not afford a set of hypotheses capable of being tested, a higher level of legitimacy is sought for it by placing science at its heart or as its modus operandi.[173] "Modern Americans cling to scientific rhetoric no matter what the issue."[174] Indeed, "scientific sanctification" validates many conservative beliefs by attributing scientific credibility to their biblical interpretations.[175] What is seen in reality, then, is that by shifting attention from issues of faith and value to those of scientific interpretation, the scientific creationists have "reduced the Bible to the level of a science [text]."[176]

Since mainstream Christians and Jews do not see the Bible and evolutionary theory as inconsistent, modern creation science is not a contemporary issue of great moment.[177] Rather, they understand that science, itself, can neither tackle and resolve the moral issues of the day nor serve as a template for living life to the fullest. Put simply, "whether rejected or accepted, evolution cannot speak to the vital issue of right and wrong."[178]

Scopes and its aftermath

When in 1925 in Dayton, Tennessee, a high school science teacher, John T. Scopes, taught a class on evolutionary theory, a national debate was thereby triggered over the origins of humans which—in turn—forced the Nation to confront not only its fears and suspicions of scientific knowledge, but its application and uses as well.[179] In essence, the "Scopes Monkey Trial" pitted religion, and a fundamentalist view of divine creation (e.g., creationism) against scientific thought on evolution. It became a harbinger of the utilization of evolutionary biology that did not begin however until after World War II.[180] William Jennings Bryan represented the fundamentalist cause and argued for a strict, literalist approach to interpreting the Bible. Clarence Darrow, as opposing counsel, was more interested in promoting secularism than individual freedom.[181] Bryan worried that the public school teaching of Darwinism—with its emphasis on the argument that humans were products of a random, survival-of-the-fittest evolutionary process, would fuel "militarism, imperialism [and] the exploitation of labor eugenics."[182]

In 1925, the Tennessee Legislature became the first state in the Nation to enact a law against the teaching of evolution in the public schools. Not only was Darwinism banned, but all teaching concerned with human evolution as well and criminal sanctions were imposed for violations. Originally initiated by the ACLU as a means of invalidating the state's anti-evolution statute as a violation of the First Amendment, Bryan and Darrow elevated their legal arguments to issues of high drama and emotion: religion and morality. In the end, Scopes lost and was found guilty by a jury and the court imposed a fine of $100.00. On appeal, the Supreme Court of Tennessee went back to the original legal issue—that is, whether the anti-evolution statute was inconsistent with the state constitution's religion clause which forbade preferences being given, by law, "to any religious establishment or mode of worship." With but one dissent, the court held that the challenged legislation was constitutional. Yet, on a technicality, Scope's conviction was reversed. Since, under the Tennessee Constitution, any fine greater than $50.00 could be assessed only by a jury, it was held that the trial judge had no jurisdiction to impose the $100.00 fine.[183] The historians of the 1950s and the commentators of the 1930s saw the Scope trial at two levels: both groups agreed that it was a defeat for fundamentalism, while the commentators of that period during which the trial occurred saw it as a "media spectacular."[184]

In the end, then, perhaps the Scopes trial can be viewed properly as "a step in the triumph of reason over revelation and science over superstition."[185] Stated otherwise, the enduring importance of Scopes is that it embodied the quintessential "American struggle between individual liberty and majoritarian democracy, and cast it in the timeless debate over science and religion."[186] The Scopes controversy continues to persist even today.[187] It is recast now as creation science (as opposed to creationism) versus evolution.[188]

The continuing debate: strategizing against evolution

It was not until 1968, and the case of Epperson v. Arkansas,[189] that the federal constitutionality of prohibiting the teaching of evolution in public schools was decided by the United States Supreme Court. Here, again, the ACLU joined in seeking a declaratory judgment against a 40-year-old anti-evolution statute which had never been used. With but one dissent, the Court held that the statute was void because it sought to establish a religion and thus violated the Establishment Clause.[190] "Religious purpose alone became the Court's basis for striking the law."[191] Stated simply, it was held that there could be no state prohibition against teaching a scientific theory or doctrine for reasons that would counter the fundamental principles of the First Amendment.

In 1987, in the case of Edwards v. Aguillard, the United States Supreme Court held that a creationism law in Louisiana forbidding the teaching of the theory of evolution in public elementary and secondary schools, unless accompanied by instruction in the theory of creation science, was invalid facially as violative of the Establishment Clause of the 1st Amendment.[192] The purpose of the challenged legislation was to discredit evolution by counterbalancing its teachings at every turn with the teaching of creationism—either of which would promote the beliefs of certain religious groups.[193]

With the ultimate demise of the anti-evolution statutes through Epperson, opponents of the theory of evolution have two, possibly three, strategies in their present battle to eviscerate or bury the theory. First-line attacks have centered on supporting attempts to exclude evolution from being taught in the classrooms altogether—asserting as such that the teaching of evolutionary theory promotes the religion of secular humanism.[194] Accordingly, its inclusion in public school science curricula violates the Establishment Clause of the U.S. Constitution. Courts have rejected this view generally—holding that the theory of evolution is scientific and, thus, not to be taken as a religious belief.[195]

The second strategy has focused on efforts to either compel the teaching of creationism as another valid scientific theory on the origins of life or, alternatively, to discredit the validity as well as the importance of the theory of evolution in the sciences. This strategy has been advanced by efforts to legislate in some states Balanced Treatment Acts designed to require public schools to give balanced treatment to creation science with evolution science.[196] This approach has also not been successful.[197] Interestingly, in June 2008, the

Governor of Louisiana signed into law the Louisiana Science Education Act which allowed the state the dubious honor of being the first state to pass an anti-evolution academic freedom law.[198] Designed to "promote students' critical thinking skills and open discussion of scientific theories" in relation to the teaching of science in public elementary and secondary schools on such topics as "evolution, the origins of life, global warming and human cloning," the law allows the use of supplemental texts to achieve this goal.[199]

Another clever approach—and no doubt the third strategy—to advancing the creation science movement, was seen in 1999, with the actions of the Kansas State School Board in adopting a new statewide science curriculum which wipes out virtually all mention of evolution and related concepts such as natural selection, common ancestors, and the origins of the universe.[200] While the science standards neither prohibited the teaching of creationism, they discouraged clearly the teaching of evolution. Even though these standards were but guidelines, thus allowing each school board within the state the freedom to decide whether to continue to teach evolution, the State School Board had the final authority to determine the content of standardized tests. Accordingly, it was decided—with the 2000–2001 school year, that both the 7th and 10th grade state science examinations would not contain questions regarding the origin of life, the earth, and the universe. The practical effect of this decision is that the teaching of evolution in the classroom is now discouraged, at best, and—at worst—eliminated totally.[201]

In November 2000, a new state board of education was elected in Kansas. It proceeded to reject the 1999 science standards and went on to adopt in February 2001, new standards which identified evolution as one of the unifying concepts of science.[202] These standards direct students who have completed the twelfth grade of education to acquire an understanding of biological evolution and the origin and evolution of the earth and the universe. The statewide science examination will, furthermore, contain specific questions on evolution.[203] Automatically, every four years, the science standards will be reviewed.[204]

One overriding point remains clear: since the U.S. Supreme Court failed to address clearly in Edwards v. Aguillard the multiple relationships and interactions of religion, science, and secular humanism within the bounds of public school education, unending controversy will continue.[205] Indeed, all of the Supreme Court's decisions since the Tennessee Supreme Court's decision in Scopes v. State have failed to slow the spread of creationism. Rather, they have encouraged fundamentalists, more and more, to abandon evolution-teaching public education for creation-affirming church affiliations or home schooling where their faith, and that of their children, can be nurtured and sustained.[206]

New outreaches and challenges

Even with the "failures" of public education to accommodate fundamentalism in curricular offerings, with higher education, however, a most interesting occurrence is being recorded: that is, religion—as an academic subject—is no longer confined to divinity schools and Sunday pulpits. Today, it is probed, and its relevance examined, in undergraduate and graduate programs in sociology, political science, international relations, business, and medicine.[207] Rather surprisingly, this new-found student interest in the field of religion and the quest to make its tenets applicable to the contemporary problems of daily professional living is having the effect of reshaping the content and the direction of the whole of the social sciences.[208] The extent to which explicit religious arguments should be introduced into public debate remains an open-ended issue however.[209]

Interpreting, reconciling, or stabilizing

In the May 1959, Rede Lecture at The University of Cambridge, C.P. Snow articulated his thesis: that contemporary (post-war) society was composed of two competing and often clashing cultures—the (literary) intellectuals and the scientists.[210] Since science was not a subject presented easily to the public through literature (e.g., journals and magazines) the self-proclaimed intellectuals ignore the value and importance of the ideas and values science sought to promote. Thus, the scientific ethic remained largely invisible as an intellectual, moving activity.[211]

In the second edition of The Two Cultures published in 1963, Snow suggests the emergence of a new third culture which will close the communications gap between the literary intellectuals and the scientists and will, further, be recognized as new public intellectuals or synthesizers. As such, they will be interpreters of the ideas and values of the continuing scientific revolution.[212]

Today, Snow's third culture has undergone a radical transformation—for literary intellectuals no longer communicate at any sustained level with scientists; rather, scientists communicate directly with the general public. In the past, the traditional intellectual media played what has been termed "a vertical game"—with journalists writing up and professors writing down.[213] In contemporary society, "third-culture thinkers tend to avoid the middleman and endeavor to express their deepest thoughts in a manner accessible to the intelligent reading public."[214] Indeed, what in the past was seen as "science," is now "public culture,"[215] for science is the news.[216] Yet, having the capacity to synthesize scientific knowledge remains an enormous problem for the average citizen.[217]

Borrowing from Snow's ideas, perhaps religion could serve as a stabilizer or interpretative "third culture" between Law and Medical Science. Others would no doubt see this idea as but an aspirational goal arguing, as such, that religion is a destabilizing force since most of the tenets of main-line religious faiths are, as observed, still rooted in and tied to historical biblical precedents which, in turn, lack a contemporary "real-world" focus for application.

A democratic and political process tied more to television sound bites than intelligent and informed deliberations among its citizens is a process guaranteeing itself of lethargic inactivity if not stagnation. It is for the judiciary to fill the breach and continue its role as interpreters of the Common Law and when need be, architects of the new Age of Biotechnology. Ideally, when individual cases of profound disagreement arise over issues of medical science, courts and legislatures should remain passive and allow resolution of these disputes within each concerned family unit and, where possible, their church or community of faith.[218] Oftentimes, the at-risk family and its religious support groups are unable to cope with understanding the ramifications of ultimate decisions regarding medicine. "Meditating structures"[219] can only go so far in discerning and promoting legal justice—or, the obligation to support the common good.[220] The common good is shaped by the legislatures and the courts and—ultimately—it remains for an enlightened judiciary to interpret its course. It is regrettable, but a fact in contemporary society, that every complex moral issue is more often than not, transformed into a legal issue.[221] Since law and morality intersect in daily life, it is not surprising that the courts are called upon to arbitrate.[222] Invariably, law supports some visions of how life should be lived within the community while, at the same time, undermining others.[223]

A synergistic partnership

Religion, and its denominational theologies, set normative standards for ethical conduct and, thus, serve as a construct for social decision-making. Alternatively, as suggested, these norms and constructs can be seen properly as a third culture—interpreting, reconciling, and stabilizing law and medical science. Yet, if the view is accepted that the "bedrock of moral order is religion,"[224] it must follow that law and science not only build upon it but are linked irretrievably to it in all of their present policies and actions.

The alternative hypothesis suggests the synergistic forces of law, religion, and science combine in a dynamic partnership to form a communitarian alliance dedicated to providing a framework in which man can pursue the peace of ordered harmony which allows for a balanced happiness in his social, spiritual, and physical relationships.[225] Within the alliance, the rank or equality of status depends largely upon the frame of reference taken for each problem presented.

Historically, there can be no disputation of the first order significance of the moral and ethical theories and principles derived from religion. Indeed, it has been suggested that without religious beliefs, moral teachings merely "hang in the air" without any foundation.[226] In contemporary society, however, law—as has been suggested—must assume the primary role of directing and stabilizing all courses of human affairs—fortified in interpretative analysis, to be sure, by ethical and moral principles. In public matters, however, if not a Jeffersonian "wall of separation" between matters of church and state, then at least a Madisonian "scrupulous neutrality" must be maintained if faithfulness to the original intent of the framers of the Constitution is to be respected.[227]

While some Americans believe in "The Living Constitution" as a "morphing document" evolving from age to age according to majority wishes[228]—expressed and manifested ideally, as such, through a "deliberative" democratic process[229] (sadly, not guided by informed judgment)—the central weakness to this theory of living constitutionalism is that there is no one guiding principle for it to follow.[230] In contemporary issues of bio-medicine, there is little "rational" deliberation by the populace. This condition, in turn, forces the judiciary—as interpreters of the laws and the social conscience—to define and inevitably test current medico-legal issues by the text and legislative history of the Constitution thereby providing, ideally, both predictability and stability to both an evolving and highly contentious area of the law.[231]

Compatibilities and incompatibilities

The duality of man or the recognition of his spiritual and material sides, has not been the grounds upon which contemporary science has advanced. Rather than challenge and attack this concept, science has merely set it aside and defined as non-scientific all inquiries into spiritual matters.[232] As the scientific dialogue has assumed increasingly that man is no more than matter and energy, dualism has nearly disappeared.[233] Yet, throughout modern science, there remains a continuing search for an intersection point between values and empiricism.[234]

Perhaps the noblest and most practical point of balance between religion and science should be love, justice, or humaneness—for, its achievement by man promotes the essence of faith by instilling meaning and value to the life-experience and also enhances one's overall physical well-being. Stated otherwise, the fulcrum of this balancing test between religion and science is the achievement of a point of equilibrium that promotes policies and shapes direct actions that minimize suffering and improve the social well-being of all men.[235]

There is a common misperception that religion needs only faith in order to sustain itself. The correct understanding is that "religion requires belief and belief is built on knowledge."[236] Within differing contexts, both science and theology, then, seek truth and wise judgment.[237]

Toward reconciliation

Not every scientist must become a believer nor every believer embrace science totally in order for there to be a reconciliation between science and faith. While viewed from vastly different perspectives, the biblical and the scientific description of the creation of the universe and the beginning of life or earth present identical realities. Once these perspectives are identified, they can coexist rather comfortably. If an acceptance of the need to read and understand the Bible on the Bible's terms—complete with subtextual levels of interpretation—is understood and science then admits it is powerless to either confirm or deny a purpose for life, a true reconciliation between science and faith will be achieved.[238]

Scientific investigation is in fact very similar to religious experience. In science, the defining event is when that which was unknown becomes visible and even clear. In spirituality, experiences with meaning, purpose, and teleology are foundational. Thus, semantic differences remain small between scientific insight and what is termed—in the language of religion—revelation.[239]

A *unified goal and response*

The theologies of the world religions not only demand an answer but also prompt a response to the problem of suffering—for they assist in seeking an explanation to, or rationalization of, suffering. In one very real sense, then, the New Biology is considered properly as a theological response to the enigma of human suffering. The medical scientists and physicians endeavor to cure. Through therapeutics and investigation, the purpose of religion and medical science is the same: to minimize or ameliorate suffering.[240]

It remains ultimately for law to serve as a primary mechanism for effecting this duality of purpose through wise and humane legislation, administrative policy-making, and judicial interpretations designed to assume both distributive and corrective justice in the delivery of health care and the advancement of medical science[241] which, in turn, promote the personal dignity, value, and integrity of the human person.[242]

Notes

1   *See generally* Hugh Heclo, *An Introduction to Religion,* ch. 1 in RELIGION RETURNS TO THE PUBLIC SQUARE: FAITH AND POLICY IN AMERICA (Hugh Heclo & Wilfred M. McClay eds. 2003); *Symposium on Religion in The Public Square,* 17 J. L., ETHICS & PUB. POL'Y 307 (2003).

2   Larry Copeland, *Church-and-State Standoffs Spread over USA,* USA TODAY, Sep. 30, 2003, at 15A.

3   *See e.g.,* Stephen R. Glassworth v. Roy S. Moore, 229 F. Supp. 2d 1290 (M.D. Ala. 2002), aff'd 335 F.3d 1282 (11th Cir. 2003); Van Orden v. Perry, U.S.L.W. 1308 (Nov. 25, 2003).

4   *See e.g.,* Newdow v. United States Congress, 328 F.3d 466 (9th Cir. 2003), *cert.* granted in part *sub nom.,* Elk Grove Unified School District v. Newdow, 72 U.S.L.W. 3266 (Oct. 14, 2003).

On June 14, 2004, the U.S. Supreme Court held that Michael A. Newdow had no standing to sue the school district where his daughter attended elementary school, on her behalf, to ban the words, "under God," from the Pledge of Allegiance. 542 U.S. 1 (2004). Interestingly, an April 2004 Gallup Poll revealed only 8% of the public wanted the "under God" clause removed from the Pledge—with 91% wishing to retain it. *See* Charles Lane, *Justices Keep 'Under God' in Pledge,* WASH. POST, Jun. 15, 2004, at A1.

On March 11, 2010, the 9th Circuit Federal Court of Appeals ruled in two cases that: the words, "under God," in the Pledge of Allegiance is not an unconstitutional endorsement of religion but—rather a phrase invoking patriotism and thus a ritual, not a prayer (Newdow v. Lefevre *et al.,* 598 F.3d 638 (9th Cir. 2010)) and that the National motto, "In God We Trust," printed on coins and currency, is patriotic and ceremonial and therefore not religious (Newdow *et al.* v. Rio Linda Union School Dists. *et al.,* 597 F.3d 1007 (9th Cir. 2010)). *See also* Douglas W. Kmiec, *Oh God! Can I Say That in Public?* 17 J. L. ETHICS & PUB. POL'Y, 307 (2003).

5 *See generally* James Moore, *Charles Darwin*, ch. 16 and Peter J. Bowler, *Evolution*, ch. 17 in SCIENCE AND RELIGION: A HISTORICAL INTRODUCTION (Gary B. Ferngren, ed. 2003).

6 Claudia Kalb, *Faith and Healing*, NEWSWEEK, Nov. 10, 2003, at 44.

7 Jim VandeHei, *A Spiritual Struggle for Democrats: Silence on Religion Could Hurt Candidates*, WASH. POST, Nov. 27, 2003, at A1. In a non-partisan Pew Research Center study conducted in June 2003, it was found that—among respondents in a poll taken—too little reference was made by politicians to religious faith and prayer. *Ibid. See also* Nancy Gibbs, *The Faith Factor*, TIME, Jun. 21, 2004, at 26; Alan Cooperman, *Religious Left Seeks Center of Political Debates: Conferees Call for Stronger Voice*, WASH. POST, Jun. 10, 2004, at A2. *See generally* William Carey, *American Democracy and The Politics of Faith*, ch. 5 in RELIGION RETURNS TO THE PUBLIC SQUARE, *supra* note 1; A. JAMES REICHLEY, FAITH IN POLITICS (2002).

8 Keith B. Reichburg, *French President Urges Ban on (Islamic) Head Scarves in Schools*, WASH. POST, Dec. 18, 2003, at A1; Keith B. Reichburg, *French Senate Approves Ban on Religious Attire*, WASH. POST, Mar. 4, 2004, at A14. *See* Robin Givhan, *The Latest Taboo in Paris*, WASH. POST, Jan. 23, 2004, at C2 (reporting on how the religious symbol ban has been broadened recently from head scarves, Jewish skull caps, and Christian crosses to include beads and bandannas).

On November 3, 2009, the European Court of Human Rights held that it was a violation of the religious and educational rights of Italian children for them to attend classes in which a crucifix hangs on the wall. The Court rejected the argument by Italy that the cross had become one of the secular values of the Italian Constitution and represented the values of civil life. Lautsi v. Italy (Application #30814/06). *See generally* Nikki R. Keddie, *Secularism and Its Discontents*, 132 DAEDALUS 14 (2003).

9 Dogru v. France, 49 E. H. R.R. 8 [at 64] (2008).

Here, the plaintiff (or applicant) attempted to attend required physical education and sports classes in attire—a head scarf—which would prevent her from participating in the classes. *See* Patrick West, *A Nation in Diversity: France, Muslims and the Head Scarf*, www.opendemocracy.net/debates/article-5-57-1811.jsp.; Reuven Ziegler, *The French 'Head Scarves Ban': Intolerance or Necessity?* 40 J. MARSHALL L. REV. 235 (2006).

10 Doreen Carvajal, *Sarkozy Backs Drive to Eliminate Burka*, N.Y. TIMES, Jun. 23, 2009, at A4. On October 7, 2010, the French Constitutional Council approved a law banning full-face veils in public which will take effect later in 2011. This law is expected to be challenged in the European Court of Justice. Steven Erlanger, *France: Full-Face Veil Ban Approved*, NEW YORK TIMES, Oct. 8, 2010, at A8; *French Legislation Takes Effect Banning Full-Face Coverings*, N.Y. TIMES, Apr. 12, 2012, at A4.

In a Swiss referendum on whether to ban the building of minarets alongside mosques, 57.5 percent of those voting rejected the measure. This ballot was seen as a sign of continued unrest in Western Europe over continued Muslim immigration. Christian voters appear increasingly eager to preserve the traditional ways and unwilling to jeopardize a national attitude supportive of church steeples and quiet conformity. Edward Cody, *Switzerland Votes to Prohibit the Building of Mosque Minarets*, WASH. POST, Nov. 30, 2009 at A10.

11 Jeremy T. Gunn, *The Complexity of Religion and The Definition of "Religion" in International Law*, 16 HARV. HUM. RTS. J. 189, 191 (2003).

12 *Ibid.* at 190.

13 *Ibid.* at 200–205.

14 380 U.S. 163, 165–66 (1965).

15 Stephen R. Glassworth v. Roy S. Moore, *supra* note 3.

16 335 F.3d 1282 (11th Cir. 2003).

17 In re Moore, Moore v. Glassworth, *cert.* denied, 72 U.S.L.W. 3309 (Nov. 4, 2003).

18 AP, *Alabama Judge Removed: Moore Installed Monument to Commandments*, WASH. POST, Nov. 14, 2003, at A1 (reporting on the removal of the Chief Justice from his office of the Supreme Court of Alabama by a unanimous Court of the Judiciary of Alabama).

19 *See generally* RONALD D. ROTUNDA, MODERN CONSTITUTIONAL LAW: CASES AND NOTES ch. 11 (6th ed. 2000).

20 Van Orden v. Perry, 351 F.3d (5th Cir. 2003).

21 2002 U.S. Dist. LEXIS 26709 (W.D. Tex., Oct. 2, 2002).

22 Van Orden v. Perry, 351 F.3d 173 (5th Cir. 2003).

23 *Ibid.* at 180.

24 *Ibid.* at 182.

25 *Ibid. See* Edith Brown Clement, *Public Displays of Affection ... For God: Religious Monuments after McCreary and Van Orden*, 32 HARV. J. L. & PUB. POL'Y 231 (2009).

26 Copeland, *supra* note 2. Previously, the Congress had enacted the Religious Freedom Restoration Act which directed the government to demonstrate a compelling interest before intruding into any sphere of religious practice. 42 U.S.C. § 2000bb *et seq.* (1994). While the free exercise clause protects absolutely religious beliefs, the state can—indeed—regulate religious conduct. In 1997, the U.S. Supreme Court, in City of Boerne v. Flores, held the Act was unconstitutional as a violation of the Establishment Clause. 521 U.S. 507 (1999).

   Subsequently, the Congress passed The Protection of Religious Exercise in Land Use and by Institutionalized Persons Act, 42 U.S.C. § 2000cc (2000) which requires not only that land use regulations that burden, substantially, religious exercise be the least restrictive means of advancing a compelling government interest, but—as well—prohibit land use regulation either disfavoring religious uses relative to non-religious uses or unreasonably exclude religious uses from a particular jurisdiction (42 U.S.C. § 2000cc(b)). The courts addressing the constitutionality of this Act have upheld it. *See* Marci A. Hamilton, *Federalism and The Public Good: The True Story Behind the Religious Use and Institutionalized Persons Act*, 78 IND. L. J. 311 (2003).

   On April 26, 2010, the U.S. Supreme Court held in a 5 to 4 decision that a lower court ruling that it was improper to allow a 6½ foot white cross erected more than 75 years ago to remain on a stretch of land in the 1.6 million acre Mojave Desert to honor the dead of World War I could not be sustained. Writing for the majority, Justice Anthony M. Kennedy concluded that the cross should be seen as not only a reaffirmation of Christian beliefs but often accepted as but a symbol to show honor and respect for heroism. Under these circumstances, the government is not restrained by the Constitution to avoid totally the role of religion in society. The degree to which a governmental accommodation is to be found in all cases for the display of religious symbols without violating the Constitution's prohibition on the endorsement of religion remains unclear. Salazar v. Buono, 130 S. Ct. 1803 (2010).

27 Copeland, *supra* note 2. In a September 2003, poll of 1,003 adults conducted by USA TODAY/CNN/Gallup, it was determined that 70% of the respondents approve of the placement of Ten Commandments monuments in public places. *Ibid.*

28 Stephen R. Glassworth v. Roy S. Moore, *supra* note 3.

29 Van Orden v. Perry, *supra* note 20.

30 Copeland, *supra* note 2.

31 Stone v. Graham, 449 U.S. 39, 41 (1980).

32 Stone v. Graham, *ibid.* at 42 (their use in teaching a secular study of comparative religion, history or civilization is acceptable).

33 Allegheny County v. Greater Pittsburgh ACLU, 492 U.S. 573, 591 (1988).

34 330 U.S. 1 (1947).

35 330 U.S. at 15–16, *aff'd*, Illinois ex rel. McCollum v. Board of Education, 333 U.S. 203 (1948).

36 Wallace v. Jaffee, 472 U.S. 38 at 52 (1984).

37 129 S. Ct. 1125 (2009).

38 *Ibid. See generally* Richard W. Garnett, *Religion, Division and the 1st Amendment*, 94 GEO. L. J. 1667 (2006).

39 *See generally* GEORGE P. SMITH, II, THE NEW BIOLOGY: LAW, ETHICS AND BIOTECHNOLOGY (1989), Monograph, OF PANJANDRUMS, POOH-BAHS, PARVENUS, AND PROPHETS: LAW, RELIGION AND MEDICAL SCIENCE (2005).

40 *See generally Symposium*, R. Kent Greenawalt, *Establishing Religious Ideas: Evolution, Creationism, and Intelligent Design*, 17 NOTRE DAME J. L. ETHICS & PUB. POL'Y, 321 (2003).

41 George P. Smith, II, *Genetics, Eugenics and Public Policy*, 1985 SO. ILL. L. REV. 435.

42 *See generally* Eric Gregory, *Religion and Bioethics*, in A COMPANION TO BIOETHICS at ch. 5 (Helga Kuhse & Peter Singer, eds., 2nd ed. 2009); George P. Smith, II, *Intrusions of a Parvenu: Science, Religion, and The New Biology*, 3 PACE L. REV. 63 (1982).

43 George P. Smith, II, *Biotechnology and The Law: Social Responsibility v. Freedom of Scientific Inquiry*, 39 MERCER L. REV. 437, 460 (1988).

44 *Ibid.*; George P. Smith, II, *Manipulating The Genetic Code: Jurisprudential Conundrums*, 64 GEO. L. REV. 697, 733 (1976).

I am, of course, expanding the "unalienable" rights to life, liberty, and happiness set out in the Declaration of Independence to include, modernly, the right to access good genetic health since being healthy is required usually for total happiness. *See* George P. Smith, II, *Human Rights and Bioethics: Formulating a Universal Right to Health, Health Care, or Health Protection?* 38 VANDERBILT J. TRANSNAT'L L. 1295 (2005).

45 AUDREY R. CHAPMAN, UNPRECEDENTED CHOICES: RELIGIOUS ETHICS AT THE FRONTIERS OF GENETIC SCIENCE 19 (1999).

46 *Ibid.*

47 *Ibid.*

48 *Ibid.* at 24, 25.

49 *Ibid.* at 25.

50 *Ibid.* at 31, 32.

51 *Ibid.* at 32. Various reports, policy statements, and studies have been commissioned by eight major North American Protestant denominations (including the Methodist, Episcopal, Lutheran, Presbyterian, and Baptist churches) which address the religious and ethical ramifications of the science of genetics. *Ibid.* at 34 *passim.*

52 *See generally* KEVIN D. O'ROURKE & PHILIP BOYLE, MEDICAL ETHICS: SOURCES FOR CATHOLIC TEACHING (2nd. ed. 1993). *See also* Tim Townsend, *Bishops Not Indulgent on Infallibility*, WASH. POST, Feb. 20, 2010, at B12 (reporting on a meeting of the U.S. Catholic Bishops where a document was approved which condemned certain reproductive technologies—including artificial insemination—as not "morally legitimate" ways to combat infertility).

53 CHAPMAN, *supra* note 45 at 40.

54 *Ibid.* at 37.

55 RICHARD A. McCORMICK, THE CRITICAL CALLING: REFLECTIONS ON MORAL DILEMMAS SINCE VATICAN II at 267 (1989).

Alterations of infrahuman life—if judged to be advantageous to a fuller human life— may be allowable under the Roman Catholic faith. Rihito Kimura, *Religious Aspects of Genetic Information* in HUMAN GENETIC INFORMATION: SCIENCE, LAW AND ETHICS at 157 *passim* (CIBA Foundation ed. 1990). *See also* GENETIC ENGINEERING: ETHICAL AND SOCIAL DIMENSIONS (Albert S. Moraczewski, ed. 1983).

56 *See* Sarah Delaney, *Pope Condemns Cloning of Human Embryos & Organ Transplant Technology*, WASH. POST, Aug. 30, 2000, at A18.

Further clarification of the Vatican's position on human cloning came in August 2003, by the President of the Pontifical Council for the Family when he stated such endeavors should be banned internationally as "crimes against the human persons" because they are against the very right to human life and true individuality. Cindy Wooden, *Human Cloning Would Be a Crime against People*, CATHOLIC STANDARD, Aug. 14, 2003, at 3. And, in 2008, The Congregation for The Doctrine of The Faith issued a new Instruction as a supplement to its 1987 Instruction, *Donum Vitae*, organized as such to address recent progress in biomedical research (*e.g.*, human embryo and stem cell research). *See* *www.vatican.va/roman_curia/congregations/cfatih/*documents/rc_con _cfaith_doc2 ... (accessed Dec. 16, 2008).

57 *Supra* note 45 at 45.

58 *Ibid.* at 44–46.
59 David H. Smith, *Creation, Preservation and All The Blessings*, 81 ANGLICAN THEOL. REV. 567 (2001).
60 *Ibid.* at 568, 569. *See generally* IAN BARBOUR, RELIGION IN AN AGE OF SCIENCE (1990).
61 H. TRISTRAM ENGLEHARDT, Jr., BIOETHICS AND SECULAR HUMANISM: THE SEARCH FOR A COMMON MORALITY 4, 16 (1991).
62 *Ibid.* at 61.
63 *Ibid.*
   Indeed, secular fundamentalists maintain religion should never be seen as a legitimate component of *realpolitik*. David Waters, *'God Gap' impedes U.S. Foreign Policy, Study Says*, WASH. POST, Feb. 24, 2010, at A2.
64 *Supra* note 61 at 8.
65 *See* ROBERT WRIGHT, THE EVOLUTION OF GOD (2009). *See also supra* note 45 and accompanying text on the challenges of adapting religion to a modern, biotechnological society.
66 Samuel E. Stumpf, *Theology and Jurisprudence*, 10 VAND. L. REV. 885, 886 (1957).
67 Jerome Hall, *Religion, Law and Ethics—A Call for Dialogue*, 29 HASTINGS L.J. 1257, 1267 (1978).
68 ST. AUGUSTINE, THE CITY OF GOD, book xix, c.1 at ps. 112–14 (John Healey trans. 1931).
69 Hall *supra* note 67 at 1270.
70 *Ibid. See generally* MARTIN RHONHEIMER, NATURAL LAW AND PRACTICAL REASON: A THOMIST VIEW OF MORAL AUTONOMY (Gerald Malsbary trans. 2000).
71 HAROLD J. BERMAN, THE INTERACTION OF LAW AND RELIGION 83 (1974).
72 *Ibid.* at 11.
73 *Ibid.* at 25.
74 *Ibid.* at 79.
75 HAROLD J. BERMAN, FAITH AND ORDER: THE RECONCILIATION OF LAW AND RELIGION 19 (1993).
76 *Ibid.* at 391.
77 *See* JOSEPH FLETCHER, MEDICINE AND MORALS (1954). *See also* George P. Smith, II, *Stop in the Name of Law!*, 19 ANGLO-AMERICAN L. REV. 55 (1990).
78 *See generally* George P. Smith, II, *Setting Limits: Medical Technology and The Law*, 23 SYDNEY L. REV. 283 (2001).
79 MICHAEL NOVAK, ON TWO WINGS: HUMBLE FAITH AND COMMON SENSE AT THE AMERICAN FOUNDING 27 (2002). *See also* A. JAMES REICHLEY, FAITH IN POLITICS ch. 3 (2002).
80 NOVAK, *ibid.* at 28–29.
81 *Ibid.* at 30.
82 *Ibid.* at 30, 33.
83 *Ibid.* at 70.
84 *Ibid.* at 77. While the framers valued the contribution religion made to morals, "they distrusted faith, the transcendent dimension of religion, the yearning for the divine likely to express itself in prophecy, theology, or mysticism." William Carey McWilliams, *American Democracy and The Politics of Faith* ch. 5 in RELIGION RETURNS TO THE PUBLIC SQUARE *supra* note 1 at 147.
85 FRED M. FROHOCK, HEALING POWERS 140 (1992). *See generally* R. Kent Greenawalt, *Diverse Perspectives and The Religion Clauses: An Examination of Justifications and Qualifying Beliefs*, 74 NOTRE DAME L. REV. 1433 (1999).
86 *Ibid. See* ARTICLES OF FAITH, ARTICLES OF PEACE: THE RELIGIOUS LIBERTY CLAUSES AND THE AMERICAN PHILOSOPHY (J. Hunter & O. Guinness eds. 1990).

87 FROHOCK, *supra* note 85. *See generally* DAVID L. FAIGMAN, LABORATORY OF JUSTICE ch. 10 (2004); HERBERT HOVENKAMP, SCIENCE AND RELIGION IN AMERICA 1800–1860 (1978).

88 *Ibid. See Symposium, Religiously Based Morality: Its Proper Place in American Law and Public Policy*, 36 WAKE FOREST L. REV. 217 at 401 *passim* (2001). *See also* John Witte Jr., *The Theology and Politics of The First Amendment Religion Clauses: A Bicentennial Essay*, 40 EMORY L. J. 489, 491–99 (1990) (presenting an excellent study of the bifurcated heritage of church-state theories and laws). He terms the early historical conflict as one between strict separatists and non-preferential accommodationists. *Ibid.* at 490–91.

89 David Novak, *Law: Religious or Secular?* 86 VA. L. REV. 569, 570 (2000). *See* R. Kent Greenawalt, *Religion as a Concept in Constitutional Law*, 72 CAL. L. REV. 753 (1984). *See generally* PHILIP KURLAND, RELIGION AND THE LAW (1962); R. Kent Greenawalt, *The Use of Religious Convictions by Legislators and Judges*, 36 J. CHURCH & STATE 541 (1994).

90 Novak, *ibid.* at 371.

91 *See* CHARLES E. RICE, BEYOND ABORTION: THE THEORY AND PRACTICE OF THE SECULAR STATE 135 (1979).

92 Ronald Reagan, *Politics and Morality are Inseparable*, 1 NOTRE DAME J. L. ETHICS & PUB. POL'Y 7 (1984). *See generally* James Carroll, *Why Religion Still Matters*, 132 DAEDALUS 9 (2003).

93 Michael Walzer, *Drawing the Line: Religion and Politics*, 1999 UTAH L. REV. 619. *See generally* R. KENT GREENAWALT, RELIGIOUS CONVICTIONS AND POLITICAL CHOICE (1988).

94 *Ibid.* at 623.

95 STEPHEN L. CARTER, THE CULTURE OF DISBELIEF: HOW AMERICAN LAW AND POLITICS TRIVIALIZE RELIGIOUS DEVOTION 9 (1993).

96 Michael Walzer, *supra* note 93 at 624. *See generally* ROBERT D. PUTNAM & DAVID E. CAMPBELL, AMERICAN GRACE: HOW RELIGION DIVIDES AND UNITES US (2010).

97 Walzer, *ibid.* at 630.

98 *Ibid. See generally* Michael W. McConnell & Richard A. Posner, *An Economic Approach to Issues of Religion*, 56 U. CHI. L. REV. 1 (1989).

99 MICHAEL L. PERRY, LOVE AND POWER: THE ROLE OF RELIGION IN AMERICAN POLITICS 77 (1991). *See also* CHAPMAN, *supra* note 45 at 17.

100 MICHAEL L. PERRY, *ibid.* at 78.

101 *Ibid.* at 124, 125.

102 Novak, *supra* note 89 at 575, 576.

A survey by the Pew Forum on Religion and Public Life found 25 percent of approximately 4,000 Americans interviewed sometimes integrate their Christian faith beliefs with "competing" spiritual beliefs (such as reincarnation) seen in Eastern and New Age faiths. *See* NICHOLAS WADE, THE FAITH INSTINCT: HOW RELIGION EVOLVED AND WHY IT ENDURES (2009).

103 Novak, *supra* note 89 at 576.

104 *Ibid.* at 576, 577.

105 *Ibid.* at 580. *See also* JOHN W. GOUCH, THE SOCIAL CONTRACT: A CRITICAL STUDY OF ITS DEVELOPMENT (2nd ed. 1957).

106 Novak, *supra* note 89 at 593.

107 *Ibid.* at 572. A two-year study by the Chicago Council on Global Affairs concluded that religion should be made an integral part of U.S. foreign policy. Present policies are handicapped—the study found—by both a narrow and ill-informed Western secularism which, in turn, feeds religious extremism. Waters, *supra* note 63.

108 Novak, *ibid.* at 572.

109 *Ibid.* at 573. *See generally* Pierre Schlag, *Law as the Continuation of God by Other Means*, 85 CAL. L. REV. 427 (1997).

110 Novak, *supra* note 89 at 574.

111 *Ibid.* at 575.

112 *Ibid.* at 595, 596.

113 *Ibid.* at 596. *See* RONALD DWORKIN, LAW's EMPIRE 407 (1986).

114 EDWARD J. LARSON, SUMMER FOR THE GODS 14 (1997).

115 *Ibid.* at 16. The theory of evolution focuses on changes in life once begun rather than the origins of life.

116 *Ibid.* at 17. *See generally* MICHAEL R. ROSE, DARWIN'S SPECTRE: EVOLUTIONARY BIOLOGY IN THE MODERN WORLD chs. 7, 11 (1998).

117 CHAPMAN, *supra* note 45 at 169.

118 CORNELIUS G. HUNTER, DARWIN'S GOD 145, 159 (2001).

119 *Ibid.* at 160.

120 *Ibid.* at 159. *See generally* JOHN F. HAUGHT, DEEPER THAN DARWIN: THE PROSPECT FOR RELIGION IN THE AGE OF EVOLUTION (2003).

121 STEPHEN J. GOULD, THE STRUCTURE OF EVOLUTIONARY THEORY chs. 2–7 (2002). *See generally* JAMES B. CONANT, ON UNDERSTANDING SCIENCE: AN HISTORICAL APPROACH (1947).

122 *Ibid.* at 172 (citing PHILIP HEFNER, THE HUMAN FACTOR: EVOLUTION, CULTURE AND RELIGION at 37 (1993)).

123 *Ibid.* at 173 (citing P. HEFNER, *ibid.* at 156).

124 CHAPMAN, *supra* note 45 at 175.

125 *Ibid.* at 178.

126 *Ibid.*

127 *Ibid.*

128 *Ibid.*

129 *See* JAMES M. GUSTAFSON, INTERSECTIONS: SCIENCE, THEOLOGY AND ETHICS (1996). CHAPMAN, *supra* note 45 at 199–204.

130 CHAPMAN, *supra* note 45 at 15 (relying upon the philosophy of Daniel Callahan).

131 *See generally* ROGER L. SHINN, THE NEW GENETICS: CHALLENGES FOR SCIENCE, FAITH AND POLITICS (1996).

132 BERNARD J. FICARA, EVOLUTION: FACT, FICTION OR FANCY ch. 21 (2001).

133 John Tagliabue, *Pope Bolsters Church: Support for Scientific View of Evolution*, N.Y. TIMES, Oct. 25, 1996, at 1.

134 *Ibid.* at A12.

135 FICARA, *supra* note 132 at 124. *See* MICHAEL RUSE, THE RELATIONSHIP BETWEEN SCIENCE AND RELIGION (2001). *See also* JOHN PAUL II, ON SCIENCE AND RELIGION (Robert J. Russell, William R. Stoeger & George V. Coyne eds. 1990).

136 CHAPMAN, *supra* note 45 at 235.

137 J.A. MOORE, FROM GENESIS TO GENETICS at 190, 191 (2002).

138 Edmund D. Pellegrino, *Theology and Evolution in Dialogue*, 79 Q. REV. BIOLOGY 385, 389 (1997).

139 *Ibid.* at 389.

140 World in Brief, *Pope, in Remarks on Evolution, Says World is 'Intelligent Project,'* WASH. POST, Nov. 10, 2005, at A23.

141 George Johnson, *For the Anti-Evolutionists, Hope in High Places*, N.Y. TIMES, Oct. 2, 2005, at 3.

142 Editorial, *Thorny Issues of Evolution Tops Papal Student Reunion Agenda*, THE IRISH NEWS Ltd., Sep. 5, 2006, at 10.

143 *Ibid.*

144 Ian Fisher, *Professor-Turned-Pope Leads a Seminar on Evolution*, N.Y. TIMES, Sep. 2, 2006, at A3.

145 N.Y. TIMES, Sep. 11, 2006, at A3 (unauthored byline accompanying picture of the Pope).

146 RATZINGER, *infra* note 150 at 178, 258. *See* Editorial, IRISH TIMES, *supra* note 142.

147 *Supra* note 144.

148 Editorial, *supra* note 142.

149 *Supra* note 144.

150 JOSEPH CARDINAL RATZINGER, TRUTH AND TOLERANCE: CHRISTIAN BELIEF AND WORLD RELIGIONS at 257 (trans. Henry Taylor, 2003).

151 *Ibid.* at 179, 258.

152 *See* www.papalencyclicals.net/Pius12/P12HUMAN.HTM (accessed Jun. 18, 2007).

153 *Ibid.*

154 *Ibid.*

155 Owen D. Jones & Timothy H. Goldsmith, *Law and Behavioral Biology*, 105 COLUM. L. REV. 405, 499 (2005). *See* Smith, *supra* note 78, *Judicial Decisionmaking in The Age of Biotechnology*, 13 NOTRE DAME J. LAW, ETHICS & PUB. POL'Y 34 (1999).

156 RATZINGER, *supra* note 150 at 257.

157 *Ibid.*

158 *Ibid.*

159 KARL RAHNER, THE CHRISTIAN OF THE FUTURE 35 (trans. W.J. O'Hara, 1967). *See also* http://www.religion-online.org/shouchapter.asap?ttle=524&c+534 (accessed Jun. 30, 2007).

160 *Ibid.* at 36.

161 *Ibid.*

162 PHILLIP E. JOHNSON, DARWIN ON TRIAL (1991).

163 *See* INTELLIGENT DESIGN CREATIONISM AND ITS CRITICS: PHILOSOPHICAL, THEOLOGICAL, AND SCIENTIFIC PERSPECTIVES (Robert T. Pennock, ed. 2001). *See generally* Greenawalt, *supra* note 40.

164 BRIAN J. ALTERS & SANDRA M. ALTERS, DEFENDING EVOLUTION IN THE CLASSROOM: A GUIDE TO THE CREATION/EVOLUTION CONTROVERSY (2001). *See* Edward B. Davis & Robin Collins, ch. 25, *Scientific Naturalism* in SCIENCE AND RELIGION: A HISTORICAL INTRODUCTION, *supra* note 5 (analyzing the advocates of intelligent design attacks on scientific naturalism or the claims that "all objects, processes, truths, and facts about nature fall within the scope of scientific method") at 322.

165 Beth McMurtrie, *Darwinism Under Attack*, CHRON. HIGHER ED., Dec. 21, 2001, at A8. *See generally* Francis Beckewith, *Science and Religion Twenty Years after McLean v. Arkansas: Evolution, Public Education, and The New Challenge of Intelligent Design*, 26 HARV. J. L. & PUB. POL'Y 455 (2003).

166 Pennock, *supra* note 163.

167 JOHN C. WHITCOMB & HENRY M. MORRIS, THE GENESIS FLOOD (1965). *See* DOROTHY NELKIN, THE CREATION CONTROVERSY: SCIENCE OR SCRIPTURE IN THE SCHOOLS (1982).

168 Judith Villarreal, *God and Darwin in the Classroom*, 64 CHIC.-KENT L. REV. 335, 345 (1988).

169 ARLIE HOOVER, THE CASE FOR TEACHING CREATION (1981).

170 Villarreal, *supra* note 168 at 350.

171 *Ibid.* at 351. *See* HUGH ROSS, THE GENESIS QUESTION: SCIENTIFIC ADVANCES AND THE ACCURACY OF GENESIS ch. 11 (1998). *See also* RONALD COLE-TURNER, THE NEW GENESIS: THEOLOGY AND THE GENETIC REVOLUTION (1993). *See also* Bill Broadway, *Redefining Omniscience: Theologians Who Contend That God Doesn't Know the Future Face Fervent Criticism—and Expulsion from Evangelical Group*, WASH. POST, Nov. 8, 2003, at B9 (reporting on how the theory of open theism constitutes, for some, an egregious departure from orthodoxy and, as such, requires those who advance it be excluded from membership in the Evangelical Theological Society).

172 STEVEN GOLDBERG, SEDUCED BY SCIENCE 33 (1999).

173 *Ibid.* at 35, 36.

174 *Ibid.* at 36.

175 *Ibid.* at 37.

176 *Ibid.* at 25. *See* RONALD L. NUMBERS, THE CREATIONISTS (1992).

177 *Ibid.* at 38, 39.

178 *Ibid.* at 39. *See* RAYMOND A. EVE & FRANCIS B. HARROLD, THE CREATIONIST MOVEMENT IN MODERN AMERICA (1991).

179 Scopes v. State, 154 Tenn. 105, 289 S.W. 363 (1927).

180 Gilbert Merritt, *From the Scopes Trial to the Human Genome Project: Where is Biology Taking the Law?* 67 U. CIN. L. REV. 365, 368 (1999).

181 Edward J. Larson, *The Scopes Trial and The Evolving Concept of Freedom*, 85 VA. L. REV. 503, 519 (1999).

182 *Ibid.* at 508. *See generally* FAIGMAN, *supra* note 87 at ch. 6.

183 Larson, *supra* note 181 at 512.

184 EDWARD J. LARSON, SUMMER FOR THE GODS 239 (1997). *See generally* EDWARD A. WHITE, SCIENCE AND RELIGION IN AMERICAN THOUGHT: THE IMPACT OF NATURALISM (1952).

185 LARSON, *ibid.* at 227.

186 *Ibid.* at 265. *See generally* JOHN H. BROOKE, SCIENCE AND RELIGION: SOME HISTORICAL PERSPECTIVES (1991).

187 *See e.g.*, Jon Christensen, *Teachers Fight for Darwin's Place in U.S. Classrooms*, N.Y. TIMES, Nov. 24, 1998, at F3.

188 Villarreal, *supra* note 168 at 345; Dan Sheid, *Evolution and Creationism in The Public Schools*, 9 J. CONTEMP. L. 81, 85–87 (1983).

189 393 U.S. 97 (1968).

190 Larson, *supra* note 181 at 524.

191 *Ibid.* at 525.

192 482 U.S. 578 (1987).

193 For an analysis of whether creation science is really science or merely the religious doctrine of divine creation repackaged in jargon, together with arguments for creationism from the Establishment Clause and the Free Exercise Clause of the Constitution, *see* CHARLES FRIED, SAYING WHAT THE LAW IS: THE CONSTITUTION IN THE SUPREME COURT ch. 5 (2004); FAIGMAN, *supra* note 87 at 318–23.

   See generally Jay D. Wexler, *Darwin, Design, and Disestablishment: Teaching the Evolution Controversy in Public Schools*, 56 VANDERBILT L. REV. 751 (2003). *See also* BERT THOMPSON, THE SCIENTIFIC CASE FOR CREATION (1985).

194 Wendell Bird, Note, *Freedom of Religion and Science Instruction in Public Schools*, 87 YALE L. J. 515 (1978).

195 Colleen McGrath, *Redefining Science to Accommodate Religious Beliefs*, 45 N.Y. L. SCH. L. REV. 297, 303 (2001).

196 *Ibid.* at 303. *See* ARK. CODE ANN. § 80–1663 (1981); 17 LA. REV. STAT. ANN. § 286 (1981); TENN. CODE ANN. § 49–2008 (1973).

197 McGrath, *supra* note 195 at 305–9. *See* McLean v. Arkansas, 529 F. Supp. 1255 (E.D. Ark. 1982), often referred to as "Scopes II," where state legislation mandating balanced treatment of creation science and evolution science in public school curricula was held unconstitutional thus thereby dealing a death blow to the teaching of creationism and, by implied reference, the teaching of Intelligent Design. Beckewith, *supra* note 165 at 458 *passim*.

198 LA. REV. STAT. 17:285.1 (2008).

199 *Ibid. See generally* Adam Nossiter, *Boycott by Science Group Over Louisiana Law Seen as Door to Teaching Creationism*, N.Y. TIMES, Feb. 17, 2009, at A14.

200 Hanna Rosin, *Creationism Evolves: Kansas Board Targets Darwin*, WASH. POST, Aug. 8, 1999, at A1. *But see* Larry Witham, *49 States Mandate Teaching Evolution*, WASH. TIMES, Apr. 8, 2000, at A3 (reporting, however, that Louisiana, Mississippi, Georgia, Alabama, Florida, and Arkansas have very brief and restricted standards in regards to the teaching of evolution).

201 McGrath, *supra* note 195 at 319.

202 *Ibid.* at 328.

203 *Ibid.*
204 *Ibid.*
205 Villarreal, *supra* note 168 at 374.
206 Larson, *supra* note 181 at 261.
    The Religious Land Use and Institutionalized Persons Act of 2000, *supra* note 26, not only forbids governmental land use regulations burdening the religious exercise of a person or religious assembly but extends this protection to schools operated by religious groups. 42 U.S.C. § 2000cc (a)(1). *See* Caroline Adams, *The Constitutional Validity of The Religious Persons Act of 2000*, 70 FORDHAM L. REV. 2361 (2002). *See generally* R. Kent Greenawalt, *Hands Off! Civil Court Involvement in Conflicts Over Religious Property*, 98 COLUM. L. REV. 1843 (1998); McConnell & Posner, *supra* note 98.
207 Teresa Watanabe, *Faiths Social Reach: Academia Is Getting Religion*, WASH. POST, Nov. 9, 2000, at A18.
208 *Ibid.*
209 GOLDBERG, *supra* note 172 at 130.
210 CHARLES P. SNOW, THE TWO CULTURES AND THE SCIENTIFIC REVOLUTION (1959). *See generally* Stephen P. Weldon, *Postmodernism* in SCIENCE AND RELIGION ch. 30, *supra* note 5.
211 SNOW, *ibid.*
212 CHARLES P. SNOW, THE TWO CULTURES: AND A SECOND LOOK (1963). *See* Carl Sagan, *Describing the World As It Is, Not As It Would Be* in THE WRITING LIFE: WRITERS ON HOW THEY THINK AND WORK at 309–11 (Marie Arana ed. 2003) (arguing for a concerted national effort to write clearly about science and popularize it through books so that every citizen can, in turn, understand it).
213 JOHN BROCKMAN, THE THIRD CULTURE at 18 (1995).
214 *Ibid.*
215 *Ibid.*
216 *Ibid.*; Sagan, *supra* note 212 at 311.
217 *Ibid.* at 28.
218 DOUGLAS W. KMIEC, CEASE-FIRE ON THE FAMILY: THE END OF THE CULTURE WAR 55 (1995).
219 PETER L. BERGER & RICHARD J. NEUHAS, TO EMPOWER PEOPLE: FROM STATE TO CIVIL SOCIETY 148–49 (1996). *See generally* GEORGE P. SMITH, II, FAMILY VALUES AND THE NEW SOCIETY: DILEMMAS OF THE 21st CENTURY (1998). *See also* George P. Smith, II, *Monograph*, CHALLENGING FAMILY VALUES IN THE NEW SOCIETY 18 (1996).
220 KMIEC, *supra* note 218 at 97.
221 M. Cathleen Kaveny, *Law, Morality and Common Ground*, AMERICA 7 (Dec. 9, 2000).
    Indeed, Justice Antonin Scalia terms the fixation Americans with the law as a "material obsession." ANTONIN SCALIA, A MATTER OF INTERPRETATION: FEDERAL COURTS AND THE LAW 3 (1997).
222 *Ibid. See generally* R. Kent Greenawalt, *The Use of Religious Convictions by Legislators and Judges*, *supra* note 89.
223 *Ibid.*
224 Reagan, *supra* note 92. *See generally* R. Kent Greenawalt, *The Role of Religion in a Liberal Democracy: Dilemmas and Possible Solutions*, 35 J. CHURCH & STATE 503 (1993).
225 *See* ST. AUGUSTINE, *supra* note 68.
226 Peter Singer, WRITINGS ON AN ETHICAL LIFE xviii (2000).
227 *See* Witte, *supra* note 88. *See generally* GOLDBERG *supra* note 172 at ch. 8; R. KENT GREENAWALT, RELIGIOUS CONVICTIONS AND POLITICAL CHOICE (1988). *But see* Jacqueline Salmon, *Scalia Defends Public Expression of Faith*, WASH. POST, Jan. 13, 2003, at B1 (reporting on Justice Scalia's concerns that too many court decisions have, in recent years, outlawed expressions of religious faith in public events).
228 SCALIA, *supra* note 221 at 46, 47.

229 CASS R. SUNSTEIN, THE PARTIAL CONSTITUTION chs. 4–6 (1993).

230 SCALIA, *supra* note 221 at 44, 45.

231 *See ibid., supra* note 221 at 44 *passim.*

232 GOLDBERG, *supra* note 172 at 18.

233 *Ibid.*

234 *Ibid.* at 135. *See generally* GUSTAFSON, *supra* note 129.

235 Smith, *supra* note 77. *See also supra* notes 67, 68.

236 GERALD SCHROEDER, THE SCIENCE OF GOD 18 (1997).

237 JOHN POLKINGHORNE, BELIEF IN GOD IN AN AGE OF SCIENCE 92 (1998). *See* BARBARA BRADLEY HAGERTY, FINGERPRINTS OF GOD (2009) (maintaining that science and faith are not mutually exclusive and instead of dispelling the spiritual, science is cracking it open for all to see); Gregory, *supra* note 42.

238 SCHROEDER, *supra* note 236 at 21, 141.
    Science has already sought to close biblical ranks by recognizing there was not only a beginning to the universe but that life began on earth rapidly following water and not through millennia of random sets of reactions. *Ibid.* at 29. *See also* ARTHUR PEACOCKE, PATHS FROM SCIENCE TOWARDS GOD: THE END OF ALL OUR EXPLORING chs. 1, 2 (2001).

239 *See* SCHROEDER, *supra* note 236; ARTHUR PEACOCKE, THEOLOGY FOR A SCIENTIFIC AGE (1993).

240 HEALTH/MEDICINE AND THE FAITH TRADITIONS: AN INQUIRY INTO RELIGION AND MEDICINE at 209 (Martin E. Marty & Kenneth L. Vaux, eds. 1982). Interestingly, eighty-four percent of Americans think that praying for the sick improves their chances of recovery. Claudia Kalb, *supra* note 6 at 46.

241 George P. Smith, II, *Distributive Justice and Health Care*, 18 J. CONTEMP. HEALTH L. & POL'Y 421 (2002). *See generally* GEORGE P. SMITH, II, GENETICS, ETHICS AND THE LAW, 164–65 (1981).

242 J. ROBERT NELSON, ON THE NEW FRONTIERS OF GENETICS AND RELIGION 162 (1994). *See generally* J. I. JOSÉ LAVASTIDA, HEALTH CARE AND THE COMMON GOOD: A CATHOLIC THEORY OF JUSTICE (2000).

4 Human rights, health care, and bioethics

Introduction and historical overview

While the modern Law of Human Rights may have a short, formative period of no more than three centuries, both the principle and the history of the Dignity of Man—together with his common citizenship in society—can be seen for thousands of years. Indeed, almost from the very beginnings of recorded humanity, the quest for a validation of human rights has been found, not so much perhaps in reason, as with an instinctive feeling of what is both right and good.[1] Thus, it has been said, "Human rights have always existed with the human being," as with the concept of human dignity.[2]

Under an interpretation of human rights, they are seen as "non-positivistic, principled, legal limits to what states, state actors, and state agents can do to their citizens."[3] As such, they impose no obligations on states; rather, they impose limits to state action.[4] This American view is drawn from the philosophy of the Bill of Rights and rooted in a neo-Lockean conception of the rule of law as a "commitment to a determinate set of legal rules."[5] In the international human rights community, however, a contrary view is taken—a view which holds to the notion that these rights either obligate state action under certain circumstances or, alternatively, obligate restraint by the state.[6]

Although a concrete notion of human rights appears absent from the Greek and Roman legal systems as well as the Chinese and other ancient civilizations,[7] certain claims to parental authorship have—over time—been tied to Magna Carta 1215 and the Bill of Rights 1689, as well as the American Declaration of Independence 1776, and the French Declaration of the Rights of Man and of The Citizen 1789.[8] Yet, from the standpoint of historical accuracy, the French Declaration is seen correctly as the first document of its character to reference contemporary social, economic, and cultural rights styled originally as the rights to education, work, property ownership, and social protection.[9]

Even though viewed as a type of generalized philosophical manifesto for the Western World, the French Declaration was not embraced by subsequent European constitutions.[10] Indeed, these new constitutions were seen as not only less pragmatic as the Declaration but they also were prone to de-emphasize "the philosophy of inalienable rights."[11] Rights were, thus, constitutional in origin. In America, as seen, however, rights were held to be not societal "gifts," but natural or inherent.[12]

The European constitutions of the nineteenth century were the frameworks or mechanisms for declaring rights to be protected constitutionally within legal boundaries.[13] Put simply, then, it was solely within the legislative power where fundamental rights were not only declared but limited[14] Latin American constitutionalism de-emphasized the "inalienability of rights" and—instead—during the nineteenth and twentieth centuries, chose to reference only those laws established by state authorities.[15]

In attempting to distinguish human rights from fundamental constitutional rights, socialist jurisprudence sought to ignore any inherent or natural rights theories and treated them as but philosophical rights—this, while recognizing the constitutionally created rights as political in origin.[16] Even though constitutions drafted during the post-socialist period failed to follow the socialist concept of granted right, there remained a dilemma: how to develop a "middle-ground approach" which would validate the idea that "a consensus reached by the people at the constitution's adoption is the result of their recognition of some commonly accepted values."[17] It was all too apparent to those drafting new constitutions that securing fundamental recognition of a selection of core rights was not guaranteed by a designation that these rights were "natural."[18] Indeed, throughout the subsequent history of human rights, "cultural relativism" has been a dominant force with which to reckon—for, the values of some people are not always capable of being judged by the norms shared by others.[19]

Even with vagueness and imprecision as the all-too-often banner of contemporary human rights, a trend toward the "internationalization of human rights movements" is evidenced.[20] Yet, such a trend by no means can be seen as an integration of internationalized human rights with international human rights movements. Rather, it must be accepted as but a "toleration for human rights monitoring by governmental and non governmental organizations and accession to the most important human rights treaties."[21]

Seeking a consensus

The need for a consensus on the universality of human rights—their international declaration, recognition, and protection—arose modernly as a consequence of the ravages of World War II. The Axis Powers' savage trampling on human rights, the holocausts of the gas chambers of Auschwitz and Dachau, and the use of the atom bomb on Hiroshima galvanized an international response to universalize a legal process for protecting human rights in the United Nations adoption in 1948 of The Universal Declaration of Human Rights.[22] While the 1945 Charter of the United Nations re-affirmed "faith in fundamental human rights, in the dignity and worth of the human person, in the equal rights of men and women," this was found to be rather vague regarding the encouragement of respect for human rights. This deficiency was corrected on December 10, 1948, when the U.N. General Assembly adopted the Universal Declaration and, at least on paper, established the universalization of basic human rights.[23]

The Organization of American States' action, also in 1948, in issuing The American Declaration of The Rights and Duties of Man,[24] complemented the Universal Declaration. Together, both documents became the bulwark for recognizing—internationally—human rights and fundamental freedoms. They are also seen as the source for other conventions which further defined and elaborated the rights stated originally within these two instruments— with the most significant being the 1966 International Covenant on Economic, Social and Cultural Rights (ICESCR),[25] and the 1966 International Covenant on Civil and Political Rights (ICCPR).[26]

Article 1 of the 1945 United Nations Charter affirms the dignity and worth of the human person as the cornerstone of human rights. This precept is buttressed by the Universal Declaration in Article 22 where economic, social, and cultural rights are recognized as "indispensable for a person's dignity and the development of his personality." Thus, it is seen, that autonomy—and its exercise—is central to recognition and implementation of the very goal of maintaining human rights. Indeed, "the free and full development" of personality in the community can never be achieved, as Article 29 of the Universal Declaration sets out, unless one is seen as an autonomous individual.

Interestingly, while the Universal Declaration has no force as a binding treaty, it has encouraged—nonetheless—"a culture of human rights" and thereby served as a framework for expanding and recreating the very boundaries of human rights—this by means of a "vast array of non-governmental organizations, and civil society bodies, committed in very practical ways, to upholding universal rights at home and abroad."[27]

The purpose of this Chapter is to explore the extent to which a universal right to health, health care or health protection is being shaped—and to some degree and level, recognized—under the rubric of a social or cultural entitlement within the law of human rights. The conclusion to be reached is that current issues of indeterminacy, justiciability, and progressive realization present serious roadblocks to the goal of codifying and then implementing an international right to health. While measured progress in meeting these first two challenges is occurring, the most contentious impediment remains: namely, determining the extent to which a sustained level of economic stability must be attained, in the first instance, before a state can seek to recognize and enforce a right to health at any minimum or maximum level. Stated otherwise, economic self-interest must be recognized as the primary vector of force gauging the extent to which a state will honor the enforcement of a human right to health, health care, or health protection.

Applying international law

Issues of justiciability and indeterminacy

The international law of human rights is shaped—initially—by states assuming obligations measured as such in various pertinent international instruments. While these documents do reference individual rights in every instance, a state's obligation and the rights of individuals are neither correlative nor necessarily even in the same legal order. Because of this reality of international lawmaking, three perspectives have developed—and are used alternatively as dictated by the particular circumstances—to evaluate the integrity of international human rights agreements.

Under the first perspective, human rights are viewed essentially if, indeed not exclusively, as interstate matters. Accordingly, international human rights create two sets of duties: the duty of every state-party to act as it promised and, the corresponding right of the other state-party to have the original promise kept. An individual has no international legal rights nor remedies in the international legal order and is but an "incidental beneficiary" of rights and duties between the state-parties.[28]

Some interpret justiciability as a principle that allows a judicial body to address complaints alleging violations of a legal right while others expand the meaning to include the "possibility" to be heard before, for example, what was formerly the European Commission of Human Rights,[29] but which has been replaced by a newly constituted European Court of Human Rights.[30] Defined broadly, then, as "the susceptibility of a right to third-party adjudication,"[31] justiciability varies in scope and application from one decision-making body to another—all because of the heretofore lack of uniformity or consistency in global judicial decision-making.[32]

A move toward consistency was taken in 1998 when the 11th Additional Protocol to The European Convention for The Protection of Human Rights and Fundamental Freedoms entered into force.[33] Prior to this Protocol, by ratifying the European Convention on Human Rights (ECHR), the only mandatory procedure required of states was adherence to the interstate complaints procedure of the European Commission of Human Rights and the Committee of Ministers—at the time, the highest political body in the Council of Europe.[34] Since individual complaints procedure and jurisdiction before the European Court of Human Rights were wholly optional, the parties thus had the option of recognizing them through voluntary declarations—and, then, usually for but a limited period.[35]

Under the newly established permanent European Court of Human Rights, optional claims were eliminated.[36] This, in turn, had the direct effect of requiring individual complaints and interstate complaint procedures by all state parties to be brought before an independent court.[37] In turn, the Commission of Ministers is now eliminated from the decision-making processes and charged with the responsibility for supervising, at the national level, the execution of the Court's judgments.[38]

Divested largely of political influence, as well as streamlined and accelerated, the system has seen an increase in individual complaints.[39] Indeed, in the five years since 1998 and Protocol 11's entering into force, roughly 135,000 applications have been lodged.[40] This figure is higher than the overall total of all such applications submitted previously in over 40 years.[41]

Although mandatory since the establishment of the ECHR, interstate complaints procedures against other states for human rights violations have rarely been pursued.[42] Interestingly, only 12 interstate complaints were filed in the 50-year history of the ECHR's existence.[43]

The second view held is that, in addition to creating rights and duties for party states, international human rights agreements confer upon the individual, rights against the state under international law—these in addition to rights ensuring to his benefit under his national constitutional legal system. Even though enforceable only by inter-state remedies or by governments or international bodies acting in his behalf, the individual does, it is contended, have international legal rights under this view.[44]

A good example of this perspective in action may be seen in the British 1998 Human Rights Act which implements the 1950 ECHR in English domestic law.[45] While not incorporating the ECHR into domestic law, the Act allows the Convention, however, to be relied upon directly in British domestic courts. Indeed, under so-called "Convention rights," certain provisions of the Convention and some of its protocols are given a "defined status" in English law.[46] What the ECHR does is to guarantee a number of rights without limit or restriction.[47] Thus, when a citizen's rights and freedoms are violated, under Article 13 of the Convention, they are given an effective remedy before a national authority.[48]

Finally, the third perspective advocates a privatization theory or a position which holds that as to legislating party-states, the states have legislated "human rights" into international law—thus conferring upon those rights the status of affirmative independent values.[49] This view is advanced as a basis for acknowledging a right to health be incorporated fully, both in principle and in operation, as part of the domestic national legal system. Such an incorporation would thereby create a public obligation on national governments to implement that right as well as structure a private legal remedy for its enforcement in its domestic courts, administrative tribunals, and other public authorities.[50]

Multiple international investigative or settlement bodies complicate the issue of justiciability. For example, the ICESCR designates the Economic and Social Council (ECOSOC), the Commission on Human Rights and particular specialized agencies—International Labor Organization, the United Nations Educational, Scientific and Cultural Organization (UNESCO), Food and Agricultural Agency, and the World Health Organization (WHO)—as oversight bodies for individual human rights complaints.[51] When the jurisdiction of the Committee on Economic, Social and Cultural Rights is brought into play on the issue of individual complaints,[52] the determination of issues of justiciability becomes even more clouded. Additionally, to some extent, economic, social, and cultural rights claims are also subject to review under their respective treaties by the Human Rights Committee, the Committee on the Elimination of Racial Discrimination, and the Committee on the Elimination of Discrimination against Women.[53]

Current efforts by a newly structured working group of the U.N. Commission on Human Rights are tackling this very contentious issue of whether a new complaints mechanism which seeks to codify all those economic, social, and cultural human rights—together with civil and political ones as well—can be presented under one individual complaints procedure.[54] It is argued that since all human rights are universal and interdependent, they should be enforced uniformly under one mechanism.[55]

Skepticism has been expressed whether such a mechanism is practical and not Utopian since the ICESCR never intended the rights and obligations contained in it "to be susceptible to judicial or quasi-judicial determination."[56] Indeed, the drafters of the Universal Declaration of Human Rights, the International Covenant on Civil and Political Rights and the International Covenant on Economic, Social and Cultural Rights "well understood the differences between economic, social and cultural rights, on the one hand, and civil and political rights, on the other."[57]

Prevailing authority holds that both social and cultural rights are not—generally—and the right to health in particular, justiciable and thus unsuitable because of their very indeterminacy as bases for judicial review.[58] Put simply, since the U.N. provides no specific procedures for complaints for violations of health rights, as well as other economic, social, and cultural rights, these rights are, thus, not justiciable.[59]

In order to shape access to health care resources—which would thus advance a claim to an ultimate aspirational goal of a right to health—a workable definition of what precisely a right to health includes must be given. Article 3 of the Convention on Human Rights and Biomedicine mandates only equitable access to health care of appropriate quality. Of course, this does not mandate what form of health care is accessible or appropriate.[60] Indeterminacy, thus, is a serious central weakness to stabilizing the very right to access health care and is coupled with the realization that there is neither a moral nor a legal standard that gives universal meaning to a right to health.

Non-treaty bases for implementing human rights

Traditional support for formulating a general, non-treaty-based international law of human rights is to be found in customary law, authentic interpretation, and general principles.[61] Customary international law is seen as supplying a comprehensive set of norms held applicable to all states. Indeed, it has been maintained that the range of rights enumerated in the 1948 Declaration of Human Rights should now be seen as accommodating all of the desired human rights principles.[62] Others contend the International Covenants on Economic, Social and Cultural Rights as well as the one on Civil and Political

Rights,[63] have shaped the customary acceptance of some 16 groups of human rights more or less found in the covenants, themselves.[64] While in the past, customary law was developed through the emergence of practice joined by a sense of legal obligation or *opinio iuris*, today there has been a movement from empirical or inductive verification to interpretative verification. Accordingly, the words of text of a U.N. declaration or treaty provision are tested in order to determine whether the normative claims set forth there are, by conduct, being upheld.[65]

Inasmuch as the rules and principles built upon the Universal Declaration of Human Rights are recognized as authoritative interpretations of the U.N. Charter obligations of Articles 55 and 56, all member states are bound— under this view of authentic interpretation—to conform their treaty obligations and practice with relevant organizations of the U.N. in ways promotive of human rights.[66]

Using the general principles of law recognized by civilized nations— developed as such in domestic law—and then transferred to the international plane and applied to relations between states, give yet another anchor for human rights obligations through rules of *jus cogens*.[67]

A final source for validation of international human rights, regarded by some as the most important part of contemporary lawmaking here, is referred to as the "soft law" of human rights. This term includes policies and mechanisms for standard setting designed as either a final or intermediate consensus; for it is with the process of standard setting and monitoring where most political action occurs.[68]

Limits of practical applicability

The general rules of international law may be seen probably as failing to establish an individual right of action before a domestic court—unless domestic law provides specifically for this.[69] As debilitating a weakness as this may be for enforcing human rights and setting penalties for their breach, perhaps the central road block to an effective blueprint for action is the U.N. Security Council's enforcement lethargy. Thus, in addition to recognizing a right of protection for human rights, an "obligation to intervene" for humanitarian purposes must be imposed as well.[70]

Presently, the voluntary system of compliance and self-policing efforts by individual states, coupled with the Security Council's lack of decisiveness, guarantees the self-interests of each state will shape and control its ultimate response to an enforcement or violation of human rights. Coupled with the passivity of the Security Council is the lack of jurisdictional authority by the International Court of Justice to deal with serious human rights infractions.

Another inherent weakness is to be seen in the absence of a general system of ethics under the very concept of human rights. In order to achieve a system of this nature, structures would have to be designed in such a way as to impose far-reaching obligations on the individual to other individuals which is, of course, as has been seen, alien to the classical nature of international law. State obligations are established under the concept of human rights, with there being no inclusion of individual duties to other human beings. The demand made in Article 1 of the Universal Declaration on Human Rights that all beings "should act towards one another in a spirit of brotherhood" is far too broad to be seen as a visible mechanism for imposing concrete duties. "The fact that human rights create individual duties"[71] is quite rational. This is the case because "the function of human rights is to create State obligations, and not to create general ethics. They are minimum standards for acceptable governance and a means of empowerment against oppression by States."[72]

In the final analysis it appears as though contentious debate will continue over succeeding years to focus nevertheless on whether economic, social, and cultural rights are as pressing as civil and political rights.[73] Some would seek to prioritize rights—arguing there are varying moral weights attached to them. Others contend no ranking can be made of fundamental rights and, indeed, none should be honored before others.[74] Seeking universality in application of human rights requires all states to respect a defined set or core of minimum standards of behavior. So long as they meet these standards, adjustments might, in turn, be allowed for differing legal, moral, and cultural value systems within each state.[75]

Specific protections for human rights in the age of biotechnology

In November 1996, the Council of Europe adopted, and in April 1997, signed the Convention for The Protection of Human Rights and the Dignity of the Human Being with Regard to the Application of Biology and Medicine: Convention on Human Rights and Bioethics.[76] Patterned after the human rights approach of the European Convention on Human Rights and Fundamental Freedoms of 1950 (ECHR),[77] the Bioethics Convention seeks to establish a direct relationship between bioethics and human rights. While the ECHR uses a holistic personality-identity framework for focusing on the value of the human being and the dignity and value of humanhood, the Bioethics Convention endeavors to enlarge and build upon this concept of respect, dignity, and protection and to apply it to human substances as well, thereby safeguarding genetic heritage.[78]

The Convention on Human Rights and Biomedicine is similar to the Universal Declaration of Human Rights in its aspirational goal to recognize "the importance of insuring the dignity of the human being" in its Preamble and Declaration in Article 1 that holds the parties "shall protect the dignity and identity of all human beings." Yet, in the Explanatory Report to the Convention, emphasis is placed on the conclusion that the essential value to be upheld and used to interpret the Convention is the protection of human rights and dignity—with the principle of respect for human dignity being central to Articles 15 (regarding scientific research), 17 (safeguarding the protection of those unable to consent to research upon them) as well as 21 (prohibiting the commercialization of human genes and human reproductive cloning). On the issue of human cloning, the draft Protocol to the Convention states with clarity the need to be guided by the understanding that "the instrumentalisation of human beings" is contrary to human dignity.[79] In addition, Article 1 suggests that the concept of human dignity may be used to protect those nascent human life forms which are not yet eligible for protection under a human rights analysis.[80]

Although this Convention is primarily for European Community members, countries—such as the United States—which have observer status in the Council of Europe and acted as participants in the Convention's preparation, are invited to become signatories. The truly fascinating point to be made in comparing U.S. federal precepts (*e.g.*, principles of autonomy, beneficence, and justice) with regard, for example, to research involving human subjects with those espoused by the Convention, itself, is the level of striking similarity found between the two.[81] This fact, in turn, supports the point that contemporary norms for global bioethical decision-making are beginning to take shape and be recognized under the very dynamic concept of transnational human rights.

The UNESCO Declaration

When evaluating UNESCO's Universal Declaration on the Human Genome and Human Rights,[82] the concept of human dignity is seen as the linchpin of the Declaration, itself. Indeed, of the 25 articles compromising the document, the first four are set under the heading, "Human Dignity and the Human Genome." Article 2 affirms:

(a) Everyone has a right to respect for their dignity and for their rights regardless of their genetic characteristics.
(b) That dignity makes it imperative not to reduce individuals to their genetic characteristics. ...

Following through with the need to maintain the human genome in its natural state and prevent its commercialization (Art. 4), dignity is referred to subsequently in seven other articles. Article 6 prohibits "discrimination based on genetic characteristics" which infringe human dignity; Article 10 forbids research on the human genome which fails to respect human dignity, and other practices (*e.g.*, human cloning) "contrary to human dignity" (Art. 11); "advances in biology, genetics and medicine" are to be made available to all "with due regard for the dignity ... of each individual" (Art. 12); a framework for free genomic research is to be provided in a way which safeguards "respect ... for human dignity" (Art. 15) and thereby raises awareness of "responsibilities regarding the fundamental issues relating to the defense of human dignity" that arises from human genetic research (Art. 21). In Article 24, the International Bioethics Committee is mandated to provide oversight "regarding the identification of practices that could be contrary to human dignity" (*e.g.*, germline interventions).[83] Essentially, then, the Declaration seeks to but establish a legal framework for international research.[84]

A new bioethics instrument

UNESCO's continuing effort to give both substantive and practical value to the basic principles of Bioethics as linchpins for safeguarding advances in genetic science is seen in its study of the need for and development of a Universal Instrument in Bioethics[85] which culminated on January 28, 2005, when UNESCO's International Bioethics Committee finalized its Preliminary Draft Declaration on Universal Norms on Bioethics.[86] This instrument was adopted by acclamation, subsequently, by the member states of UNESCO on October 19, 2005, as the Universal Declaration on Bioethics and Human Rights.[87] In declaring its aim to provide a framework for setting forth universal principles and procedures to assist states in developing legislation and policies in bioethics,[88] the Declaration seeks, specifically, to "promote equitable access to medical, scientific and technological developments"[89] consistent with safeguarding respect for human dignity and protecting human rights and fundamental freedoms.[90]

Enunciating a Principle of Social Responsibility codified in Article 14, the Declaration directs decisions and practice in science and technology should seek to advance the common good by providing "access to quality of health care and essential medicines,"[91] "access to adequate nutrition and water,"[92] improved living conditions,[93] eliminating the marginalization of persons,[94] and reducing poverty and illiteracy.[95] Building on this delineation of social responsibility, Article 15 underscores the notion that the benefits of scientific research should be shared "with society as a whole"—and particularly "with developing countries"—in order to advance, among other interests, "access to quality health care"[96] and "support for health services."[97]

While most of the principles set forth in the Declaration are by no means original—but, indeed, derivative of existing international instruments[98]—the strength of the Declaration is to be found in its efforts to integrate declaratory bioethical principles within a human rights framework.[99] The extent to which bioethics is seen properly as an "independent, normative discourse [apart] from international human rights" is open to current debate.[100] What is certain, however, is the real risk that bioethics could become irrelevant in social justice debates if it is not anchored to a substantive body of law—more specifically, International Human Rights.[101]

As with any United Nations Declaration, the Declaration on Bioethics and Human Rights is non-binding and comprises "soft law instruments" intended, as such, to encourage—not oblige—"states to enact enforceable rules inspired by the common standards" set forth in various other U.N. Declarations such as the foundational Universal Declaration of Human Rights.[102] This Declaration on Bioethics must be viewed, in the final analysis, as a noble effort to assist states in their *combined* efforts to not only advance responsible biomedical research and clinical practice[103] but, in doing so, to be true to, and consistent with, the law of international human rights.[104] If this goal is achieved, the Declaration will not only have validated the inextricable relationships between dignity and human rights with access to health care but, indeed, activated a vital alliance among them.[105]

The scope of human dignity

Human dignity, as a concept, is open to abuse and certainly misinterpretation. It can not only oversimplify complex issues, but can also encourage a form of paternalism totally incompatible with the very spirit of self-determination.[106] Oftentimes, it is seen as the primary source of human rights. While, at other times, it is viewed as but a species of it or a framework for defining the subject of human rights. Still, in other applications, human dignity defines objects to be protected—with the effect being that in some situations it may thus limit individual rights of autonomy and self-respect.[107] It has been asserted that "any violation of human rights *implicitly* violates human dignity."[108]

Dignity may also be thought of as a claim for a basic degree of respect as individual human beings; and is accordingly a driving or defining force in shaping well-being.[109] As such a mechanism for action, it may be understood further "as that which protects self-respect, which in turn permits self-conscience and self-identity, which, in turn, requires the promulgation of rights."[110] Always at the very crux of defining and advancing human well-being, however, are to be found health and human rights.[111]

The right to health, health care, or health protection

As early as the fourth century B.C., Aristotle wrote reportedly of an absolute right by citizens to that measure of good health as society is able to give.[112] Over the course of time, the notion of a right to health or to health care as a human right has gained some level of credence when it considered as a corollary to an understanding of the duty and responsibility of states to advance the enjoyment of those freedoms and entitlements considered to be a right of each human.[113] Yet, as has been seen, the battle for *universal* recognition and enforcement of human rights has been largely aspirational and unenforceable.[114] That said, an interesting perspective in law reform is, nonetheless, beginning to take hold and is being led by a prominent Australian jurist.

In the 55th Hamlyn Lecture, Justice Michael D. Kirby of the High Court of Australia, observed that the trend toward globalism dictates human rights law, as a part of the larger body of international legal principle, be used to fill gaps in the common law decision-making process or when ambiguities in written law need to be resolved.[115] Indeed, "as national and international determinations come to influence courts in many lands, global sources will supplement purely local ones in judicial reasoning, especially when the judge is faced by a novel problem."[116] Contemporary constitutional interpretation more and more requires reference to international law and normative values—this, in order to avoid intellectual isolation by the judiciary.[117] The extent to which there is an active or passive interaction between international law and national law remains an issue of great moment.[118]

Definitional uncertainties

Defining and enforcing civil and political rights in the world community has taken—and continues to take—tenacity and great patience. The record of achievement has, at best, been quite irregular. An even greater challenge is to be seen in shaping a meaningful, identifiable, operational, and enforceable right to health within the ambit of economic and social rights.

To make a right to health more than merely aspirational, a first step is to develop a workable definition of what precisely such a right includes. What, for example, does "enjoyment of the highest attainable standard of health"—as used in the preamble of the World Health Organization's 1946 Constitution, mean? Article 55 of the U.N. Charter dedicated the United Nations to promoting solutions for international health problems. What is the nature and scope of these problems? The Universal Declaration of Human Rights structures a right to enjoy "a standard of living adequate for the health and well-being of individuals and their families" (Art. 25). What are the requisites of health necessary for a state of well-being?[119] Interestingly, the ICESCR does not define the right to health and treats it in general, rather than in specific, terms.[120]

Some rights within the Covenant are "recognized,"[121] while others need only be "respected,"[122] "ensured,"[123] or "guaranteed."[124] The highest ordering of state responsibility under the Covenant, then, is to be found under the terms, "to ensure" and "to guarantee;" for they are not subject to the standard of "progressive realisation."[125] While the right to the highest standard of health is, as seen, only "recognized," this was done in the drafting of the Covenant to assure wider acceptability to States unwilling, initially, to assume specific responsibilities—it is, however, given a stronger ordering by the enumeration of various, non-exhaustive steps for its realization.[126]

In actuality, a fundamental right to health suggests something that usually cannot be guaranteed at all—namely, perfect health. Not only does this state or condition vary from person to person, but from country to country and is thus truly an indeterminant variable.[127] In the relevant international human rights instruments pertinent to shaping a right to health,[128] a right to health is seen as corresponding to a shorthand term for "the right to the highest attainable standard of health"[129]—with the right to health care seen as an inherent part of the right to health.[130] Caution must always be taken to avoid broadening the scope of this right to include "almost everything."[131]

There is agreement, however, that there are basic underlying preconditions which influence health and indeed become part of this right to health. They include: adequate nutrition, safe drinking water, sanitation, safe working conditions or occupational health, and a healthy environment.[132]

Without doubt, many of these preconditions overlap with the Covenant for Economic and Cultural Rights.[133] They, in turn complement and strengthen what has been termed "core health care elements" such as safeguarding maternal and child health care (including family planning), immunizing against major infectious diseases and the appropriate treatment of common diseases and injuries.[134]

As seen, Article 3 of the Convention on Human Rights and Biomedicine mandates equitable access to health care of appropriate quality.[135] This, of course, does not resolve in any manner the defining issue of what form of health care is accessible and appropriate.[136] Nor does this mandate allow for any recognition of the fact that the strength and availability of health care services depend upon, in reality, not only the resource bases available to those within domestic health care systems[137] but the social settings in which health demands arise.[138] Consequently, individual claims to appropriate health care is often seen as incompatible with communitarian obligations to preserve the general good.[139]

The Universal Declaration of Human Rights and the two Covenants can be understood—at best—as referencing the *right* to health as but an "imperfect obligation."[140] And, under the principle of cultural relativism, serious doubts remain as to whether all of the rights in the Declaration are encoded culturally in one context or are subject to differing applications within the varying world cultures, themselves, especially since notions of right and wrong vary across transnational boundaries.[141]

Shaping a right to health care

Because of these profound uncertainties, it has been suggested that it is misleading to refer to a governmental obligation to guarantee a person's good health.[142] Rather, it is better and more accurate to refer to a right to health protection[143] which would include a right to health care and a right to live under healthy conditions.[144] Yet, it has been seen that a strong conceptual framework for both identifying and analyzing those essential societal factors representing the conditions under which people can be healthy is lacking.[145] Others suggest that a right to health does exist in the abstract but disagree as to the practical consequences of its recognition.[146] Consistent with all of these concerns, the World Health Organization concluded recently that it made poor economic sense to provide comprehensive medical services for everyone. Accordingly, poorer countries should be helped to carry out low-cost programs to tackle illnesses such as malaria, while wealthier countries should learn how to prioritize the care they offer. Again, the components of qualitative health care availability are seen as being shaped by a clear understanding of resource availability within each state.[147]

The ESCR Comment

The United Nations Committee on Economic, Social and Cultural Rights (ESCR) which is charged with monitoring the implementation of the

ICESCR, issued—in 2000—General Comment No. 14: The Right to the Highest Attainable Standard of Health.[148] While proclaiming health as "a fundamental human right indispensable for the exercise of other human rights," the ESCR structures the right within broad norms, state obligations, violations, and implementations.[149]

Among the core state obligations designed as such to guarantee a minimal level of health are four: non-discriminatory access to health services—especially for vulnerable or marginalized groups; adequate food sources that are enriched nutritionally; basic shelter which accommodates sanitation; and potable water and use of essential drugs.[150] The development of national public health strategies which seek to address health concerns regarding reproduction and maternal health, immunization, infectious disease control, and ready access to health information are of central importance.[151]

While impressive, the General Comment must surely have been seen as more aspirational than determinative—for, the indisputable fact remains: these lofty (albeit noble) pronouncements on state obligations remain non-justiciable. In addition, the bottom line may well be that the members of the transnational community simply—by and large—refuse to invest the necessary economic capital sufficient to guarantee the components of the right to health as seen by the ESCR. Enforcement of such broadly defined and indeterminate rights are not thought practical.

Since the United States, as observed previously, has not ratified the ICESCR, the General Comment has neither force nor effect on its international responsibilities. In point of fact, the United States may be seen as probably violating the right to health—surely not because it spends too little on health care and public health, but rather because its resources are distributed inequitably.[152]

Insurmountable difficulties?

For any working definition of a right to health, health care, or health protection to have contemporary relevance, it must first include recognition of an obligation of the state "to ensure the conditions necessary for the health of individuals."[153] As observed previously, there is no consensus on what minimal conditions are necessary for health[154]—this, because of the almost inextricable relation its recognition as a perfect or imperfect right has with the level of cultural and economic development of each state within the world community.[155] Inevitably, then, individual claims to health right protections must be balanced within a utilitarian construct against societal or communal needs.[156] The result of this often means that equity is forsaken for economic stability.

Organizationally, at the supranational level of administration, the internal weaknesses of the U.N. Security Council and the International Court of Justice for enforcing violations of human rights are compounded—in specific health policies—by the WHO inability to assume a decisive leadership role. Indeed, the WHO has been reluctant to utilize its legal powers—or to adopt legal principles—which implement directly health care strategies. It has chosen instead to adopt a functional or technical approach to health care matters—thereby developing a well regarded and limited reputation for the collection of data and for technical standardization of international health regulations.[157]

Recommendations, resolutions, codes of conduct and technical standards, then, comprise the arsenal used by the WHO to impact health issues transnationally.[158] Whether this is viewed as an effective, systematic, and assertive approach to problem-solving is questionable. Absent use of the treaty-making process, however, it is feared the leadership ability of WHO and, for that matter, other international organizations, will remain limited—this, due inherently to the continuing domination of independent states.[159]

An uncertain future

Regardless of which approach is taken to resolving the complex definitional issues of human rights and their scope, the overriding need is for more explicit implementation standards to be articulated and developed in order to reflect the dynamic quality of a contemporary human rights doctrine.[160] The very imprecision in problems of definition as well as measurement, monitoring, and enforcement have been roadblocks to applying useful economic, social, and cultural rights. Indeed, some consider them insuperable obstacles.[161] Until all countries ratify the ICESCR, establish the domestic capability to monitor the successful enjoyment of these covenant rights and create a complaint and investigative process when allegations of human rights violations occur, no resounding progress or success will be recorded.[162]

Concrete steps have been taken to address many of these concerns. Central to this agenda for change has been the 11th Additional Protocol to The European Convention for the Protection of Human Rights and Fundamental Freedoms which has streamlined a new complaint procedure for individual human rights complaints and interstate complaint procedures for all state parties.[163] In addition, the Commission on Human Rights and other specialized agencies[164] provide a venue for individual human rights complaints. The current efforts of a Working Group of the U.N. Human Rights Commission to study and resolve, hopefully, the issue of whether human rights are universal and, thus, should be enforced under on mechanism, can have nothing but a salutary effect on clarifying the issues of justiciability.[165]

Whether justiciability of economic, social, cultural, and health rights is achieved (as it has been for civil and political rights)[166] in the future, depends in very large measure upon the willingness of the courts to recognize and apply them. Perhaps as important is whether there is a demonstrable level of economic prosperity achieved nationally which accommodates a recognition, and a guarantee, of these rights.[167] Even though a discernible trend is seen toward such a recognition,[168] the fact remains that without a sustained level of economic stability, justiciability will not be validated for claims to either a right to health, health care, or health protection. To be remembered is the fact that Art.2(1) of the ICESCR allows the realization of rights set out within it by the state signatories "progressively" *and* "to the maximum of a State's available resources." Thus, this principle of progressive realization has the very real effect of emasculating any concerted and sustained attempt to structure a universal right to health—this, because the justifiable differences among states (timely or otherwise) in this area of concern are based upon their varying respective degrees of political will and levels of economic resources.[169] So long as their compliance efforts move "progressively" toward the goal of realizing the Article 12 right to health, no violations are registered.[170]

Perhaps the self-defeating weakness of the whole enforcement structure is its reliance upon a voluntary system of compliance and self-policing efforts by individual states. Inevitably, self-interest shapes and controls the ultimate response to a violation of human rights as well as health care protections which are an inherent part of those basic rights.[171]

Notes

1 Fali Nariman, *The Universality of Human Rights*, 50 REV. INT'L COMM. JURISTS 9, 11 (1993).

2 Avery Dulles, *Human Rights: Papal Teaching and The United Nations*, AMERICA 14 (Dec. 5, 1995). *See generally*, H.C. PAYNE, ETERNAL CRUCIBLE: A NEW COSMOLOGY, ch. 27 (1974).

3 Robin West, *Human Rights, the Rule of Law, and American Constitutionalism*, ch. 4 at 93 in PROTECTING HUMAN RIGHTS: INSTRUMENTS AND INSTITUTIONS (Tom Campbell, Jeffrey Goldsworthy & Adrienne Stone, eds. 2003).

4 *Ibid.* at 93.

5 *Ibid.* at 95.

6 *Ibid.* at 93.

7 Michael D. Kirby, Paper, *The Right to Health Fifty Years On—Still Skeptical?* Bagnoud Center for Health and Human Rights, Harvard University School of Public Health, Cambridge, Massachusetts, Dec. 4, 1998, at pp. 5, 6, quoting Isaiah Berlin, I BERLIN, *Two Concepts of Liberty* in FOUR ESSAYS ON LIBERTY 118, 129 (1970).

8 Kirby, *ibid.* at 5, 6 *passim. See generally*, R. H. Helmholz, *Magna Carta and the iuis commune*, 66 U. CHI. L. REV. 297 (1999); Akhil R. Amar, *The Bill of Rights as a Constitution*, 100 YALE L. J. 1131 (1991).

9 *Ibid. See* P. G. LAUREN, THE EVOLUTION OF INTERNATIONAL HUMAN RIGHTS (1998); Stephen P. Marks, *From the Single Confused Page to the Decalogue for Six Billion Persons: The Roots of the Universal Declaration of Human Rights in the French Revolution*, 20 HUMAN RIGHTS Q. 459, 472 (1998). *But see* Hugo Adam Bedau, *Anarchical Fallacies: Bentham's Attack on Human Rights*, 22 HUMAN RIGHTS Q. 261 (2000).

10 Rett R. Ludwikowski, *Constitutionalization of Human Rights in Post-Soviet States and Latin America: A Comparative Analysis*, 33 GA. J. INT'L. & COMP. LAW 1, 20 (2004).

11 *Ibid.*

12 *Ibid.*

13 *Ibid.*

14 *Ibid. See generally* JEFFREY GOLDSWORTHY, THE SOVEREIGNTY OF PARLIAMENT: HISTORY AND PHILOSOPHY (1999).

15 Ludwikowski, *supra* note 10 at 21.

16 *Ibid.*

17 *Ibid.* at 22.

18 *Ibid.*

19 *Ibid.* at 23.

20 *Ibid.* at 40.

21 *Ibid.* at 41–42.

22 G.A. RES. 217A (III), U.N. GAOR, 3d Sess., U.N. Doc. A/810 (1948).

23 Nariman, *supra* note 1 at 12. *See generally,* Mary Ann Glendon, *Knowing The Universal Declaration of Human Rights,* 73 NOTRE DAME L. REV. 1153 (1998).

24 O.A.S. Doc. OEA/ser.L./V./I.4.

   The Convention contains 26 rights and freedoms—21 of which are found, in similar phraseology, to provisions within the International Covenant on Civil and Political Rights. HENRY J. STEINER & PHILIP ALSTON, INTERNATIONAL HUMAN RIGHTS IN CONTEXT 642 (1996).

25 993 U.N.T.S. 3. The United States is not a party.

26 999 U.N.T.S. 171. The United States is a party, subject to several reservations, understandings, and declarations.

   For some, the whole international law of human rights is viewed as having developed essentially by these two covenants. *See, e.g.,* D. P. FORSYTHE, THE POLITICS OF INTERNATIONAL LAW 177 (1990).

   Other notable regional conventions include the 1989 Convention on Rights of the Child; the 1984 Convention Against Torture and Other Cruel, Inhuman or Degrading Treatment or Punishment; the 1979 Convention on The Elimination of All Forms of Discrimination Against Women; and the 1965 Convention on the Elimination of All Forms of Racial Discrimination. *See* Dinah Shelton, *Challenges to the Future of Civil and Political Rights,* 55 WASH. & LEE L. REV. 669 (1998).

27 Kirby, *supra* note 7 at 17, 23. *See also* STEINER & ALSTON, *supra* note 24 at 563–69. *See generally* 1 MILTON I. ROEMER, NATIONAL HEALTH SYSTEMS OF THE WORLD (1991).

28 Louis Henkin, *The Philosophy of Human Rights* in THE PHILOSOPHY OF HUMAN RIGHTS at 137–38 (Milton E. Winston, ed. 1989). *See generally,* A. CASSESE, HUMAN RIGHTS IN A CHANGING WORLD (1994).

29 BRIGIT C.A. TOEBES, THE RIGHT TO HEALTH AS A HUMAN RIGHT IN INTERNATIONAL LAW 168 (1999).

30 Treaty 155 in the European Treaty Series (ETS) amending the European Convention on Human Rights Treaty 005 in the ETS.

   Protocol 11 amended The European Convention for The Protection of Human Rights and Fundamental Freedoms and came into effect November 1, 1998. *Ibid.* It directs all state-parties to accept a complete overhaul of the Convention control mechanisms with the creation of a single Court of Human Rights replacing, as such, The European Commission and Court. It is hoped that—with time and implementation—this Protocol will go far in clarifying issues of justiciability.

31 TOEBES, *supra* note 29.

32 *Ibid.* at 169.

   Others view justiciability as a concept referring—primarily—to what is permissible in a state's domestic law or as tied to the issue of what rights (or disputes about them) are recognized, and thus justiciable in a mechanism capable of adjudicating them. When mechanisms or procedures are found lacking, disputes are seen as non-justiciable. And, interestingly, no provision is made by the majority of states for domestic adjudication of economic, social, and cultural rights. Michael J. Dennis & David P. Stewart, *infra* note 51 at 473, 474. *See also* Brigit Toebes, *Towards an Improved Understanding of The International Human Right to Health,* 21 HUMAN RIGHTS Q. 661, 671 *passim* (1999); HUMAN RIGHTS: NEW DIMENSIONS AND CHALLENGES 135 *passim* (Janusz Symonides, ed. 1998).

33 *Supra* note 30.

34 MANFRED NOWAK, INTRODUCTION TO THE INTERNATIONAL HUMAN RIGHTS REGIME 161 (2003).

35 *Ibid.* Interestingly, Turkey and a number of other states, took decades before recognizing these optional procedures. *Ibid.*

36 *Ibid.* at 164, 165.

37 *Ibid.*

38 *Ibid.*

39 *Ibid.* at 164.

40 *Ibid. See generally* HUMAN RIGHTS: INTERNATIONAL PROTECTION, MONITORING, ENFORCEMENT (Janusz Symonides, ed. 2003).

41 NOWAK, *supra* note 34 at 164.

42 *Ibid.* at 165.

43 *Ibid.* at 166. *See generally* ANNE F. BAYEFSKY, HOW TO COMPLAIN TO THE U.N. HUMAN RIGHTS TREATY SYSTEM (2003).

44 Louis Henkin, *supra* note 28.

45 213 U.N.T.S. 221 (1950), entered into force, Sept. 3, 1953.

46 K.D. Ewing, *The Human Rights Act and Parliamentary Democracy*, 62 MOD. L. REV. 79, 82 (1999). *See* Richard A. Edwards, *Deference under The Human Rights Act*, 65 MOD. L. REV. 859, 860 (2002) (observing that while the extent of judicial deference to the other branches of government is under current debate, it nonetheless is a firmly established feature of judicial review in cases involving the British Human Rights Act). *See also* Paul Craig, *The Courts, the HRA and Judicial Review*, 117 LAW Q. REV. 589 (2000). *See generally* K. D. Ewing, *The Case for Social Rights*, ch. 16 PROTECTING HUMAN RIGHTS: INSTRUMENTS AND INSTITUTIONS (Tom Campbell, Jeffrey Goldsworthy & Adrienne Stone, ed. 2003).

47 *See e.g.*, the right to life (Art. 2); the right not to suffer torture or inhuman degrading treatment (Art. 3); the right not to be held in servitude (Art. 4); the right to liberty (Art. 5); the right to a fair trial (Art. 6); protection against the retrospective application of the criminal law (Art. 7); the right to protection of private life (Art. 8); rights to freedom of conscience and religion (Art. 9); expression (Art. 10), and association and peaceful assembly (Art. 11); and the right to marry and found a family (Art. 12). Some of these rights are— to be sure—qualified: among them being those relating to privacy, conscience and religion, expression, and association and assembly. *Supra* note 17; Ewing, *supra* note 46 at 80.

48 Ewing, *supra* note 46 at 80. *See generally*, Mark Elliott, *The Demise of Parliamentary Sovereignty? The Implications of Justifying Judicial Review*, 115 L. Q. REV. 119, 126 *passim* (1998).

49 Henkin, *supra* note 28 at 138–39. *See infra* notes 115–18. *See* ANDREW CLAPHAM, HUMAN RIGHTS IN THE PRIVATE SPHERE (1993).

50 Philip W. Bates, *Health Law, Ethics and Policy: Challenges and New Avenues for the 21st Century and New Millennium*, 18 MED. LAW 13, 21 (1999). *See* FRANCISCO F. MARTIN, CHALLENGING HUMAN RIGHTS VIOLATIONS: USING INTERNATIONAL LAW IN U.S. COURTS (2001); Richard B. Lillich, *Damages for Gross Violations of International Human Rights, Awarded by U.S. Courts*, 15 HUMAN RIGHTS Q. 207 (1993). *See also* TIMOTHY S. JOST, DISENTITLEMENT? THE THREATS FACING OUR PUBLIC HEALTH-CARE PROGRAMS AND A RIGHTS-BASED RESPONSE 24–30 (2003) (discussing the extent to which, in America, there is a constitutional right to health).

51 Michael J. Dennis & David P. Stewart, *Justiciability of Economic, Social and Cultural Rights: Should There be an International Complaints Mechanism to Adjudicate the Rights to Food, Housing and Health?* 98 AM. J. INT'L 462 at 506 (2004).

52 *Ibid.*

53 *Ibid.* at 504.

54 *Ibid.* at 462.

55 *Ibid.* at 463.

56 *Ibid.* at 515.

57 *Ibid.*

58 TOEBES, *supra* note 29 at 169.

59 *Ibid.* at 181.

60 Convention for the Protection of Human Rights and Dignity on the Human Being with Regard to the Application of Biology and Medicine: Convention of Human Rights and Medicine, Apr. 4, 1997, art. 3, Eur. T.S. No. 164, 36 I.L.M. 817 (1997) [hereinafter Convention on Human Rights and Biomedicine].

61 R. J. VINCENT, HUMAN RIGHTS AND INTERNATIONAL RELATIONS 227 (1986).

62 *Ibid.* at 215.

63 *See generally*, FORSYTHE, *supra* note 26.

64 Rolf Künneman, *A Coherent Approach to Human Rights*, 17 HUMAN RIGHTS Q. 323, 324–25 (1995).

65 *Supra* note 61 at 216–20.

66 *Ibid.* at 223.

67 *Ibid.* at 224.

68 *Ibid.* at 223.

69 Bruno Simma, *International Human Rights and General International Law: A Comparative Analysis*, in IV COLLECTED COURSES FOR THE ACADEMY OF EUROPEAN LAW, Bk. 2, 153, at 231 (1993). *See* Jordan J. Paust, *The Other Side of Right: Private Duties under Human Rights*, 5 HARV. HUMAN RIGHTS J. 51 (1992).

70 Simma, *ibid.* at 232.

71 Künneman *supra* note 64 at 339.

72 *Ibid.*

73 Helena M. Cook, *International Human Rights Mechanisms*, 50 REV. INT'L. COMM. JUR-ISTS 31, 38 (1993).

74 *Ibid.* at 38.

75 *Ibid.* at 40. *See also* LAWRENCE O. GOSTIN & ZITA LAZZARINI, HUMAN RIGHTS AND PUBLIC HEALTH IN THE AIDS PANDEMIC 29 (1997).

76 Eur. T.S. No. 164, 36 I.L.M. 817 (1997); *see supra* note 60.

77 213 U.N.T.S. 221.

78 Eibe Riedel, *Global Responsibilities and Bioethics: Reflections on The Council of Europe's Bioethics Convention*, 5 IND. J. GLOBAL LEGAL STUD. J. 179, 182 (1997).

79 Deryck Beyleveld & Roger Brounsword, *Human Dignity, Human Rights and Human Genetics,* 61 MOD. L. REV. 661, 663–64 (1998).

   Inasmuch as the original Biomedicine Convention contained no direct ban on human cloning, a protocol to this effect was drafted prohibiting "any intervention seeking to create a human being genetically identical to another human being, whether living or dead." Jan. 12, 1998, Eur. T.S. No. 168, at Art. 1 as cited in Shelton, *supra* note 26 at 680, f.n.70.

80 Beyleveld & Brounsword, *ibid.* at 664. *See* Maurice A.M. de Wachter, *The European Convention on Bioethics*, 27 HASTINGS CENTER RPT. 13 (Jan.-Feb. 1997).

81 F. William Domel & Duane Alexander, *The Convention on Human Rights and Biomedicine of The Council of Europe*, 7 KENNEDY INST. ETHICS J. 259, *passim* (1997).

82 BIO-97/Conf. 201/CLD.6, Final Report (July 25, 1997).

83 Beyleveld & Brounsword, *supra* note 79 at 664, 665. *See generally* Roberto Andorno, *Dignity and The Person in The Light of International Biomedical Law*, 1 MEDICINE & MORALS 91 (2005).

84 B.A. BRODY, THE ETHICS OF BIOMEDICAL RESEARCH: AN INTERNATIONAL PERSPECTIVE (1998). *See also* Michael D. Kirby, *Challenges of The Genome*, 20 U. NEW SO. WALES L. J. 537 (1997).

85 SHS/EST/02/CIB-9/5 Paris, 15 November 2002. Preliminary Report on the Possibility of Elaborating a Universal Instrument on Bioethics, Working Group of the IBC (International Bioethics Committee). *See also*, Council of Europe Draft Additional Protocol to the Convention on Human Rights and Biomedicine on Biomedical Research, CDBI/INF

(2001) 5, which seeks to provide protection on human experimentations. Strasbourg, July 18, 2001 [bioethics/texts/publics/draftprotocolresearch (2001) 5a]. *See generally*, Allyn L. Taylor, *Globalization and Biotechnology: UNESCO And An International Strategy to Advance Human Rights and Public Health*, 25 AM. J. LAW & MED. 479 (1999).

86 SHS/EST/CIB-EXTR/05/CONF.202/2, Paris, Feb. 9, 2005.

Interestingly, the Committee—differing with the style of the U.N. charge to it—recommended the document be entitled, "Universal Declaration on Bioethics and Human Rights." Explanatory Memorandum on The Elaboration of The Preliminary Draft Declaration on Universal Norms on Bioethics, SHS/EST/CIB/05/CONF.202/4 Paris, Feb. 21, 2005, (paras. 9–12). *See generally* George P. Smith, II, *Bioethics and Human Rights: Toward a New Constitutionalism*, 13 CONST'L L. & POL'Y REV. 68 (2011).

87 Press Release, UNESCO, UNESCO's General Conference adopts Universal Declaration on Bioethics and Human Rights (Oct. 19, 2005), *available* at http://tinyurl.com/do886.

The complete Declaration may be accessed at *http://portal.unesco.org/shs*/en/file_download.php/46133e1f4691e4c6e57566763d474a4dBioeticsDeclaration_En.pdf or, alternatively, at: *http://unesdoc.unesco.org/images/0014/001428/142825e.pdf#page=80*.

88 Art. 2 (a).

89 Art. 2 (f).

90 Art. 3 (l).

91 Art. 14 (a).

92 Art. 14 (b).

93 Art. 14 (c).

94 Art. 14 (d).

95 Art. 14 (e).

96 Art. 15 (b).

97 Art. 15 (d). *See also* Art. 24 (2).

98 *See e.g.*, European Convention on Human Rights and Biomedicine; the Universal Declaration on The Human Genome and Human Rights.

99 *See* Thomas A. Faunce, *Will Human Rights Law Subsume Medical Ethics? Intersections in The UNESCO Universal Bioethics Declaration*, 31 J. MEDICAL ETHICS 173 (2005); GEORGE P. SMITH, II, HUMAN RIGHTS AND BIOMEDICINE (2000).

100 Michael D. Kirby, *Human Rights and Bioethics: The Universal Declaration of Human Rights and UNESCO Declaration of Bioethics and Human Rights*, 25 J. CONTEMP. HEALTH L. & POL'Y 309, 325 (2009).

101 *Ibid. See generally* LAW, HUMAN RIGHTS AND THE BIOETHICS DISCOURSE ch. 6 (Michael Freeman, ed. 2008).

102 Roberto Andorno, *Global Bioethics at UNESCO: In Defense of The Universal Declaration on Bioethics and Human Rights*, 33 J. MEDICAL ETHICS 150, 152 *passim* (2007).

103 Art. 18. *See* O. Carter Snead, *Assessing the Universal Declaration on Bioethics and Human Rights*, 7 NAT'L CATH. BIOETHICS Q. 53 (2007) (observing that the Declaration affirms the central importance of respect for the life of human beings and is anchored in the concept of human dignity).

104 *See e.g.*, Art. 3, Human Rights and Dignity; Art. 10, Equality; Art. 11, Non-discrimination; Art. 14, Social Responsibility. *See generally* GEORGE J. ANNAS, AMERICAN BIOETHICS: CROSSING HUMAN RIGHTS AND HEALTH LAW BOUNDARIES (2005); SMITH, *supra* note 99.

105 *See supra* notes 99, 100, 102, and ANNAS, *ibid.*

106 Beyleveld & Brounsword, *supra* note 79 at 662.

107 *Ibid.* at 665. For an extended analysis of human dignity as a duty-led or rights-led concept, *see ibid.*, at 667–73.

108 *Ibid.* at 665. *See* Andorno, *supra* note 83.

109 MYRES S. McDOUGAL, *ET AL.*, HUMAN RIGHTS AND WORLD PUBLIC ORDER 10, 146 (1980).

110 Alice Ely Yamin, *Defining Questions: Situating Issues of Power in the Formulation of a Right to Health Under International Law*, 18 HUMAN RIGHTS Q. 398 (1996).

111 Jonathan M. Mann, Lawrence O. Gostin, *et al.*, *Health and Human Rights*, 1 HEALTH & HUMAN RIGHTS 7, 19 (1994).

Individual conscience is seen, interestingly, as an emerging norm in the international law of human rights. ROBERT F. DRINAN, CAN GOD AND CAESAR COEXIST? BALANCING RELIGIOUS FREEDOM IN INTERNATIONAL LAW 24 (2004).

112 E.B. BRODY, BIOMEDICAL TECHNOLOGY AND HUMAN RIGHTS 13 (1993).

113 *Ibid.*

114 GEORGE J. ANNAS, SOME CHOICES: LAW, MEDICINE AND THE MARKET 256 (1998).

115 MICHAEL KIRBY, JUDICIAL ACTIVISM: AUTHORITY, PRINCIPLE AND POLICY IN THE JUDICIAL METHOD 74 (2004).

116 *Ibid.* at 75.

117 Justice Michael Kirby, The Seventh Annual Grotius Lecture: "The Growing Use of International Human Rights Law in the Elaboration of Municipal Constitutions," The American Society of International Law, 99th Annual Meeting, Mar. 30, 2005, Washington, D.C.

118 *See generally, supra* note 46.

119 *See* GOSTIN & LAZZARINI, *supra* note 75 at 27–31.

120 *Ibid. See* PAUL SIEGHART, THE LAWFUL RIGHTS OF MANKIND 130 (1985) (acknowledging the European Social Charter (Art. 11), and the African Charter, (Art. 16), also recognize the rights of everyone to the enjoyment of the highest or best attainable standard of health—both physical and mental). *See* 21 I.L.M. 58 (1982). *See also* M. C. R. CRAVEN, THE INTERNATIONAL COVENANT ON ECONOMIC, SOCIAL AND CULTURAL RIGHTS (1995).

121 Art. 12(1) (right to health).

122 *See e.g.*, Art. 13(3) liberty of parents regarding certain aspects of their children's education; Art. 15(3) freedom of scientific research.

123 *See e.g.*, Art. 3 (equal rights of men and women), Art. 8 (trade union rights).

124 *See e.g.*, Art. 2(2) non-discrimination, Art. 7(a)(1) prohibition of gender discrimination in employment.

125 TOEBES, *supra* note 29 at 293.

126 *Ibid.* at 293–332.

127 *Ibid.* at 16. *See also* Symonides, *supra* note 32 at 132–35.

128 TOEBES, *supra* note 29 at 28 *passim*, 245, 246.

The instruments are: The WHO Constitution; The Universal Declaration of Human Rights; The Covenant on Elimination of All Forms of Discrimination Against Women; and The Convention on The Rights of The Child. *See supra* note 26.

129 TOEBES, *supra* note 29 at 17, 18.

130 *Ibid.* at 19.

131 *Ibid.* at 259.

The right to health is seen, essentially, as a right of access to health services. DAVID P. FIDLER, INTERNATIONAL LAW AND PUBLIC HEALTH: MATERIALS ON AND ANALYSIS OF GLOBAL JURISPRUDENCE 302–9 (2000).

132 TOEBES, *supra* note 29 at 122, 272.

It has been argued that the right to health, as a social human right to health, is linked—perhaps inextricably—to "the right to an adequate standard of living and right to food." NOWAK, *supra* note 34 at 143.

133 TOEBES, *supra* note 29 at 122, 272.

134 *Ibid.* at 284.

135 Eur. T. S. No. 164, 36 I. L. M. 817 (1997). *See* JAMES E. CHILDRESS, PRACTICAL REASONING IN BIOETHICS 249–50 (1997) (arguing for equitable access to health care).

136 Dieter Giesen, *Health Care as a Right: Some Practical Implications*, 13 INT'L J. MED. & L. 285, 290 (1994). *See generally*, MEDICAL ETHICS, ch. 3 (R.M. VEATCH, ed. 2nd ed. 1994).

137 RICHARD A. EPSTEIN, MORTAL PERIL: OUR INALIENABLE RIGHT TO HEALTH? 417 (1997).

138 ANNAS, *supra* note 114 at 254.

139 BRODY, *supra* note 112 at 29.

140 Kirby, *supra* note 7 at 20.

141 Kirby, *supra* note 7 at 18; STEINER & ALSTON, *supra* note 24 at 192–94; VINCENT, *supra* note 61 at 37–38.

142 *But see* CHILDRESS, *supra* note 135 at 241 (arguing for a political-legal right to health care).

143 *Health, Human Rights and International Law*, 82 AM. SOCY. INT'L. L. PROC. 122 (1988).

144 Virginia Leary, *The Right to Health in International Human Rights Law*, 1 HEALTH & HUMAN RIGHTS 25, 31 (1994). *See generally* HEALTH AND HUMAN RIGHTS (Jonathan M. Mann, *et al.*, eds. 1999).

145 Jonathan M. Mann, *Medicine and Public Health, Ethics and Human Rights*, 37 HASTINGS CENTER RPT. 6, 8 (May–Jun. 1997).
    For all the definitional uncertainty, it has been asserted the right to health is seen as embodying both freedoms and entitlements: freedom to the control of one's health and body together with the right to be free from interference with medical treatment and an entitlement to participation in a system of health protection which affords all individuals under it a right to attain the highest levels of health. NIHAL JAYAWICKRAMA, THE JUDICIAL APPLICATION OF HUMAN RIGHTS LAW: NATIONAL REGIONAL AND INTERNATIONAL JURISPRUDENCE ch. 32 at 883 (2002).

146 ECONOMIC, SOCIAL AND CULTURAL RIGHTS: PROGRESS AND ACHIEVE-MENT 201 (Ralph Beddard & Dilys M. Hill, eds. 1992).

147 Ian Murray, *World Body Calls for Healthcare to be Rationed*, THE (LONDON) TIMES, May 12, 1999, at 2.

148 General Comment 14, E/C.12/2000/4, 4 Jul. 2000, available at www.unhchr.ch/tbs/doc.nsg/

149 *Ibid.* Sadly, Art. 12 (2) of the International Covenant is far too general to provide clear insight into concrete actions states parties need to take in order to be in compliance. DAVID P. FIDLER, INTERNATIONAL LAW AND INFECTIOUS DISEASES 188 (1989). *See also* Meier, *supra* note 60 at 156 (observing that little guidance is provided to the states regarding the scope of their obligations under the right to health under the ESCR).

150 *Supra* note 148.

151 *Ibid.*

152 Lawrence O. Gostin, *The Human Right to Health: A Right to the "Highest Attainable Health,"* 31 HASTINGS CENTER RPT. 29, 30 (Mar., Apr., 2001).
    Indeed, the World Health Organization ranked performance of the U.S. health care system 37th among all nations due to disparities by race and income. *See* Eleanor D. Kinney, *The International Human Right to Health: What Does This Mean for Our Nation and World?* 34 IND. L. REV. 1457 (2001). *See generally* Ronald Dworkin, *Justice in The Distribution of Health Care*, 38 McGILL L. J. 883 (1993); Smith, *supra* note 86.

153 GOSTIN & LAZZARINI, *supra* note 75 at 29.

154 Mann, *supra* note 145 at 6, 8.

155 Kirby, *supra* note 7 at p. 18.

156 GOSTIN & LAZZARINI, *supra* note 75 at 4, 33–34; BRODY, *supra* note 112; HEALTH AND HUMAN RIGHTS 54–55, *supra* note 144.

157 Alison Lakin, *The Legal Powers of the World Health Organization*, 3 MED. L. INT'L. 23, 24 (1997). *See generally*, Yutaka Arai-Takahashi, *The Role of International Health and The WHO in The Regulation of Public Health*, ch. 4 in LAW AND THE PUBLIC DIMENSION OF HEALTH (Robyn Martin & Linda Johnson, eds. 2001); Elsa Stamatopoulou, *The Development of United Nation's Mechanisms for the Protection and Promotion of Human Rights*, 55 WASH. & LEE L. REV. 287 (1998).

158 Lakin, *ibid.* at 24, 33–34.

Newly revised International Health Regulations (IHL) which entered into effect in 2007 are a noble effort to effect a multilateral agreement geared at facilitating co-operation through information-sharing in disease control by prescribing (voluntary) obligations for WHO member states to meet. There is, however, no effective enforcement mechanism to ensure compliance with these regulations. The effectiveness of the work of the WHO is limited severely by this state-centered model of voluntary disease control. The enforcement powers of the WHO would be strengthened immeasurably if the World Trade Organization's dispute settlement system was to be adopted. David P. Fidler, *et al.*, *Strategies for Implementing the New International Health Regulations*, 86 BULL. WORLD HEALTH ORGAN. 215 (2008). *See* Belinda J. Bennett, *Globalization Rights? Constructing Health Rights in a Shrinking World*, ch. 1 in BRAVE NEW WORLD OF HEALTH (Belinda Bennett, *et al.*, eds. 2008).

159 Lakin, *supra* note 157 at 24, 33–34.
160 GOSTIN & LAZZARINI, *supra* note 75 at 35.
161 *Ibid.* at 35.
162 *Ibid.*
163 *See supra* notes 36–38.
164 *See supra* note 51.
165 *See supra* notes 54–55.
166 TOEBES, *supra* note 29 at 231, 232, 345.
167 *Ibid.* at 349. *See also* Symonides, *supra* note 32 at ch. 3.
168 TOEBES, *supra* note 29 at 349.
169 Meier, *supra* note 60 at 159.
170 *Ibid.*
171 GOSTIN & LAZZARINI, *supra* note 75 at 8, 9. *See* TIMOTHY S. JOST, READINGS IN COMPARATIVE HEALTH LAW AND BIOETHICS, ch. 1 (2001). *See generally* Harold H. Koh, *How Is International Human Rights Law Enforced?* 74 IND. L. J. 1397 (1999).

5 Allocating health care resources

Technology and mortality

So long as individuals continue to persist in their desire to attain a degree of immortality by sustaining human life to the limits that science allows,[1] the American health care system—termed "technologically driven [and] death-denying"[2]—will continue to tweak and re-chart the frontiers of medical science. At the end-stage of life, marginal improvements will, assuredly, continue to be made even though they may be seen—by the patient—as worthless from a qualitative standard of reference and, from a societal point of view, extraordinarily expensive.[3] In 2008, a study on the cost of end-of life treatment found both dramatic and alarming variations in not only the amount and intensity of care, but the actual cost of providing care in the last two years of life throughout the United States. As might be expected, Medicare expenditures for chronic illness (e.g., diabetes, cancer, and heart disease) were, during this time frame, significant—varying from an average of $52,911 spent for medical patients at the U.C.L.A. Medical Center to $28,763 for those who used St. Mary's Hospital (the Mayo Clinic) in Minnesota.[4]

With more than 90 million Americans living with chronic disease, and seven out of ten actually dying from these illnesses, it is not surprising to find that most of Medicare spending on these patients is for actual hospital care during the final period of life.[5] Set within a culture of aggressive patient-centered care demanded by patients, themselves, which has its very roots in "defensive medicine" designed to forestall medical malpractice suits[6]—physicians are drawn inevitably into a vortex of socio-medico-legal stresses calibrated by ethical values and principles. Until mortality is accepted, costs will never be contained.[7] Thus, the challenge of contemporary health care distribution is to structure a framework for normative decision-making whereby the goal of distributive justice is achieved equitably for as many citizens as possible—both at the *micro* or individual patient level, and the *macro* or national level.[8] *Micro* issues are often regarded as "patient selection issues," or "choices among patients," concerning the resources available for specific kinds of health care services.[9] *Macro* issues are focused on highly political matters such as the amount to which a nation is devoting its health care resources to primary and preventive care—as opposed to new biotechnology medicine—as well as budget percentages being expended by hospitals.[10]

Modern focus and reform efforts

The United States devotes 16% of its gross domestic product to medical care, more *per capita* than any other nation in the world—but lags in overall health, ranking 29th in infant mortality, 48th in life expectancy and 19th out of 19 industrialized nations in preventable deaths.[11] As health care costs continue to rise faster than the rate of inflation, Medicare continues to contribute billions to growing budget deficits as it inches toward insolvency.[12] Compounding matters, Medicare continues to accelerate its engine-power for underwriting "the most wasteful, inefficient system of health-care payments in any advanced industrial country" by maintaining a reward system where practitioners and hospitals alike are remunerated according to the volume of procedures they undertake rather than successful patient outcomes.[13] Indeed, the current system has been termed "hospital centric" in that the system—itself—is not activated until an individual becomes sick.[14] At that point in time, enormous sums of money are then invested in order to restore health.[15] What needs to be done is to build primary care as the core for health care.[16]

Since, in the Medicare program, rates for reimbursement are below actual costs, the effect of this situation is to drive hospitals and doctors to undertake more and more tests and procedures in order to meet their bills. At the same time, this very procedure becomes a strategy for "defensive medicine" designed, as such, to meet—if not blunt—potential lawsuits for claims of malpractice[17] and accordingly preclude "evidence-based medicine" which has the more positive effect of prescribing medicine based solely on known benefits and risks.[18]

Evidence-based medicine

While recognizing the centrality of individualized patient care and the uniqueness of quality and value-of-life judgments for each case, evidence-based medicine (EBM) seeks, nonetheless, to apply that which is considered the best available scientific evidence to medical decision-making. By implementing this goal, EBM endeavors to not only assess the risks but the benefits of treatment or non-treatment.[19] Rather than merely make conclusionary medical judgments based on generally accepted medical "opinion," physicians practicing EBM must support their orders by appropriate reference to (current) scientific studies—all with the goal of ensuring best prediction of medical treatment outcomes. At the institutional level, EBM guidelines are mandated and include the production and use of regulatory procedures which are value-based.[20]

Instead of relying on patient testimonials, case studies and expert opinion—all subject as such to inherent biases in both observation and reporting—EBM attempts to first categorize, and then rank, clinical evidence based upon the level of freedom from biases presented in the clinical evidence, itself. Randomized double-blind placebo-controlled trials which involve a homogenous patient population as well as medical condition are considered the "gold standard" for therapeutic EBM decision-making.[21]

Embraced by medical practice empiricists, health economists, policy-makers and managers, as a useful construct for measuring performance as well as rationing scarce medical resources,[22] EBM is—for this very reason—viewed with suspicion by many.[23] In addition, there is an overriding concern that EBM discounts the value of clinical experience in assessing the basic question of what is the best course of treatment for an individual patient.[24]

Alternative reform measures

An alternative approach designed to reform the present chaos of medical malpractice litigation would design a new social pool which would provide a source for patients injured by medical error to draw upon. Rather than be dependent upon lay juries, adjudication of claims of this nature would be done by medical experts who—unlike present tort litigators—would not receive a third of the damages under such malpractice judgments.[25] By placing a "relatively small tax on all health insurance premiums" the pool would be funded sufficiently. By socializing the risk, all too many avarice-driven trial lawyers would be eliminated from the malpractice scenario altogether. Under this model, the harshest penalty for a malpractice conviction would be medical license forfeiture.[26]

Some of the other suggestions for health care reform include adopting a "value index" for Medicare designed to essentially reward those providers who give "safe, high-quality care with excellent service at a reasonable cost."[27] The central equation would thus become "Value equals Quality divided by Cost" and have direct ties to EBM and merge, ideally, into "bundling" which was begun in 1991 with Medicare.[28] Starting with common conditions such as heart failure, lung disease, and diabetes together with some common procedures such as hip and knee operations and open heart surgery, bundling forces these medical services to be outcome-oriented rather than tethered to individual procedures.[29] Under bundling, a single flat rate is charged for each episode of patient care—this, *in lieu* of a separate charge for various services rendered.[30]

The American Medical Association is cautious about giving a total endorsement of bundled payments because of concerns that, if implemented widely, bundled payments could well lead to hospital-controlled payments to physicians.[31] One estimation is that, if used nationally, bundling payments in both inpatient and outpatient settings could reduce total medical costs by 5.5 percent.[32]

Conflicts in distribution

Because of rising health care costs during the past 20 years, societal concern has focused on whether the world's health care resources are being distributed fairly and wisely. More and more, contemporary medicine demands of its practitioners—particularly those in America—that the principle of justice be made a distinct factor in the decision-making process.[33] Increasing governmental pressures continue to stress the need to follow cost control policies, eliminate waste and inefficiency and—as noted—implement the principle of distributive justice in patient care. As a consequence of these three competing policy concerns, more and more, patient interests become secondary to health care delivery.[34] The central conflict for physician-gatekeepers, thus, is to assure and maintain a patient-centered ethic in their professional work while, at the same time, from a *macro* economic standard, safeguard their responsibility to preserve society's resources.[35] Ancillary to this conflict is the harsh reality that implementing distributive justice at the patient bedside, without any real societal consensus on how it is defined and practiced, most often means that an arbitrary process is put in place which depends upon—to a very large extent—the individual value system of the person assigning worth to the medical intervention or procedure put in issue.[36]

In considering applications of distributive justice, then, physicians are required to evaluate this operative principle at two levels: the statistical patient or the identifiable patient.[37] The more direct example of statistical applications of distributive justice is seen within the process of establishing guidelines for utilization review.[38] Not a new phenomenon, the utilization review process was done traditionally on a retrospective basis as a way for health care insurers to review claims for treatment on the basis of medical necessity. As such, utilization review is not only a cost containment strategy but one of quality of control implemented by managed care organizations to assure that health care is more affordable.[39] Utilization review compares requests for medical services, or "utilization," to treatment guidelines deemed appropriate for such services—especially in Medicare and Medicaid.[40]

Modernly, utilization review is being used as both a concurrent and prospective review—with the concurrent review being acknowledged as a strategy tied to monitoring in-patient treatment level-of-care review, continued-stay reviews, and discharge planning.[41] Prior to costs being incurred with the commencement of patient services, prospective utilization review simply requires physicians to obtain authorization first from the relevant managed care organization before admittance to a hospital.[42]

Vastly different in its ultimate effect from a retrospective system, in a concurrent or prospective review system—when a denial of coverage is made—the most likely consequence of denial is that the patient will simply forgo the medical procedure in question. In effect, prospective review places a managed care organization or its director of utilization review in the role of substituting their non-medical judgments for that of an attending physician and thereby determining the course and scope of medical treatment without a level of medical or expertise intellectual discernment to determine the extent to which there is a medical necessity for treatment.[43]

Gatekeeping issues

As observed, physicians are—of necessity—the primary gatekeepers to the health care distribution industry; for they are responsible for not only limiting or, as the case may be, facilitating medical tests but treatments as well as consultations and—most importantly—initial admissions to the health care institutions, themselves.[44] There are three traditional gatekeeping roles for physicians: the *de facto* role which imposes upon them a responsibility to practice medicine which is both beneficial and effective for the patient; that of negative gatekeeping which operates under a prepayment system and, in turn, requires a physician to limit, within the rules of the system, the use of health care services; or positive gatekeeping, where the physician encourages patient use of the health care system for either personal or corporate profit.[45]

Allocating and rationing health care

Regardless of which of these three roles are assumed by the gatekeepers, primary issues of allocation and rationing are central to all of them; for, health care involves a competition for limited resources and therefore—at one level or other—forces a cost-benefit approach which balances reasonable individual needs against the availability of medical resources.[46] In the face of ever mounting distribution costs, it is the elderly, in specific, who become major players in the health care drama for which they are cast in alternating roles as victims and as villains.[47] The health care system helps to prolong their lives, yet at the same time, puts more and more dollars into geriatric spending.[48] The controlling ethical issue implicit here involves the fair distribution of public resources among different age groups.[49]

Forms of rationing

Lacking a clear and unambiguous definition of rationing, it may nonetheless be seen as a process whereby some are—temporarily and against their wishes—left without types of health care that would otherwise provide a benefit to them.[50] In addition to referring to these general limitations, rationing may encompass, as well, very "specific treatment decisions for particular patients" at the bedside.[51] Alternatively, rationing is seen as a means of providing every citizen with a guaranteed level of basic health care—this, by excluding from coverage those treatments considered to be "outside" the package.[52] One point in this analysis is certain: rationing is the central health care policy issue of the day.[53]

Long viewed as haphazard and unprincipled, rationing occurs today as it always has.[54] Yet, the term is softened considerably by referring to it as merely allocations of health care resources[55] tied, inescapably, to a foundation in risk-benefit analysis.[56] Among the approaches to rationing used widely are:

- a 'first come, first served' system of queues;
- random selection (which takes no account of the gravity of either the patient's conditions or of the medical benefit);

- ability to pay;
- *triage* systems based on medical urgency; and
- more recently, systems tied to computations of Quality Adjusted Life Years (QALYs). ...[57]

A central concern with rationing, as seen, is devising a distribution system that is fair and equitable.[58] In the current American health care system, the ability-to-pay is used as an implicit rationing device; yet, a lack of consensus in values and norms prevents a specific method to achieve the ends of rationing health care services.[59] "Thus, the debate is no longer whether health care should be rationed, but rather, how to ration it equitably."[60]

Health care decisions, in the control of third-party payers, have distorted the ability to make real choices.[61] Cost containment issues in geriatric health care have also changed the role of physicians, and forced them, as observed, to become reluctant medical gatekeepers.[62] Inherent in health care decisions is the conflict between saving costs and obtaining quality health care.[63] In essence, "rationing has come to represent discrimination in access to health care services on the basis of socio-economic status."[64]

Rationing must be viewed as more than limiting care, for it is a means of providing care where resources are managed and preserved.[65] Rationing is also access control, which is dependent upon the medical good, the patient's values, and the needs of society itself.[66] Here, justice involves a constant balancing between the good of the individual and the needs and welfare of society.[67]

Valuations and allocations

The allocation of health care resources "involves a societal determination of what resources should be devoted to a particular program."[68] Perhaps the best examples of age-based allocation schemes are to be found in the experiences in other countries, where cost containment initiatives result in indirect limits on care for the elderly.[69] Utilizing cost containment initiatives or following a cost-benefit approach to distributing health care resources is, however, neither practical nor sound ethically; this, because either policy seeks to reduce or convert all health benefits to dollar amounts. In turn, both seek, awkwardly, to convert what might be considered quality of life benefits into hard, uncompromising economic terms.[70]

One method proposed as a solution to this inequality of the cost-benefit analysis seeks to evaluate the quality-adjusted life-years (QALYs) produced for each available health care dollar.[71] The goal of this resource allocation strategy, then, is to maximize the most QALYs for each available health care dollar.[72] There is a central weakness to this method, however, because considering the limited remaining life-years of the elderly—individually and as a group—and calculating their QALYs is highly problematic. The reason for this situation is that QALY measure only treatment endpoints without taking into consideration either the proportional loss or the gain in the quality of one's life. Accordingly, a group of elderly individuals needing a surgical procedure will not fare as well using the QALY approach as a younger group of patients— this being rather obvious inasmuch as the older patients in the group have fewer remaining years to live.[73]

An alternative to QALYs

An alternative to QALYs has been suggested in what is termed, "the saved young life equivalent" (SAVE).[74] Although, arguably, still reducing individuals to numbers, this approach seeks a unit of measurement in which saving a young person's life and restoring him to full health is the controlling paradigm. This position is justified on the grounds that most people would regard this goal, itself, as the maximum benefit an individual can gain.[75] An assessment of comparative treatment values is thus made "in terms of how many expected outcomes of each treatment would be equivalent to SAVE."[76]

Instead of trying to structure a model that seeks to incorporate a defensible method of pricing life and health, QALYs are thought to be a more feasible means of prioritizing health care services. The goal of trying to obtain the most QALYs from a health care system does not force a search for an answer to the central question: namely, what amount of money should be spent per QALY. Thus, QALYs will be of considerable use in those contexts in which the question of the amount of resources to spend on health care has presumably been answered; that is, when there is a health budget to stay within specified treatment caps such as in the British National Health Service, an American prepaid plan, or in a rational Medicare plan operating in the twenty-first century.[77] Indeed, some speculate that soon within this century, QALYs will be accepted totally and used in planning and organizing health services.[78]

QALYs under British Health Care

QALYs are used extensively in the United Kingdom by the National Institute of Health and Clinical Excellence (NICE)—the body charged with providing guidance on what treatments should be covered, or underwritten by the National Health Service (NHS).[79] Although no absolute threshold for applying the QALY metric was set by the NHS in 2004, it was unlikely to have rejected treatment costs between £5,000 and £15,000 solely on the basis of cost. Yet, special reasons would have had to be shown to gain approval for use of a medical technology costing over £25,000 to £35,000 per QALY.[80] Interestingly, in 2008, NICE did set a limit—in American dollars—of approximately $49,000 as the allowed cost from public monies for treatment of advanced kidney cancer.[81] Advanced treatment by the drug, Sutent—which would exceed this limit and only provide some six months of additional life— was accordingly denied. Journalists in Britain and the United States were highly critical of this being a flagrant example of a policy lacking in compassion and regard for life.[82]

While availability of treatment or restricted access to it in principle will not be denied because of age, NICE guidelines do allow for it to be referenced when one or more of the following apply:

- There is no evidence that age is a good indicator for some aspect of patients' health status and/or the likelihood of adverse effects of the treatment.
- There is no practical way of identifying patients other than by their age (for example, there is no test available to measure their state of health in another way).
- There is good evidence, or good grounds for believing that, it is likely that, because of their age, patient will respond differently to the treatment in question.[83]

Public opinion in the UK holds to the notion that while, ideally, there should be no age discrimination in the delivery of health care services under the NHS, when limitations must be imposed, and—specifically—determinations made regarding organ transplant recipients and the use of extra governmental support of NHS programs, a preference should be given to uses aiding children.[84]

Intergenerational justice

The concept of intergenerational equity arises from the association between the increased number of persons over 65 years, the probability that they are frequently using health care resources, and the resultant increase in health care costs.[85] The government is not able to bear, without restraint, the growing social and economic health care costs associated with the elderly. In America, during the presidency of Ronald Reagan, federal funding failed, for the first time, to keep pace with demand—as the demand for resources far out-distanced the available supply.[86] Every dollar given to programs for the elderly meant one less dollar for other groups. Addressable economic issues included then, as now, the proper delivery of care, the allocation of resources, effective and affordable methods of insurance, and defining research priorities.[87]

The fastest growing population in the United States and worldwide are people over the age of 65.[88] A corresponding shrinkage occurs in the population under 65 years of age who will have to bear burdens of providing for the prior and future generations.[89] Furthermore, the elderly are disproportionate consumers of health care as hospitalization of elderly persons on the average costs three times more per health care dollar than those under 65 years of age.[90] Rationing of health care resources for them is distinguished from cost containment measures which result in a withholding of medical services considered to be of no "expected patient benefit."[91] Thus, age rationing occurs only in those cases "where elderly patients, are denied access to medical services that are expected to benefit them."[92]

There is some merit to the argument that the elderly must be compensated for their work earlier in life and not be required to make additional health care sacrifices.[93] Due to their advanced years, the elderly earn some degree of public sympathy and respect because of what they have accomplished before approaching the end of their lives.[94] In coming to this end, they have discharged already many of the obligations that society has required and should not bear a disproportionate burden in their later years.[95]

Arguably, there is a shared intergenerational duty between both the elderly and those who are younger. Assurances against neglect and abuse come from the moral obligations and relationships that the young have with the elderly.[96] At the same time, the elderly are stewards of a world they helped fashion and their purpose should be to aid the young and future generations to come.[97] Therefore, the proper role for all societal groups should recognize a life cycle where the elderly have come before the young and made life easier for those who follow, while the young have the burden of supporting the elderly when they are unable to take care of themselves. The extent of that burden remains the open and truly vexatious question of this century.

Although recognizing *de facto* rationing as a current feature of contemporary health care delivery systems, any further expansions of it should be delayed, it has been suggested, until the irrationalities of the current national system are resolved.[98] This suggestion is impractical simply because rationing is seen as an inextricable (if not unavoidable) given in the present system and its "irrationalities" are beyond correction within any reasonable period of time. Others might suggest that this effort to distribute scarce resources in an equitable manner, that is, rationing, is not irrational at all.[99] The harsh reality of enforcement in health care resource allocation can be seen vividly as an ethical conundrum when either a health care system or a hospital seeks to limit the actual range of treatments available to a patient—this, because either the limitations, in and of themselves, or actions taken to exceed them, can result in meaning that the physician is acting unethically.[100]

Because health care services, providers of health care, and the means to pay for these services are all scarce, procedures must be established and followed to allow for a fair distribution of them. As observed, physicians engage regularly in rationing by their regulation of the extent of participation in Medicare as well as in health maintenance organizations (HMOs).[101] Historically, during times of military engagement, field physicians decided routinely whom they would treat because they were "salvageable" and those from whom treatment would be withheld until the others were treated. Some were even denied treatment because of the futility of such actions. And, even today, emergency medicine—as practiced in emergency wards of major hospitals and in times of local or state disaster—utilizes the principle of *triage*.[102] A strong argument could be advanced that, indeed, the very bedrock of modern rationing is to be found, to one degree or other, within the principle of *triage*. Surely an analogy can be seen between a military battlefield and the crisis in health care management because, in both, efforts must be made to balance the costs with the benefits of all actions taken.[103]

Structuring a decisional framework

Establishing fair procedures for the allocation of health care resources is a crucial goal for contemporary society to set and, hopefully, achieve. Accordingly, fairness is to be defined and shaped by four conditions: public accessibility to "limit-setting decisions," their policies and rationales; clarity in policy rationales which explain how "value for money" is met in distributing health care resources within a society where there are reasonable resource constraints on the resources themselves; a framework for principled decision-making which provides a means for resolution of disputes; and a regulatory process which not only assures public access to the initial "limit-setting decisions," but an equitable mechanism for challenging the reasonableness of contested health care distribution decisions.[104]

"Most people," it has been said, "are ignorant about most matters."[105] This is true particularly with regard to the health care market where consumers are found to be lacking in basic information about not only the quality, but the price of medical services. This ignorance, in turn, means consumers lack the expertise to evaluate the professional qualifications of health care providers as well as to evaluate necessary information regarding the range of alternative treatments available to them. Even when price information is available, health care consumers have difficulty assessing and, indeed, comprehending what the data means and how it impacts on their accessing health care.[106]

Since the efficient use of medical resources dictates that both consumers and health care providers weigh the costs and the benefits of alternative medical treatments, the failure to access health care information regarding these options means—essentially—that physician preferences for particular medical procedures trump the ideal of informed patient consent.[107] In turn, this means that the physician solidifies his position of power as the primary gatekeeper to health care resources.

Restoring trust

Sadly, as a direct consequence of the multiple and conflicting roles a physician is cast in or forced to choose because of either the particular managed care program he is practicing under or the professional ethic he espouses, medicine is no longer being seen as caring for people. Rather, the politics of economic self-interest compromise—if not extinguish—the sacred trust patients once placed in their physicians. Stated otherwise, the system promotes the use of expensive, invasive and at-risk treatments and places little effort in patient care.[108] It has been suggested that a new ethic needs to be recognized and embraced by physicians—one that shifts from using medicine if it might assist to one that promotes use only when it will.[109]

In the final analysis, what is called for is fair democratic procedures designed to allow average citizens to be sufficiently informed and knowledgeable in order to make choices among just alternatives for health care resource allocations.[110] Aided by careful cost-effectiveness and cost-benefit analyses, tied—as such—to those discernible values ranked clearly as beneficial and those regarded as costly, such a process can in fact work.[111]

Granted, a sustained public dialogue to reach a *consensus* on how medical resources ought to be distributed is unlikely.[112] Yet, today—in very large part owing to President Barack Obama's effort to establish a universal health care program in America—a very public conversation is being conducted throughout the Nation on this issue.[113] Even with passage, in March 2010, of the Patient Protection and Affordable Care Act and The Health Care and Education Reconciliation Act, implementation of this legislation will be staggering.[114] No matter within what policy forum the health care resource debate occurs—local, state, or national—a fundamental balancing test will, of necessity, be employed; one that weighs, in an equitable and reasonable manner, individual or *micro* needs with larger societal or *macro* standards of economic efficiency.[115] By seeking to integrate moral and ethical reasoning with quantitative or economic formulations of needs and resources, the opportunities for a stronger and more contemporary standard of distributive justice will, ideally, be both enhanced and stabilized.[116]

If agreement could be reached for setting principles of distributive justice which, in turn, would establish a mechanism for determining how to set fair limits to health care, societies would then be empowered to check all social decisions and practices against the principles in order to determine whether they conformed to them. In cases where decisions, policies, and practices failed to conform, they would be held unjust and subsequent actions then taken to change them. When disagreements arose over interpretation of principles or facts, legal procedure for resolving such disputes would be sought.[117]

Ideally, the establishment of a national minimum standard of health care delineating, as such, what an adequate level of care should be for managed care organizations, the managers within it and the physicians who are practicing under it would be a positive step toward resolving present inadequacies in the system. Once such a standard is in place, there will be some level of expectation that competition will "take place not on establishing the leanest rationing strategy the market will bear (however ethically problematic it may be), but on delivering the agreed minimum standard efficiently."[118] This standard would demand of the physician an ethical obligation to his individual patients "to interpret it in the light of the patient's circumstances and make certain it was offered to them."[119] Realistically, designing a satisfactory mechanism for defining a morally acceptable threshold standard of care is problematic.[120] Reaching a political consensus on this challenge is even more daunting when the level of public "understanding"—and, indeed, lethargy—is realized.

Seeking a balanced understanding

In the final analysis, it is quite possible (and probable) that society has come to review health care as little more than a commodity—a service—much as other commodities in a market economy and for which specific and harsh rationing decisions are imposed on physicians. The direct consequence of this societal re-direction means the cornerstones of professional medical ethics—beneficence, patient autonomy, and justice—will yield to "social good and economic need."[121] The whole art of healing, once seen as a partnership between the healer and nature, itself, is also thus recast as an effort to redesign nature—improving upon it, and aiming it in new startling directions heretofore not found in its history.[122]

The choice implied, inherently, in the rationing of medical goods and services, "will reveal more about the kind of people we are, and wish to be, than it would about the ideas we profess."[123] Indeed, there is a growing national belief in, and acceptance of, the inevitability of rationing and an awareness of the attendant ethical issues and dilemmas deriving therefrom within the patient–physician relationship[124]—issues arising inescapably from the very nature of managed care which, itself, challenges the foundational basis of relationship-centered care.[125]

From a transnational perspective, perhaps it is more realistic—when considering the extent to which there should be a governmental obligation to guarantee a citizen's good health—to refer to a right to health protection, with this including a right to access health care together with a right to live under healthy conditions.[126] Ideally, guaranteeing access to health care resources is the foundation upon which all other assertions of health care "rights," and their permutations are built. Lacking a strong determinative framework for both identifying and analyzing the essential societal factors representing the conditions under which people can access health care, it is thought unrealistic and impractical to acknowledge an absolute right to health care.[127] International legislative templates go only so far in shaping a response to this issue. Rather, the dynamics of gatekeeping ethics and the centrality of the medical healing partnership between patient and physician must be seen as the paramount elements in assuring distributive justice both in the national and transnational health care delivery system.[128]

Notes

1 GEORGE J. ANNAS, STANDARD OF CARE: THE LAW OF AMERICAN BIOETHICS 214 (1993).
2 *Ibid.* at 211.
3 *Ibid. See also* DANIEL CALLAHAN, WHAT KIND OF LIFE: THE LIMITS OF MEDICAL PROGRESS (1990); Daniel Callahan & Sherwin B. Nuland, *The Quagmire: How American Medicine is Destroying Itself*, THE NEW REPUBLIC 16 (Jun. 9, 2011).
4 Robert Pear, *Researchers Find Huge Variations in End-of-Life Treatment*, N.Y. TIMES, Apr. 7, 2008, at A17 (drawing this story from the DARTMOUTH ATLAS OF HEALTH CARE) (2008).
5 *Ibid.*
6 *Ibid.*
7 ANNAS, *supra* note 1 at 216.
8 *See generally Symposium, Ethics of Health Care Law Reform*, 12 J. HEALTH CARE L. & POL'Y 1 (2009).

9 John F. Kilner, *Allocation of Health Care Resources* in 2 ENCYCLOPEDIA OF BIOETHICS at 1067, 1075 (rev. ed. 1995).

10 *Ibid.* at 1067.

11 Ceci Connolly, *U.S. 'Not Getting What We Pay For,'* WASH. POST, Nov. 30, 2008, at A6.
   One report sets the percentage of Gross Domestic Product spent on healthcare at 16.2%, or $2.3 trillion a year. Lesley Alderman, *Doctors Offer Thoughts on Cutting Health Care Costs*, N.Y. TIMES, Mar. 27, 2010, at B5.
   By 2020, the Nation's health care costs will rise to $4.6 trillion; account for about $1 of every $5 spent in the economy. WASH. EXAMINER, Jul. 29, 2011, at 12.

12 David Browder, *Obama's Easier Path*, WASH. POST, Sept. 13, 2009, at A25.

13 *Ibid. See generally Symposium on Health Care Technology: Regulation and Reimbursement*, 31 W. NEW ENG. L. REV. 293 (2009).

14 Connolly, *supra* note 11.

15 *See generally* Elizabeth W. Leonard, *The Public's Right to Health: When Patient Rights Threaten the Commons*, 86 WASH. U. L. REV. 1335 (2009).

16 Connolly, *supra* note 11.

17 Charles Krauthhammer, *Health Care Reform: A Better Plan*, WASH. POST, Aug. 7, 2009, at A21.
   Polled by the Massachusetts Medical Society, five out of six physicians admitted they order tests, procedures, and referrals solely as protection from lawsuits. Nationally, defensive medicine has been estimated as costing $200 billion a year. *Ibid.*

18 Ceci Connolly, *In Delivering Care, More Isn't Always Better, Experts Say*, WASH. POST, Sept. 29, 2009, at A3; Kevin Sack, *Culture Clash in Medicine*, N.Y. TIMES, Nov. 20, 2009, at A1. *See generally* Leonard, *supra* note 15.

19 Stefan Timmermans & Aaron A. Mauck, *The Promise and Pitfalls of Evidence-Based Medicine*, 24 HEALTH AFFAIRS 18 (2005).

20 David M. Eddy, *Evidence-based Medicine: A Unified Approach*, 24 HEALTH AFFAIRS 9 (2005).
   M. Gregg Bloche, *The Emergent Logic of Health Law*, 82 SO. CAL. L. REV. 389 at 455–60 (2009).

21 Timmermans & Mauck, *supra* note 19.

22 SIMON SINGH & EDWARD ERNST, TRICK OR TREATMENT: THE UNDENIABLE FACTS ABOUT ALTERNATIVE MEDICINE (2008).

23 *Ibid.*

24 D.L. Sackett, W.M. Rosenberg, *et al.*, *Evidence Based Medicine: What It Is and What It Isn't*, 312 BR. MED. J. 71 (1996).

25 Krauthhammer, *supra* note 17. A survey by the group Common Good and The Committee for Economic Development found 67% of registered voters supported the idea of having medical malpractice courts rather than non-expert civil juries and, alternatively, of imposing caps on non-economic damage awards in malpractice litigation. Editorial, *Majority to Obama: Get Serious on Tort Reform*, WASH. EXAMINER, Sept. 17, 2009, at 2.

26 Krauthhammer, *ibid.*

27 David Ignatius, *An Obama Plan B for Health Care*, WASH. POST, Jan. 24, 2010, at A17.

28 *Ibid.*

29 *Ibid.*

30 Peter S. Hussey, Christine Eibner, *et al.*, *Controlling U.S. Health Care Spending—Separating Promising from Unpromising Approaches*, 361 NEW ENG. L. J. MED. 22 (Nov. 26, 2009).

31 *Ibid.*

32 *Ibid.*

33 William S. Andereck, *Money, Medicine, and Morals* in THE HEALTH CARE PROFESSIONAL AS FRIEND AND HEALER: BUILDING ON THE WORK OF EDMUND D. PELLEGRINO 233 at 235 (David C. Thomasma & Judith L. Kissell, eds. 2000).

34 *Ibid.* at 236. *See generally* DANIEL CALLAHAN, SETTING LIMITS: MEDICAL GOALS IN AN AGING SOCIETY (1987).

35 Andereck, *supra* note 33 at 236.

One worrisome concern is that the ranks of the front-line physician gatekeepers will be depleted significantly as a consequence of the implementation of the new healthcare reform legislation. The Medicus Firm conducted a survey which found 46 percent of physicians indicated that they would either quit practicing medicine or simply retire as a consequence of Obamacare. Susan Ferrechio, WASH. EXAMINER, *infra* note 114. In 2010, for the first time, more physicians left private practice and are now employed by hospitals. Hal Scherz, *Obamacare Undermines Doctor-Patient Relationship*, WASH. EXAMINER, Apr. 13, 2011, at 24. *See also* Gardiner Harris, *Doctors Inc: A Wrenching Transition*, N.Y. TIMES, Apr. 23, 2001, at A1 (discussing the dramatic decline in family physicians since 1986).

36 *Ibid.* "Physicians want power, resources, and freedom, in part to preserve life ... and in part to advance medical knowledge through research." MARY R. ANDERLIK, THE ETHICS OF MANAGED CARE: A PRAGMATIC APPROACH 125 (2001).

37 Andereck, *supra* note 33 at 236.

38 *See* J. Scott Andresen, *Is Utilization Review the Practice of Medicine?* 19 J. LEGAL MED. 431 (1998).

39 *Ibid.* at 433–34.

40 *Ibid.*

41 *Ibid.* at 434.

42 *Ibid.* at 435.

43 *Ibid.* Capital budget committee practices at large hospitals also influence the extent and level to which distributive justice will be implemented. Proposed long-term investment projects are tested by cost-benefit models which are influenced significantly by patient value or use. Thus, if the Departments of Urology and of Radiation, in a given hospital, are generating more profit than the Department of Emergency Medicine, it makes sound fiscal sense to expand Urology and Radiation than Emergency Medicine—this, even though low socio-economic populations will not be able to access or receive enhanced levels of emergency medical care. *See* Claudia Kocher, *Hospital Capital Budgeting*, J. GLOBAL BUSINESS ISSUES 21 (Summer, 2007); Eugene R. Oberst, *Capital Budgeting Practices at Large Hospitals*, 37 THE ENGINEERING ECONOMIST 203 (1992).

44 Edmund D. Pellegrino, *Rationing Health Care: The Ethics of Medical Gatekeeping*, 2 J. CONTEMP. HEALTH L. & POL'Y 23 (1986).

45 *Ibid.* at 26–29. *See also* ANDERLIK, *supra* note 36 at 158–59. *See generally* Edmund D. Pellegrino, *Patient Physician Autonomy: Conflicting Rights and Obligations in the Physician-Patient Relationship*, 10 J. CONTEMP. HEALTH L. & POL'Y 47 (1994).

46 *See* George P. Smith, II, *Accessing Health Care Resources: Economic, Medical, Ethical and Socio-Legal Challenges* in AUTONOMY AND HUMAN RIGHTS IN HEALTH CARE at ch. 20 (David N. Weisstub & Guillermo Diaz Pintos, eds. 2008); Daniel Callahan, *What is a Reasonable Demand on Health Care Resources? Designing a Basic Package of Benefits*, 8 J. CONTEMP. HEALTH L. & POL'Y 1 (1992).

47 *See* HARRY R. MOODY, ETHICS IN AN AGING SOCIETY 4 (1992).

48 *Ibid.*

49 *See ibid.* at 5.

50 Kilner, *supra* note 9 at 1067.

51 *Ibid.* at 1067, 1075. *See also* HEALTH CARE LAW AND ETHICS at 91 (Mark A. Hall, *et al.*, eds., 6th ed. 2003).

52 ROBERT H. BLANK, THE PRICE OF LIFE 96 (1997).

53 Hall, *et al.*, *supra* note 51 at 98.

54 *Ibid.* at 96.

55 *Ibid.*

56 Kilner, *supra* note 9 at 1073; Andrew H. Smith & John Rother, *Older Americans and the Rationing of Health Care*, 140 U. PA. L. REV. 1847 (1992); Mark H. Waymack, *Old Age and the Rationing of Scarce Health Care Resources*, in AGING AND ETHICS: PHILOSOPHICAL PROBLEMS IN GERONTOLOGY 248, 249 (Nancy S. Jecker, ed. 1991).

57 *Ibid.*

58 Dorothy C. Rasinski-Gregory & Mariam Piven Cotler, *The Elderly and Health Care Reform: Needs, Concerns, Responsibilities and Obligations*, 22 WES. ST. U. L. REV. 65, 8 (1993).

59 *See ibid.* at 83–86 (noting the possibility of many different criteria such as age, disease, and entitlement).

60 George P. Smith, II, *Our Hearts Were Once Young and Gay: Health Care Rationing and The Elderly*, 8 FLA. J. L. & PUB. POL'Y 1, 39 (1996).

61 *See* MOODY, *supra* note 47 at 39.

62 Pellegrino, *supra* note 44. *See also* Edmund D. Pellegrino, *The Commodification of Medical and Health Care: The Moral Consequences of a Paradigm Shift from a Professional to a Market Ethic*, 24 J. MED. & PHIL. 243 (1999).

63 *See* Joanne Lynn, *Ethical Issues: Equitable Distribution and Decision Making*, in LEGAL AND ETHICAL ASPECTS OF HEALTH CARE FOR THE ELDERLY at 17 (Marshall B. Kapp, *et al.*, eds. 1986). *See also* Edmund D. Pellegrino, *Metaphors, Managed Care and Morality*, 3 J. CRIT. CARE NUTRITION 40 (1995).

64 Smith, *supra* note 60 at 11.

65 *See* David C. Thomasma, *The Ethical Challenge of Providing Healthcare for the Elderly*, 4 CAMB. Q. HEALTHCARE ETHICS 144, 152 (1995).

66 *See ibid.* at 155 (noting that the physician and patient must negotiate the good to be accomplished).

67 *See ibid.* at 155.

68 Smith, *supra* note 60 at 9.

69 MOODY, *supra* note 47 at 197.

70 John McKie, *et al.*, *Allocating Healthcare by QALYs: The Relevance of Age*, 5 CAMB. Q. HEALTHCARE ETHICS 534 (1996).

71 *See ibid.*

72 *See ibid.* at 535.

73 *Ibid. See also* ANDERLIK, *supra* note 36 at 55.

74 J.K. MASON, *ET AL.*, LAW AND MEDICAL ETHICS 364–86 (2002).

75 *Ibid.*

76 *Ibid.*

77 ANDERLIK, *supra* note 36 at 125. *See* JONATHAN HERRING, OLDER PEOPLE IN LAW AND SOCIETY 282–86 (2009).

78 PAUL T. MENZEL, STRONG MEDICINE: THE ETHICAL RATIONING OF HEALTH CARE 80–81 (1990). *See* Matthew Adler, *QALYs and Policy Evaluation: A New Perspective*, 6 YALE J. HEALTH POL'Y, LAW & ETHICS 1 (2006); JONATHAN BARON, AGAINST BIOETHICS 84–96 (2006).

79 HERRING, *supra* note 77 at 282.

　　Although not as comprehensive nationally in its authority as NICE, the utilization review process in managed care organizations in the U.S. provides a similar model for achieving cost containment and quality control in health care delivery. *See supra* notes 38–42 and accompanying text.

　　Under the Patient Protection and Affordable Care Act of 2010, a governmental process has been structured which requires a new administrative agency—the Independent Payment Advisory Board (IPAB)—appointed by President Obama, to assume responsibility for developing Medicare policies geared to achieving sustainable quality care within standards of cost containment. PL 111–48, 42 U.S.C. §3022 (2010). *See* Editorial, *Surprise! Obama wants to Ration your Health Care*, WASH. EXAMINER, Apr. 18, 2011, at 2.

80 HERRING, *ibid.* at 291.

81 *Ibid.* Interestingly, in the U.S., a growing effort among the chronically ill is to have the lifetime cap of $1 million—found routinely on many health care policies—lifted by Congressional action and raised to as high as $10 million. It is argued that present caps have not kept pace with health care inflation. Organ transplants—alone—can, for example, range anywhere from $250,000 to $600,000; and costs for hemophilia care can reach $750,000 annually. Christopher Lee, *More Hitting Cost Limit on Health Benefits*, WASH. POST, Jan. 27, 2008, at A3.

Under the new Health Reform Act, previous lifetime limits for medical costs will be eliminated from health insurance plans issued or renewed on or after September 23, 2010 or January 1, 2011. For those who have reached the "max out" cap but nevertheless remain eligible for health coverage, under the new Act, coverage for them must be reinstated on the first day of the health insurance plan year beginning on or after September 23 and cannot have lower limits than $750,000. By 2014, annual limits will be eliminated altogether. Carla K. Johnson, *Starting Thursday: No Lifetime Cap, Free Preventive Care Among Health Law Changes Kicking In*, WASH. EXAMINER, Sep. 22, 2010, at 1.

82 Peter Singer, *Why We Ration Health Care*, N.Y. TIMES MAG., Jul. 19, 2009, at MM38. The NHS does provide compassion, however, in its maintenance of dementia patients—with each patient costing the British economy £27,647 a year in institutional care which offers absolutely no curative treatment. Within 15 years, it is estimated that one million British citizens will suffer from dementia. Daniel Martin, *Dementia Time Bomb*, THE DAILY MAIL, Feb. 4, 2010, at 12.

83 HERRING, *supra* note 77 at 293.

84 *Ibid.* at 290, 291.

85 Rasinski-Gregory & Cotler, *supra* note 58 at 83. *See generally Symposium: Intergenerational Equity and Disconcerting*, 74 U. CHI. L. REV. 5 (2007).

86 Lawrence A. Frolik & Alison P. Barnes, *An Aging Population: A Challenge to the Law*, 42 HASTINGS L. J. 683 at 708–9 (1991).

87 CALLAHAN *supra* note 34 at 117.

88 Thomasma, *supra* note 65 at 148–49.

89 *Ibid.* at 148.

90 *See ibid. See generally* GEORGE P. SMITH, II, LEGAL AND HEALTHCARE ETHICS FOR THE ELDERLY (1996).

91 MARK R. WICCLAIR, ETHICS AND THE ELDERLY 80 (1993).

Although of no curative value, humane care of dementia patients is nonetheless provided even though it is not cost-effective. *See* Martin, *supra* note 82.

92 WICCLAIR, *ibid.*

93 *See* Thomasma, *supra* note 65 at 156 (noting that the elderly are responsible for building "the roads and bridges, symphonies, and schools we now enjoy").

94 Frolik & Barnes, *supra* note 86 at 713.

95 *See* Thomasma, *supra* note 65 at 156 (quoting, "While the elderly may gobble up inordinate relative amounts of healthcare dollars, while doing so, they are not using other resources of society—general resources use equalizes out in the end").

96 *See* CALLAHAN, *supra* note 34 at 83 (noting familial relationships and governmental such as Social Security and Medicare). *See generally* RICHARD A. POSNER, AGING AND OLD AGE (1995).

97 *Ibid.* at 82.

98 Daniel C. Maguire & Edith A. McFadden, *The Ethics of Health Care Rationing* in HEALTH CARE RATIONING: DILEMMA AND PARADOX at 149–54 (Kathleen Kelly, ed. 1994).

99 Amy M. Haddad, *Ethical Issues in Health Care Rationing* in HEALTH CARE RATIONING, *ibid.* at 11.

100 MARGARET SOMERVILLE, THE ETHICAL CANARY: SCIENCE, SOCIETY AND THE HUMAN SPIRIT 262 (2000).

101 *Supra* note 99. *See* Editorial, … *Obama wants to Ration Your Health Care, supra* note 79 (reporting on how the Independent Payment Advisory Board created by Obamacare is designed to slow the growth of Medicare costs by its ongoing evaluations of what medical treatments should be covered by national healthcare insurance). *See also* Timothy S. Jost, *The Independent Medicare Advisory Board*, 11 YALE J. HEALTH POL'Y L. & ETHICS 21 (2011).

102 George P. Smith, II, *Utility and The Principle of Medical Futility: Safeguarding Autonomy and The Prohibition Against Cruel and Unusual Punishment*, 12 J. CONTEMP. HEALTH & POL'Y 1 (1996).

103 CALLAHAN, *supra* note 3; Daniel Callahan, *Symbols, Rationality and Justice: Rationing Health Care*, 18 AM. J. LAW & MED. 1 (1992).
104 ANDERLIK, *supra* note 36 at 134.
105 RICHARD A. POSNER, THE PROBLEMS OF JURISPRUDENCE 112 (1990).
106 BARRY R. FURROW, *ET AL.*, HEALTH LAW 478 (2001).
107 *Ibid.* at 479. *See generally* SUSAN JACOBY, THE AGE OF AMERICAN UNREASON (2008).
108 GEORGE LUNDBERG, SEVERED TRUST: WHY AMERICAN MEDICINE HASN'T BEEN FIXED (2001). *See also* GEORGE J. ANNAS, SOME CHOICES: LAW, MEDICINE AND THE MARKET, ch. 4 (1998).
109 MARY R. ANDERLIK, *supra* note 36 at 5. *See also* Marian Gray Secundy & Rodger L. Jackson, *Engendering Trust in a Pluralistic Society* in THE HEALTH CARE PROFESSIONAL AS FRIEND AND HEALER, *supra* note 33 at 65.
110 JAMES F. CHILDRESS, PRACTICAL REASONING IN BIOETHICS 254 (1997).
111 *Ibid.*
112 BLANK, *supra* note 52 at 98.
113 *See* Shailagh Murray & Anne E. Kornblut, *Stark Divide on Display at Health Summit*, WASH. POST, Feb. 26, 2010, at A1; Alec MacGillis & Amy Goldstein, *Obama Offers A New Proposal on Health Care*, WASH. POST, Feb. 23, 2010, at A1.
114 Susan Ferrechio, *The Inconvenient Truths about Obamacare*, WASH. EXAMINER, Mar. 23, 2010, at 14; Alec MacGillis, *First Wave of Overhaul Will Inundate Insurers with New Rules*, WASH. POST, Mar. 23, 2010, at A8.
115 ANDERLIK, *supra* note 36 at 130.
   Seizing upon the fears of private practitioners that Obamacare regulations are too cumbersome and that reimbursements for their services will force them from their practice, hospitals are simply buying up physicians' practices thereby placing the practice of medicine nationwide under their institutional control. Scherz, *supra* note 35.
116 EDMUND D. PELLEGRINO & DAVID C. THOMASMA, A PHILOSOPHICAL BASIS OF MEDICAL PRACTICE: TOWARD A PHILOSOPHY AND ETHIC OF THE HEALING PROFESSIONS (1981).
117 Norman Daniels, *Justice, Health, and Health Care* in MEDICINE AND SOCIAL JUSTICE at 6, 14 (Rosamond Rhodes, Margaret P. Battin & Anita Silvers, eds. 2000).
118 Mary A. Baily, *Managed Care Organization and The Rationing Problem*, 33 HASTINGS CENTER RPT. 34, 40 (Jan.—Feb. 2003).
119 *Ibid.*
120 *Ibid.* at 185. *See generally* George P. Smith, II, *Human Rights and Bioethics: Formulating a Universal Right to Health, Health Care or Health Protection?* 39 VANDERBILT J. TRANSNAT'L L. 1295 (2005).
121 EDMUND D. PELLEGRINO & DAVID C. THOMASMA, FOR THE PATIENT'S GOOD: THE RESTORATION OF BENEFICENCE IN HEALTH CARE 133–47 (1988).
122 David C. Thomasma, *The Principle of Dominion* in THE HEALTH CARE PROFESSIONAL AS FRIEND AND HEALER, *supra* note 33 at 133–47. *See generally* Mark A. Hall, *The Legal and Historical Foundations of Patients as Medical Consumers*, 96 GEO. L. J. 583 (2008).
123 PELLEGRINO & THOMASMA, *supra* note 121 at 185.
124 *Ibid.*
125 David C. Thomasma, *The Ethics of Managed Care: Challenges to The Principles of Relationship Centered Care*, 25 J. ALLIED HEALTH 233 (1996). *See generally* Nan Hunter, *Managed Process, Due Care: Structures of Accountability in Healthcare*, 6 YALE J. HEALTH POL'Y, LAW & ETHICS 93 (2006).
126 GEORGE P. SMITH, II, HUMAN RIGHTS AND BIOMEDICINE 16 (2000).
127 *Ibid.*
128 PELLEGRINO & THOMASMA, *supra* note 116; PELLEGRINO & THOMASMA, *supra* note 121.

6   Public health emergencies

Introduction and overview

There are three major categories of emergency: those arising from "grave political crises" (*e.g.*, terrorist attacks, armed international conflicts); economic events—as with the Great Depression—and those which are born out of natural disasters, such as seen recently with Hurricane Katrina, as well as wider "*force majeure* events" (*e.g.*, riots, strikes).[1] Today, it has been said, correctly, that modern society faces dangers comparable to those the Nation was forced to deal with at the beginning of World War II.[2] What this means, then, is that emergencies, of one kind or other, have become almost the "coin of the realm."[3]

In emergencies of whatever character, the Nation's survival is imperiled and the Executive Branch of government must act to preserve the social order.[4] And, it has been argued that the Executive has a "penumbra of powers" in excess of the enumerated ones in Article II of the Constitution which allow him to act decisively.[5] The uppermost concern of civil libertarians have regarding the execution of these powers is that individual liberties or civil rights—particularly of minority interests, be they of an ethnic, ideological, or political character—will be subject to abuse, compromise, or even total abridgment.[6]

As early as 1824, the United States Supreme Court recognized the power of the states to compel isolation and quarantine.[7] In 1905, the Court determined, in the case of *Jacobson v. Massachusetts*, that citizens are subject to certain laws which promote the public health and safety for the benefit of the common good.[8]

Since that time, public health ethics—unlike bioethics which stresses non-malfeasance as one of the cornerstones of individual health care decisions[9]—requires inherently at-risk individuals to suffer elements of harm, through isolation, quarantine, or compulsory vaccination, in order to advance the public good and secure the public-at-large from being exposed to the spread of an infectious disease.[10]

It is thus reasoned that individual inconvenience or sacrifice is minimal when it is compared with the communal benefits of health and safety.[11]

Accordingly, under this model for health care management and decision-making, a point of balance is always sought between individual liberty interests and rights versus the communal benefits which may result from a limitation or restriction of those liberties. This balancing of individual rights typically does not outweigh community health benefits.[12]

There is, perhaps, always a fear—if not a risk—when public health strategies are in place to deal with emergencies or pandemics, that a police state could develop—this, because of unnecessarily broad and "arbitrary" powers conferred upon health officials with uneven levels of accountability.[13] Personal freedoms may be limited in time of national emergencies, but they must never be disregarded or even abrogated without a set time frame for their reinstatement at the conclusion of the crisis.

Civil libertarians have asserted that in times of emergency, the courts—exercising their powers of judicial review—should set stricter standards for review of government actions which go too far by reducing "the liberties of minorities while providing too much security for the public."[14] For them, the framework or mechanism for protection is to be found, for these minority or marginal voices, in *U.S. v. Carolene Prods. Co.*, decided by the U.S. Supreme Court in 1938.[15] The argument is thus advanced that where laws target minorities (*e.g.*, African-Americans) the courts should declare a clear preference for general laws as opposed to targeted laws—this, because general laws "require the self-interested majority to internalize costs."[16]

What is overlooked by the libertarians is that taken in isolation, virtually *all* laws "harm"—to one degree or other—a minority population.[17] Accordingly, *Carolene* should be accepted as applying only to a "discrete and insular minority" oppressed historically as a consequence of "prejudice."[18] As such, it becomes a faulty template for advancing the view that emergency powers exercised by the government must be scrutinized strictly because of the discriminatory effect of laws promulgated thereunder to certain minorities. The discrimination, such as it is because of isolation or quarantine principally, which of necessity occurs when any emergency powers are exercised, is no more disproportionate to the groups historically discriminated against than to other socio-ethnic groupings within contemporary society which have also been victimized by discrimination. The sad historical oppression of one group in the past simply should not be pivotal or determinative of the validity of constitutional powers exercised during public health emergencies in order to safeguard the common good.

The central issue in *Carolene* was whether Congress has, under the Commerce Clause, the right to regulate filled milk under the Filled Milk Act of 1923.[19] The limits of credulity are strained considerably when the holding of the Court—or, more particularly footnote four within the *Carolene* opinion—is elevated to a level of "satisfaction" by those intent on curtailing the emergency powers of the state.

Modernly, when emergency powers are claimed by the government in times of disaster, they are most generally justified under the rubric of the inherent powers of states to advance and maintain the common good[20] by exercise of its broad police powers—powers by their nature are "free from principled constraint."[21] In times of national emergencies, careful efforts by the judiciary must always be made in order to maintain constitutional integrity in the decision-making process—an integrity upheld by a ready willingness to find a "balance between the interest in liberty from government restraint or interference and interest in public safety."[22] The point of equilibrium in the balance must, of necessity, shift as threats to the common good intensify and subsequently abate over the course of time.[23]

Ideally, the point of balance to test the limits of a right and the point at which it may be re-calibrated is ideally to be "the point at which a slight expansion in the scope of the right would subtract more from public safety than it would add to personal liberty and a slight contraction would subtract more from personal liberty than it would add to public safety."[24] Not only do the weights placed on the various competing values become crucial in reaching the optimal point of balance between liberty and security interests, but the effects of these weights on the actual values of the safety measures being challenged, are as significant, if not definitive.[25] The absolute need for a point of balance was articulated in 1949 by Justice Robert H. Jackson of the U.S. Supreme Court when he cautioned that "the Constitution is not a suicide pact."[26]

This Chapter considers the extent to which public health emergencies necessitate a re-interpretation or re-shaping of the common good[27]—concluding, as such, that they most often do.[28] The next issue is to analyze the extent to which the medical principle of *triage* is a relevant construct, today, for allocating scarce medical resources.[29] Its efficacy or "codification" will be tested in The National Strategy of Pandemic Influenza[30] and, more particularly, in the plan for its execution developed by the Department of Health and Human Services.[31] It will be seen that under the rubric of cost-benefit analysis, *triage* is, indeed, a contemporary tool for distributing scarce medical resources and embodies, essentially, a correct use of utilitarian philosophy.[32]

Finally, two model legislative proposals—The Model State Emergency Health Powers Act[33] and The Turning Point Model State Public Health Act[34] will be considered to, again, test the validity of *triage*.[35] The ultimate conclusion reached, then, is that the ideal of attaining a level of Distributive Justice in allocating scarce medical resources has been achieved in the past[36] using *triage*, and can continue to be met today in times of public health emergencies by its incorporation into federal policy-making instruments as well as model state legislative proposals.

The common good

Often seen as a utilitarian ideal of attaining the greatest possible good for the greatest number of individuals,[37] the common good, for Maritain, was seen simply as "the good life of the multitude."[38] Rawls would surely have seen it as but a set of conditions allowing man to live under his own autonomous direction and finish his "projects" of choice since there is no good held in common.[39] Classically, the common good is viewed as embracing the community and its institutions as they serve the good of all citizens and not the limited or restricted goods of particular rules or classes.[40] The human good or, the good for human beings, is rooted in the nation that man is both a rational and a political animal.[41]

If, as Hegel posits, the norms and the values of ethical life form the very essence of the common good, that good—in turn—must be seen as derivative of "conditions of rationality" found within a particular system or within a set of values of given society.[42] Accordingly, determining what may be in the common good must be tied to testing the extent to which "currently share values stipulate" an action to be inclusive.[43] Individual judgments is, thus, inconsequential. Rooted in the school of conservative relativism, this position holds that individuals must respect prevailing social values. Indeed, when "questions of right" arise, they must be resolved "by recourse to prevailing values."[44]

Hegel postures, further, that within each community there is to be found "a dominant mode of self-reflection" or, "a self-image" which—in turn—"is embodied in a particular structure of norms and values."[45] Competing ideologies within any given society merely results in differing self-images.[46] Rather than accept the common good, then, as but a course of action set by one autonomous social group and thereby discount or disregard totally ideological conflicts,[47] what is needed today is a new philosophy in public health emergencies. This philosophy must recognize that the extent to which competing disagreements of the common good can only be resolved satisfactorily is "through a reconsideration of the language of which they are expressions."[48] From this philosophy will come, ideally, a new and informed level of debate and—ultimately— legislative frameworks for consensus decision-making, which set unambiguous and balanced normative standards for conduct, will emerge.

Triage: validating the balancing test as a tool for allocating scarce health care resources

Because of the limited resources and the limited surge capacity in the health care system, a pandemic raises unavoidable reference to and dependence on the principle of *triage*.[49] *Triage* is a French word which means "sorting, picking, grading or selecting according to quality."[50] As early as 1717, *triage* was applied in English in the separation of wool and coffee beans according to quality.[51] Coffee beans were separated into three classes: best quality, middling, and *triage*—or the lowest grade.[52]

Triage is defined as:

> The medical screening of patients to determine their priority for treatment; the separation of a large number of casualties, in military or civilian disaster medical care, into three groups: those who cannot be expected to survive even with treatment, those who will recover without treatment, and the priority group of those who need treatment in order to survive.[53]

Modern medical *triage* developed from the military system.[54] *Triage*, as a concept for medical treatment, was first introduced by Napoleon's chief surgeon, Baron Dominique Jean Larrey.[55] Larrey developed a system of removing soldiers from the battlefield using selection criteria, not by the soldier's rank as was formerly the practice, but the severity of the soldier's injury.[56] The baron's goal was to provide efficient medical services.[57] As a result, he sorted casualties based on medical need, with the highest priority given to those most severely wounded and the less severely injured waited to be provided medical attention.[58] At that time, the concern was to conserve the scarce medical resources, specifically, the time and energy of medical personnel.[59] At the same time the ultimate objective was a speedy restoration of the fighting function. The most salvageable were deemed those who could be rehabilitated, then, to return to fight another day and thereby preserve the common good.[60] Before French *triage*, the wounded remained on the battlefield where they fell and would only be gathered and evaluated at the conclusion of a battle (if even alive) and then sent to hospitals.[61]

During the United States Civil War, wounded soldiers were treated without regard to the type and severity of their condition.[62] In World War I, the United States took an example from the French and British armies, created a sorting station for wounded soldiers and adopted the term *triage*.[63] Ambulance drivers in World War I devised a system of prioritizing which wounded soldiers would be given treatment first and the determinative factor for selection was whether they could easily be sent back into battle.[64] Those who could not be returned to the battlefield were treated last and some were even left to die.[65] The problem was that there were insufficient numbers of health care workers and facilities to treat the wounded simultaneously; therefore, difficult choices were made and soldiers had to wait, even pay the ultimate price.[66]

Soldiers were treated under the "doctrine of common good" that winning the war was the top priority, so those who could not return to the battlefield were lower on the priority list.[67] The military *triage* systems, therefore, developed a utilitarian approach—soldiers that needed limited treatment and can be readily returned to battle were given a higher priority while those with life-threatening wounds were a lower priority.[68] According to the U.S. military policy, the purpose of *triage*-sorting is to evaluate and classify casualties for treatment and evacuation to accomplish "the greatest good for the greatest number of wounded and injured men."[69]

When presented in a hospital emergency room, then, patients are evaluated according to their medical condition and needs; in other words, the extent to which their injuries are life-threatening, urgent, semi-urgent, or in need of no care[70] and the likely outcome resulting from medical intervention.[71] Because health care workers are not able to treat everyone at the same time and medical resources are limited, *triage* allows—as seen—for the actual rationing of these medical resources to "produce the greatest good for the greatest number by meeting human needs most effectively and efficiently under conditions of scarcity."[72] *Triage* relies on the utilitarian rationale and goal of achieving the maximum amount of good.[73] In a purely utilitarian approach, actions are judged based on their benefits and whether they provide maximum utility to the general welfare, with little or no regard for moral rights.[74] Moral questions may, indeed, be seen as inappropriate—this, because in contemporary society, immorality governs interpersonal actions and is seen as a quality of personhood.[75]

Contemporary applications

The practice of disaster *triage*, defined as a "dynamic process of rapid evaluation and frequent reassessment of casualties presenting for evaluation,"[76] is, admittedly an inexact science—especially at the pre-hospital or field stage—on consensus opinion,[77] or simply a determination of what best preserves the "common good."[78] Although linked, inextricably, to utilitarianism, the philosophy of disaster *triage*—it is asserted—must be grounded in measurable or objective criteria by which a correct assessment is made of a victim's medical condition instead of evaluating its use or non-use based on the achievement of the "greatest good."[79] Efforts to standardize this level of *triage* in the field have proven difficult.[80]

One significant attempt at standardization was developed in California in 1983 and is designated *Simple Triage and Rapid Treatment* (START). Updated in 1994, and the most commonly used system today, it identifies, within one hour of a victim's trauma, three conditions which—if not treated—may lead to death: impaired breathing, head injury, and severe hemorrhage.[81] Not designed for scenarios where there are biological, chemical, or nuclear emergencies, START is faulted for its lack of differentiation regarding trauma types and estimations of prognosis or probability, therefore another *triage* system has been developed: Move, Assess, Sort and Send (MASS).[82] Critical care decisions have yet to be tested fully under this operational system[83]; but it nonetheless is a positive indication of re-assessment and as openness to change.

Criticism and disappointments

One critic of the system of *triage* has opined that today the whole process for its use has been reversed—with those having the most serious conditions being seen, evaluated, and attended to first while the "merely mutilated," or salvageable, are forced to wait.[84] That certainly appeared to be the situation, in very large part, in the aftermath of Hurricane Katrina where at one staging center those found to be in "direct need of medical attention" were rushed by ambulance to medical facilities in Baton Rouge while those "in the best shape" were sent to Thibodaux some 60 minutes outside of New Orleans and sheltered in a gymnasium.[85] In retrospect, this was the most humane and reasonable policy to follow. But, in one particular case, tragic consequences flowed from its adoption. Because of this *triage* practice in New Orleans, at one particular hospital—Memorial Medical Center—a physician and two nurses were charged with "mercy killing" for injecting four patients with lethal doses of a combination of morphine and midazolan.[86] The injections were apparently ordered as a result of a *triage* ranking that found these patients—not considered in imminent danger of dying—nonetheless incapable of sustaining themselves without considerable pain or anxiety for a protracted period in the hospital before being evacuated. Inside the hospital, itself, some 750 patients were trapped and unable to be transferred and thus subjected to a facility where temperatures were 100 degrees and there was no electricity nor waste disposal available.[87] None of the four patients had, incidentally, asked for assistance in euthanizing themselves.[88] Charges against the nurses were dropped subsequently[89] and a Grand Jury refused to indict the physician; yet three of the four patients' families have filed civil actions against her.[90]

A modified utilitarian approach through the principle of distributive justice

Because of the synergy of public health with human rights and the defense of individual rights and dignity, together with the recognition of the health of the greater community, a purely utilitarian approach to *triage* will not be adequate.[91] The utilitarian ethical theory as developed by Jeremy Bentham and John Stuart Mill is, as seen, that the principle of the greatest happiness and actions that promote the greatest happiness are of most utility and are considered right.[92] However, a major objection to utilitarianism is that as a society certain acts are valued because they are fair and just and not because they maximize happiness.[93] A concern is that the utilitarian principle of the "greatest happiness for the greatest number of people" sacrifices some members of society to serve the happiness of the majority.[94]

An alternative decision model has been suggested which would be applicable to pandemic strategies. Under it, decisions would be made "in a rational manner and guided by a spirit of humanism which minimizes human suffering and maximizes the social good of each situation, a humane standard of justice will be achieved and *triage* will operate as a complement to its attainment."[95]

The principle of distributive justice requires that "benefits and burdens ought to be distributed equitably, that resources ought to be allocated fairly, and that one ought to act in such a manner that no one person or group bears a disproportionate share of benefits or burdens."[96] A stockpile of countermeasures raises the question, of what order will citizens or patients receive these medical resources and who will make the decision of how to allocate them.[97] This is a matter of distributive justice and would require the government to make very difficult decisions and to list, in order of priority, who is to receive these resources first and who must wait.

This prioritization of citizens for the distribution of medical resources seems harsh and some may argue that patients should be provided treatment on a first-come-first-served basis or on a random selection principle, based on chance, or the idea that no one is given priority since all cannot be saved no one should be saved.[98] These are the three core principles of an egalitarian approach which attempts to promote equality among persons that require a scarce resource.[99] Because of the chaos a pandemic is likely to bring, a strategy that focuses on benefitting society at large is a useful one; however, it must also be "guided by a spirit of humanism" and not eliminate autonomy altogether in the process.[100]

In a pandemic, the influx of diseased or at-risk individuals will cause a surge on the health care system, inevitably raising the question of whether *triage* and rationing of scarce medical resources is unethical, unfair, and unjust.[101] The health care system will face "opposing moral obligations: to provide good health care and at the same time to protect the fabric of society."[102] A dire situation like a pandemic, with thousands of citizens becoming stricken with a deadly influenza virus, rationing health care and medical resources will not only be necessary, but it will be just if correctly applied.[103] Because a large-scale pandemic requires the distribution of health care and medical resources for the greater society, difficult choices will have to be made to determine who will receive certain kinds of care and treatment.[104] Health care practitioners will be forced to make difficult decisions in the way of "patient selection" for treatment and care while refusing treatment to others.[105] *Triage* will be the tool used for patient selection[106] which will also provide a method of justly distributing scarce medical resources.

Preparing for the Asian bird flu pandemic

Limited resources

It is feared that over time, the avian flu H5N1 virus will mutate into a form which will pass easily among persons throughout the world thereby triggering a pandemic.[107] This, in turn, will create a public health crisis which will be focused, in very large measure, on the distribution of scarce medical resources.

An integral part of any strategy designed to combat this crisis will be the manufacture of an effective anti-viral vaccine. But, this cannot be produced until the pandemic influenza strain emerges and is identified.[108] In the meantime prior to the production of the vaccine, the World Health Organization (WHO) recommends the anti-viral medication, Tamiflu, be prescribed.[109] The United States has stock piles of Tamiflu treatment courses for 81 million people.[110] Rather than treat only those clinically affected with the virus, present plans call for the delivery of anti-viral drugs to those within an identified or specific area of infection.[111] As of January 1, 2012, the resident population of the United States was projected by the U.S. Bureau of the Census to be 312,783,675.[112]

Estimates have been made that if an influenza pandemic were to occur, much as one did throughout the globe in 1918–19, some 62 million people, today, would succumb and die[113]—with 96 percent of these deaths occurring among developing countries.[114] Thirty-eight to eighty-nine million people in the United States would become clinically ill; eighteen–forty-two million would require outpatient care; 314,000–734,000 people would be hospitalized and 89,000–207,000 of the U.S. population would die.[115]

A pandemic strategy for the United States

On November 1, 2005, President Bush released *The National Strategy for Pandemic Influenza* which is to guide the preparedness and response of the nation to an influenza pandemic.[116] President Bush's pandemic strategy recognizes that vaccines and antiviral medications are available in limited supply.[117] The strategy sets out distribution protocols for these counter-measures.[118] The Administration plans to develop distribution mechanisms for antivirals and vaccines prior to and during a pandemic.[119] Another goal is to prioritize the allocation of vaccines and antivirals before an outbreak and update the prioritization when the pandemic arrives based on the knowledge of at-risk populations, supplies, and viral characteristics at the time of the outbreak.[120]

The following day, November 2, 2005, the U.S. Department of Health and Human Services (HHS) released its pandemic influenza plan.[121] HHS is the United States government's principal agency for protecting the health of all Americans and providing essential human services, especially for those who are least able to help themselves.[122] The two main goals of the pandemic response plan are to decrease health impacts of the pandemic such as morbidity and mortality, minimize societal and economic impacts, and thus provide a plan for guidance for state and local preparedness and response.[123]

In order to achieve these goals while working with limited resources, HHS has incorporated the concept of *triage* in its framework by suggesting priority groups of those who should receive the vaccines and antiviral medications.[124] Minimizing morbidity and mortality rates requires a conservation of those medical resources so they may be used to their full potential and resources are not wasted. An important theme that has been running through the decision-making process is that in order to limit the effects of a pandemic on society the essential functions must be preserved.[125] Beyond health care costs there will be significant social and economic impacts on the nation. People will most likely avoid areas where they are likely to be in contact with many people, such as schools, malls, theaters, bars, and stadiums, imposing large costs on vendors, workers, suppliers, and merchants. When parents do not send their children to school, they will likely stay home with the children resulting in absenteeism from their jobs, which will decrease productivity affecting our economy.[126] Trade and transport of goods, foods, and services both internationally and domestically are likely to be halted. Additionally, the tourism industry will fall victim to public fear during an outbreak. With the loss of jobs, productivity, and fear pervading the lives of citizens, the social and economic impact will be significant.[127]

The HHS pandemic flu plan provides guidance to state, local, and tribal groups for implementing plans that: define priority groups by their functions to maintain social continuity, develop a plan to identify these individuals, and establish effective and equitable distributive methods of vaccines and antivirals to these populations.[128] The states and localities are in a better position than the federal government to identify the critical functions that must be maintained to preserve the services and infrastructure, and those individuals essential to achieve that goal.[129] Though federal government cannot provide much tactical aid to each community, the federal government through HHS is striving "to mitigate the severity of a pandemic by setting standards for pandemic care, and by helping local officials understand the circumstances under which they should take dramatic action."[130]

Because much is unknown about when the pandemic will occur, what form the influenza virus causing the pandemic will take and the uncertainty of the impact of a pandemic, assumptions must be made to create a workable plan for distributing vaccines and antiviral medications based on *triage* principles and humanism. HHS has outlined its decisional framework in determining priority groups for resource allocation. First, those who will most likely become infected and die from the influenza virus must be considered.[131] Second, the health care system will experience a "surge" of patients requiring hospitalization and care into their facilities, possibly overwhelming the system.[132] Third, the workforce will suffer due to the increased absenteeism due to illness, fear of becoming infected, and caring for ill family members.[133] Fourth, there will be potential impacts on critical infrastructure such as transportation, with people not wanting to travel with others out of fear of infection, as well as utility services, to maintain continuity and safe, sanitary, and healthy conditions.[134] Finally, a realistic level of understanding needs to be shown regarding the inherent market limitations imposed upon the production capacity for vaccines.[135]

Triage *of vaccine distribution*

The priority group recommendations of HHS appears to seek to do the most good for the people for the least amount of burden on the health care resources. At the outbreak of a pandemic, those of top priority (Tier 1) under the HHS plan to receive vaccinations are the vaccine and antiviral manufacturers and those essential to their production.[136] Production of vaccines and antiviral drugs will provide for the common good in a pandemic. Next on the priority list are the medical and public health workers in direct patient contact, others responsible for direct patient care and vaccinators.[137] This will be necessary to help hospitals deal with the "surge" of ill people as well as limit the potential that healthcare personnel will not come to work out of fear of getting infected. The health care facilities will need "all hands on deck" to deal with the hospitalizations a pandemic can bring. The selection of these groups as top priority to receive vaccinations is based on one of the utilitarian principles of *triage* which is general social value.[138] The principle as applied to this situation shows that these manufacturers and medical and public health workers are "believed to have the greatest actual or potential general social worth."[139] Because the scarce resources in a pandemic will be vaccinations, antiviral medications, and health care workers, it is imperative that the production of these counter-measures continue and health care workers are available and healthy to treat ill patients.

The plan seeks to save the most lives as well as protect the health care resources from surging into the hospitals. After the vaccine and antiviral manufacturers, and the public health workers, HHS seeks to protect those persons from six months of age with influenza, high-risk conditions, or a history of pneumonia and influenza hospitalizations.[140] The goal here is to identify and prevent those most susceptible and most likely to be hospitalized or die from influenza, thereby making hospital resources available to those who are most likely to recover with treatment. By vaccinating those identified to be most susceptible to influenza, the government is using *triage* principles because it is immediately useful to those patients, and it seeks to conserve antivirals and other health care resources to those less likely to be infected by influenza.[141] In further conserving vaccine resources, the elderly in nursing homes and those with compromised immune systems are excluded from vaccination because the vaccine would not likely have a protective effect on these individuals.[142] Also, under another *triage* principle, vaccinating these individuals will have the lowest possibility of medical success and, therefore, it would be futile and a potential waste of limited resources that could be used in a patient that will benefit from the vaccination.[143] The goal of vaccination is to help those who will most benefit from a vaccine and not those who are unlikely to benefit.

The plan does provide for the vaccination of those who are in regular contact with individuals of compromised immune systems.[144] Pregnant women are in a high priority group of those vaccinated because it was observed from past pandemics that pregnant women were at high risk and that vaccinations will also protest the infant who cannot be vaccinated.[145] Since children under six months cannot be vaccinated, those in household contact with children of that age are to be vaccinated. In prioritizing these groups of individuals, the *triage* system is fulfilling the parent role principle, because both the caretakers and pregnant women have others who are dependent upon them for survival.[146] It would therefore be in the best interests of the community to allow for those individuals to continue caring for their dependents so as to conserve the resources of the health care system. Finally, public health officials playing a critical role in the pandemic response, and those key government leaders making decisions which implement the response, are to be vaccinated in order to maintain the effectiveness of the pandemic response.[147]

Tier 2 protects healthy individuals 65 and older, healthy infants six to 23 months, and those six months to 64 years with high-risk conditions of influenza.[148] These groups are at less of an increased risk than Tier 1; nevertheless, they are still at a high risk for influenza. Here, the HHS plan continues to try to solve the problem of the scarcity of health care resources by providing these high-risk groups with a preventative vaccination. It will eliminate hopefully the need for future treatment in a hospital, conserving the resources for others.[149] Included in this Tier are other public health emergency responders, public safety workers (police, fire, 911 dispatchers and correctional facility staff), utility workers (power, water and sewage), transportation workers (fuel, water, food, medical supplies) and telecommunications.[150] These workers are important for maintaining the continuity of societal functions and critical infrastructure and thus are valued contributors to society.[151] HHS here is providing a federal guideline for the states, which the states must modify to suit the needs of their communities and citizens. In order for a state to effectively determine which social functions are essential, the affected populations in the community must be encouraged to cooperate, so state officials may understand the values and priorities of the affected communities.[152] However, when states and localities develop a plan to maintain the social order in a time of crisis, it is important that the public is encouraged to cooperate and participate in its development so the public perceives the *triage* standards as fair.[153] When the public is regarded as a partner and an ally in the planning effort, public confidence and trust in the process is established.[154] When the public understands the rationale and has participated in the process by contributing their values and priorities, social disruption will be minimized during the pandemic.[155] Prior to a health emergency, the government must maintain the public's trust and achieving this trust will be more likely if the public "participated in setting the procedures and material criteria and ... in determining what to emphasize in medical utility, which functions and roles are essential in judgments of narrow social utility."[156]

Tier 3 includes other government decision-makers, funeral directors, and embalmers. However, the priority given to funeral directors and embalmers is a value judgment that the public must consider in their communities. In the federal strategy, they are seen as lower-priority individuals; however, with the anticipated mortality rate of the H5N1 virus being so significant, mortuaries are likely to also experience a "surge" of the dead if the virus remains this virulent.[157] The jobs of the embalmers and funeral directors who will be in close contact with increasing numbers of dead bodies will become all the more important for society. Families would like to provide their loved ones with a proper funeral. The position of the embalmers and funeral director in the priority list of vaccinations should be reconsidered when implemented by the states.

In 1918, "the most terrifying aspects of the epidemic was the piling up of bodies."[158] The undertakers, responsible for the bodies, were sick and overwhelmed. There was nowhere to put the bodies. Gravediggers were also sick or refused to bury influenza victims out of fear of getting sick. The bodies could not be buried because there were no gravediggers. Bodies piled up, because they could not be buried. Coffins ran out. The morgues could not accommodate all the bodies that were brought in, so bodies remained in the homes where they died. Some even put their loved ones on ice, creating unsanitary conditions to say the least.[159] People were dying so quickly that there was no way to accommodate the bodies. Learning from the past, it would be helpful to make those that deal with the dead a higher vaccination priority than under the current plan.

Finally, Tier 4 requires the vaccination of healthy persons two to 64 years of age not included in the other categories.[160] Those who request to be vaccinated would be provided with one. This plan assumes that H5N1 will not affect the young, 20–40 year olds, as occurred with the 1918 virus.[161] The death curves were not like those of usual influenza; instead, they were W shaped with deaths occurring in children under age five, the elderly aged 70–74, and those of ages 20–40.[162] Therefore, a supplemental plan must be developed if the virus shows to be one of the epidemiology of the 1918 pandemic. Vaccinations of those aged 20–40 must be of a much higher priority as it affects more people than those at the other peaks of the younger and the older.

Triage *of antiviral medications*

The priority groups for those being treated with antiviral medications are typically those most at risk of becoming infected with influenza and would create the greatest burden on the health care system and critical infrastructure.[163] A system of *triage* in the hospital when patients come in for treatment is designed to make the most efficient use of the antiviral medications and health care system resources.[164] According to the HHS strategy, those groups of first priority are the patients admitted to hospital with serious illness and at risk of death.[165] This brings in an egalitarian alternative to the *triage* principle by giving priority on the basis of general neediness—those at the top of the list are the most helpless and the most ill.

Second, in priority are the health care workers and emergency medical service providers who are in direct contact with patients.[166] Health care workers are a limited resource and, in a pandemic, health care personnel will be in great demand to treat those affected by the influenza virus. These health care providers, because of their limited availability, have a great social worth in a successful pandemic response.

Antiviral medications are then distributed to those outpatient groups at highest risk of hospitalization and death, as well as those who cannot be protected by vaccines because their immune system is significantly compromised.[167] Next, antivirals will be administered to health responders and public safety and government decision-makers to ensure that the pandemic health response continues effectively.[168] The fifth priority group includes those outpatients at increased risk: young children, those over 65 years of age, and people with medical conditions.[169]

The final five priorities include those who are not going to be vaccinated, such as those in nursing homes with compromised immune systems. Other health care workers necessary to the health care response and to prevent absenteeism and societal responders to implement the pandemic response are to be provided with antivirals. The last three on the priority list are those outpatients and health care workers not included on the list above. Again, however, those aged 20–40 are excluded from the top priority lists because of their strong immune systems. However, during the 1918 virus, the strength of the immune response itself was the killer, and not the virus, in those aged 20–40.[170] Those aged 20–40 with healthy immune systems were those most severely attacked by the 1918 pandemic, but are last on the priority distribution list of counter-measures to the virus. Those within that age group seeking to protect themselves from the virus in the prime of their lives will have to sacrifice their personal autonomy to medical treatment for others in the community.

The HHS-recommended plan takes into great consideration the limited medications that would be available in a pandemic as well as the strain on health care systems when patients flood the hospitals. One goal of the plan is to target groups that are most susceptible to illness for vaccination, and keep those individuals out of the hospital. In the event that those who are less susceptible to the virus fall ill and come to the hospital, there will be beds, nurses, antiviral medications, and other medical necessities available to them. Also, those individuals with compromised immune systems not likely to be protected by a vaccine will not be provided one, because providing those individuals with a vaccine will be futile and others who may benefit from the vaccination will not receive one.[171]

Implementation plan update

On July 17, 2007, an update was issued by the government[172] on the Pandemic Influenza Implementation Plan released originally November 1, 2005.[173] This new assessment of progress shows—rather strikingly—the weakness in the federal government's ability to both detect an outbreak of the flu or to even track the progress of it as it moves throughout the country. Developing, as well, a nationwide surveillance system able to track the directions of the pandemic as it moves throughout the world is yet to be operational.[174] Having concluded that sealing the Nation's borders in the event of an influenza pandemic will be impractical, since it will enter the country regardless of physical restrictions at border crossings, the government has nevertheless underscored its intent to limit the entry of individuals who might be infected or who would be considered suspects of carrying the virus.[175]

The government will, over time, refine the priority list for individuals who will receive the flu vaccine first when an outbreak occurs and—as well—develop more fully and then release plans for coordinated school closings between state and local governments.[176] Additional concern has been raised regarding the present capacity for all health care facilities to manage effectively the additional patient burdens arising from the influenza disease.[177] While capital investments of $1 billion have been dedicated to manufacturing new programs for flu vaccines, additional sums have been released by HHS and include $897 million to state governments for emergency preparedness of which $175 million is set aside, specifically, for the pandemic.[178]

The obvious conclusion to be drawn from this update is that while progress in preparing the Nation from the flu pandemic is being made, considerable work needs to be undertaken before all levels of government—national, state, and municipal—will be able to make a coordinated response to the pandemic. In developing effective emergency planning and preparedness an all hazards approach must be developed—one which, of necessity, includes pandemic influenza but the emergence of new diseases, terrorist attacks, and natural disasters. Accordingly, preparing for a pandemic must not be taken as a threat to or competition with other efforts directed at disaster preparedness.

Curtailing the pandemic

The World Health Organization declared on June 11, 2009, that the swine flu H1N1 outbreak had become a pandemic.[179] Previous to this event, in 2003 in Asia, the H5N1 flu emerged and killed approximately 60 percent of those infected by it.[180] Indeed, today, there is fear that the Asian flu will continue to mutate—this, because of two unresolved issues: the failure of Asian poultry production to meet public health sanitation standards for segregating chickens and ducks when they are slaughtered; and the reluctance of Asian countries to provide influenza strains without receiving compensation from pharmaceutical companies that will profit from them.[181]

The six-year active Asian flu period from 2003 to 2009 should have been an adequate time frame for the United States to prepare for the swine flu H1N1 pandemic.[182] Yet, by June 2009, serious concerns were raised over the inadequate domestic production capacity of vaccine to combat this virus.[183] Not only were clinical trials found wanting, but state laboratories were not testing the flu vaccine.[184] Five pharmaceutical companies were registered to produce 100 million doses of vaccine—with the Federal government spending $1 billion to date for the production and committing an additional $7 billion for further purchases.[185] There was no expectation by the government that there would be 100 percent coverage of any one group.[186]

The top priority group of Americans numbered 159 million, with about half of this population group including health care workers and emergency medical responders. The next segment of at-risk individuals having access to the flu vaccine was seen as pregnant women, children, and young adults from six months to 24 years and people aged 25 to 64 with medical problems such as asthma, diabetes, or heart disease. These high-risk group designations were consistent with those recommended by the Advisory Committee on Immunization Practices for the Centers for Disease Control and Prevention (CDC).[187]

By the end of January 2010, only about one-fifth of all Americans—or some eighty million people—had received a vaccination for swine flu.[188] Subsequently, the following month, the CDC announced that the H1N1 epidemic in the United States was no longer widespread; yet, no assurance was forthcoming that the country would escape a subsequent wave of swine flu.[189] Indeed, it was predicted that the H1N1 virus—or a variant of it—will, over time, infect, but not necessarily sicken, "nearly everybody on Earth who isn't already immune to it through vaccination."[190]

The CDC has come under a fair amount of justified criticism for its overall handling of the H1N1 epidemic. Not only was the CDC unable to characterize, with accuracy, the pandemic's trajectory, but it was unable to define the impact of the virus, offer suggestions for dealing with it or—for that matter—convince the public to get vaccinated.[191] At times, the recommendations of the CDC were ambiguous and erroneous. Public health authorities need to become clearer about the lexicon of uncertainty—what they know and do not know about a pandemic.[192] They also need to be transparent about how they devise their recommendations which often have to balance between infection control and the daily activities of business offices and schools. And care must be given to identifying which social distancing techniques truly help control pandemics—for example, does the closing of schools and malls minimize the spread of viruses from infected children to adults?[193]

On January 27, 2010, the Congressional Commission on the Prevention of Weapons of Mass Destruction Proliferation and Terrorism issued its report on national emergency preparedness and concluded that both the White House and the Congress should receive failing grades for their inability to build a rapid-response capability for dealing with outbreaks of disease from acts of bioterrorism as well as develop strategies and provide adequate oversight of security and intelligence agencies.[194] Finding the government faltered in developing and executing a unified response to the recent swine flu epidemic, the Commission concluded this deficiency is symptomatic of the fact that there is no real or prevailing "sense of urgency displayed towards the threat of a large-scale biological weapons attack."[195]

This distressing conclusion underscores the need to understand that emergency preparedness will never be effective if preventive plans are faulty.[196] More specifically, rather than relying upon and enacting more laws designed for managing an array of public health emergencies, primary emphasis must depend upon developing planning policies designed to prevent and contain situations of this nature before they become dangerous public health incidents and supporting these policies with appropriate resources.[197] Put simply, effective emergency preparedness "requires a well-functioning public health system" which, in turn, requires "a healthy, well-informed population."[198]

International weaknesses

Ideally within the transnational arena, the WHO should have a pivotal role to play in formulating and safeguarding a right to health or to health protection.[199] Since 1947, under the auspices of the WHO, 113 national influenza centers have become operational in 84 countries where laboratories analyze and track influenza viruses as they occur throughout the globe.[200]

Revised international health regulations (IHR) took effect in 2007 which have the aspirational effect of imposing various responsibilities on the member states of the WHO to provide notification and surveillance of infectious diseases.[201] While obligating the states to respond promptly to public health incidents, the regulations are defective for two major reasons: they provide no incentives for poorer countries to meet the public health standards set by the regulations nor do they require the member states to attack, proactively, the initial conditions which foster disease.[202]

The WHO needs to press forward as a forum, or even a catalyst, for international consensus building and regulatory harmonization in both preventing and responding to public health crises.[203] Absent an understanding of the transboundary effects of infectious disease, and a concerted economic, political, and social willingness to realize that it is in the self-interest of each state to prevent, monitor, and contain disease, the common good of the international community will forever remain in jeopardy,[204] and "the enjoyment of the highest attainable standard of health" but an illusion.[205]

Law reform through model legislation

A majority of state statutes dealing with public care and, specifically, isolation and quarantine, were enacted a number of years, if not decades ago.[206] In order to allow the states to come into the new age of bioterrorism and public health emergencies, in 2003, The National Association of Attorneys General (NAAG) urged them to amend or enact new legislation appropriate to effectuating this goal.[207] In order to "jump start" this updating process, NAAG brought forward two model proposals—the Model State Emergency Health Powers Act[208] (MSEHPA) and the Turning Point Model State Public Health Act[209] (TURNING POINT). Particular care was placed on re-defining due process rights in relation to cases where isolation and/or quarantine are ordered.[210]

The work product of the Center for Law and the Public Health at the Georgetown University Law Center, the Johns Hopkins University and the Centers for Disease Control, the MSEHPA arose as a consequence of the attacks by bioterrorists on New York City on September 11, 2001, and the subsequent realization that "a coordinated, appropriate response in the event of a public health emergency" was lacking.[211] In granting to both state governor and public health officers a wide array of specific emergency powers, the MSEHPA also seeks to strike a balance between their powers and the personal liberties and civil rights of the medical detainees.[212] Testifying to the "catalystic" effect of this model legislation, by August, 2002, some 34 states and the District of Columbia had enacted legislation which either included provisions of the MSEHPA or adoptions from it.[213] By July, 2006, the number of states subscribing to the model act had risen to thirty-eight.[214]

Public health law reform opportunities were enhanced, as well, by the completion of a collaborative work product undertaken by nine national organizations and government agencies, representatives from five states, and the Public Health Statute Modernization collaborative.[215] Termed TURNING POINT, this legislative model structures a framework by which states can measure their preparedness for public health emergencies.[216] By March 2007, some 33 states had—to one degree or other—introduced legislation based upon the Turning Point Act, but only 26 of these states have actually enacted legislation which reflect provisions or sections of TURNING POINT.[217]

While the two Acts overlap, two central and important differences are to be found regarding due process rights during an isolation or quarantine. When either of these are ordered, with notice, under the MSEHPA, a hearing must be held within a five-day period—with a ten-day maximum time being allowed for extraordinary and good cause.[218] Under TURNING POINT detainment hearings must be conducted, however, upon the filing of the petition, within a 48-hour period or within five days under extraordinary circumstances, and good cause.[219]

Regarding the evidentiary burden to be met under confinement by isolation or quarantine, the MSEHPA directs the judiciary to grant any petition made when by "a preponderance of the evidence" it is determined that either of these two acts of confinement are reasonably necessary to limit or prevent "transmission of a contagious or possibly contagious disease. ..."[220] Under the Turning Point Model Act, the court must grant any petition if "clear and convincing evidence" is presented.[221] Overall, greater protection of individual liberties and rights is achieved under TURNING POINT—this, because of the stricter due process requirements within its provisions.[222]

Although "tools of last resort," isolation and quarantine are effective public health measures.[223] When isolation is ordered, those having a specific infectious illness are separated from associating with healthy individuals—with the goal of such action being to block the spread of illness.[224] Quarantine may be defined as "the separation and restriction of the movement of persons who, while not yet ill, have been exposed to an infection agent and therefore may become infectious."[225] Absent punishment for a crime, involuntary detention must always be about establishing a justifiable balancing point that, while acknowledging the duty of the state to protect and safeguard the health and safety of the public, also is both sensitive and reasonable as to the liberty interests and due process rights of the individual detained.[226]

Other concerns and criticisms of the MSEHPA are tied to a number of issues: the extraordinarily broad discretionary powers of a governor to declare, unilaterally, without consultation with public health officials, a public health emergency. The conditions under which the declaration is made are not spelled out by usage of words such as "significant" and "substantial."[227] In addition, the expanded police powers granted to state and local governments are worrisome to those who fear misuse.

Additionally, concerns are expressed over provisions in the MSEHPA which force individuals to be vaccinated and treated or quarantined; allow the state to track and share the personal health information of citizens without their consent; and mobilize state militias to enforce and penalize those who disobey state orders.[228]

For civil libertarians, a provision within the MSEHPA that the government will—in experiencing its emergency powers—protect the civil rights and liberties to the "fullest extent possible consistent with the primary goal of controlling serious health threats" gives too far in its stated endeavors to strike an appropriate "balance" between those actions taken, during emergencies, to safeguard the common good, and those which respect the rights and liberties of citizenship.[229] The drafters of this Act contend that a right and proper balance between the execution of compulsory powers during emergencies with the rights of personal dignity has been maintained.[230] And, furthermore, they remind the nay sayers that there is no "right" to be free of any restraint, "but the right to be free of a particular restraint that is not justified under the circumstances."[231]

Both of these legislative modes—MSEHPA and TURNING POINT—rather successfully, on balance, seek to facilitate the implementation of five foundational functions of public health: preparedness (through public health emergency planning); surveillance (by establishing measures to not only detect, but track emergencies); management of property (by securing the availability of vaccines, pharmaceuticals, and hospitals); protection of persons (by compelling, when clearly necessary, vaccinations, testing, treatment, isolation, and quarantine),[232] and communicational by ensuring unambiguous and authoritative information reaches the public at large in a timely manner.[233] As such, both models provide that forum for debate called for previously to re-evaluate, re-educate, and inform public opinion to the evolving nature of the common good during these perilous times.[234]

For every fundamental right or civil liberty asserted, there is a coordinate responsibility or even a correlative duty to, when directed by the needs of the common good, realize that that right must be executed *reasonably*. A synonym for reasonableness is cost-effectiveness attained, as such, by and through a cost-benefit analysis. For purposes of this present analysis, the standard of reasonableness is found, historically, within the tents of the principle of medical *triage*. It is then adopted properly by the Executive and codified in the Pandemic Influenza Plan authored by the U.S. Department of Health and Human Services.[235] In addition, the standard is set once again within the provisions of the MSEHPA[236] and the TURNING POINT.[237] Either of these model statutes can serve as catalysts for law reform and, as such, become templates for a new level of public health awareness and repressiveness.

When executive actions or legislative schemes put forward to safeguard the public in time of emergencies and preserve the common good are tested in the courts for their legitimacy and constitutional efficacy, the wisest course of action should be that of "judicial modesty."[238] Indeed, it may be properly regarded as the "cornerstone of judicial interpretation of the Court in emergency situations."[239] Instead of holding for constitutional invalidity, the courts should decide the test case challenges on narrow statutory grounds[240] and eschew consideration of the "probabilistic" effects of restrictions on various civil liberties within the "social landscape."[241]

Endeavoring to find an accurate and fair point of equilibrium in balancing competing values should dictate courts to—rather than being tied to certainties and rules—give, instead, serious attention to risks. This is the case simply because the aim of most emergency measures is to reduce risks and not eliminate certainties.[242] Standards, then, not rules, must—perforce—shape the breadth of judicial review of the constitutionality of security measures.[243] Standards are more flexible and situational and allow for accommodation by balancing the costs versus the benefits of each case in reaching a disposition.

In America, sadly, all too often civil *liberties* are seen as synonymous with constitutional *rights*.[244] These rights may be modified—indeed, should be— when they, as rights, no longer strike a "sensible balance between competing constitutional values, such as personal liberty and public safety."[245] National emergencies force a disequilibrium in the system of liberties and constitutional rights which have the effect of placing public safety concerns above what, heretofore, were seen as unassailable fundamental values. Pragmatic courts and pragmatic social orders, then, must respond accordingly to these changed circumstances by recalibrating what has been a point of balance or equilibrium by restricting previously validated civil liberties in favor of safety[246] and maintenance of the common good.[247]

As seen, the frameworks or mechanisms to ensure the recalibration of the balancing test have been discussed and analyzed: the scope of the common good; the principle of *triage*—grounded in the philosophy of utilitarianism and cost/benefit analysis; the Pandemic Flu plan of the federal government together with the MSEHPA and TURNING POINT. What remains is for the *vox populi* to be educated to their responsibilities of citizenship which demand—in times of national and public health emergencies—that the common good be protected and secured and, further, that this responsibility justifies the curtailment of basic liberties and rights during the time of the emergency. To fail to recognize or accept this responsibility, courts the collapse of society, itself.

The good seen as overriding all members of a community or, here, the Nation—is surely security.[248] Put simply, without security, there can be no community. Stated otherwise, the greatest good for the greatest number within a given community is security. The attainment and guarantee of this good, grounded in *common sense*, must always be preferred over an abridgement or temporary suspension of civil liberties.[249] Failing to understand and, when necessary implement this policy, will—indeed—assure that the Constitution is little more than "a suicide pact."[250]

Notes

1 Oren Gross, *Chaos and Rules: Should Responses to Violent Crisis Always be Constitutional?* 112 YALE L. J. 1011, 1025 n.4 (2003).
2 RICHARD A. POSNER, NOT A SUICIDE PACT: THE CONSTITUTION IN A TIME OF NATIONAL EMERGENCY 3 (2006). *See generally* Eric A. Posner & Adrian Vermeule, *Emergencies and Democratic Failure*, 92 VA. L. REV. 1091, 1094 (2006).

For an excellent analysis of economic emergencies and states of political emergency, *see* Bernadette Meyler, *Economic Emergency and The Rule of Law*, 56 DePAUL L. REV. 539 (2007).

3 This phrase is adapted from its original Old English usage to mean that emergencies are now quite common. *See* THE CAMBRIDGE HISTORY OF ENGLISH AND AMERICAN LITERATURE (A.W. Ward & A.R. Waller, ed. 2000). *See* KENNETH R. WING, *ET AL.*, *infra* note 4, for reference citations to past emergencies as well as ongoing ones with HIV/AIDS and terrorism.

4 Meyler, *supra* note 2 at 541. *See* KENNETH R. WING, *ET AL.*, PUBLIC HEALTH LAW (2007) for analysis of past epidemics, public health emergencies, bioterrorism; RICHARD A. POSNER, CATASTROPHE: RISK AND RESPONSE 247 (2004).

5 Meyler, *ibid.* at 548. *See e.g.*, The Robert T. Stafford Disaster Relief and Emergency Assistance Act, 42 U.S.C. §§ 5121–5206 (2002) which confers upon the President broad powers in time of domestic emergencies. *But see* Mark v. Tushnet, *Emergencies and The Idea of Constitutionalism* ch. 8 in AT WAR WITH CIVIL RIGHTS AND LIBERTIES (Thomas E. Baker & John F. Stack, Jr., eds. 2005).

6 RICHARD A. POSNER, *supra* note 2 at 3. *See* Adrian Vermeul, *Posner on Security and Liberty: Alliance to End Repression v. City of Chicago*, 120 HARV. L. REV. 1251 (2007) analyzing Judge Richard Posner's judicial philosophy in two momentous decisions: Alliance to End Repression v. City of Chicago (Alliance I), 742 F. 2d 1007 (7th Cir. 1987) (*en banc*) and Alliance II, 237 F.3d 799 (7th Cir. 2001). *See generally*, RICHARD A. POSNER, LAW, PRAGMATISM AND DEMOCRACY (2003).

7 Gibbons v. Ogden, 22 U.S. 1, 203 (9 Wheat.) (1824).

In assessing the extent of federal power under the Commerce Clause of the Constitution, the Court held (as to the licensing of vessels on waters within the jurisdiction of New York) that "Inspection laws, quarantine laws, health law of every description" are within the Commerce Clause powers of Congress. *Ibid.* at 203.

8 197 U.S. 11 (1905).

9 BARRY R. FURROW, *ET AL.*, BIOETHICS: HEALTH CARE LAW AND ETHICS 4 (5th ed. 2004).

10 LAWRENCE O. GOSTIN, PUBLIC HEALTH LAW AND ETHICS 13 (2002).

11 *Ibid.*

12 *Ibid.* The cost-benefit test is foundational to the law of nuisance. *See* George P. Smith, II, *The Morphogenesis of an Historical Revisionist Theory of Contemporary Economic Jurisprudence*, 74 NEB. L. REV. 658, 698 *passim* (1995).

In public health governance law, the protection of population health is balanced against other policy objectives, normative values and interests. After establishing that the public health action being advocated has a valid epidemiological and scientific basis, the proposed action should be tested by the principle of non-discrimination and the least restrictive measure. Accordingly, health care measures whose effect will interfere in an unreasonable manner with the pursuit and exercise of liberties or rights by the public, must be executed in reasonable ways which minimize such interferences and are not seen as acts of invidious discrimination. Finding a point of equilibrium between these two policy objectives which, in turn, do not compromise legitimate efforts to advance and protect population health, is vexatious and, indeed, problematic. David P. Fidler, *Global Health Jurisprudence: A Time of Reckoning*, 96 GEO. L. J. 393, 402–3 (2008).

13 *See generally* George J. Annas, *Bioterrorism, Public Health and Civil Liberties*, 346 NEW ENG. J. MED. 1337 (2002), *Terrorism and Human Rights* ch. 3 in IN THE WAKE OF TERROR: MEDICINE AND MORALITY IN TIME OF CRISIS (Jonathan Moreno, ed. 2003). *See also* RICHARD A. POSNER, *supra* note 2 at 5 (acknowledging these concerns of restrictions on civil liberties and a climate of fear being created as a consequence of government actions during emergencies, but dismissing them largely as but "inevitable by-products" of such emergency powers).

14 Posner & Vermeule, *supra* note 2 at 1197.

15 304 U.S. 144 (1938).

16 Posner & Vermeule, *supra* note 2 at 1115. *See generally* GRIFFIN TROTTER, THE ETHICS OF COERCION IN MASS CASUALTY MEDICINE (2007).

17 Posner & Vermeule, *ibid.*

18 Carolene, 304 U.S. 144, 152 n.4.

19 Carolene, 304 U.S. 144.

20 Meyler, *supra* note 2 at 550.

21 MARKUS D. DUBBER, THE POLICE POWER: PATRIARCHY AND THE FOUNDATIONS 180 (2005).

22 POSNER, *supra* note 2 at 31.

23 *Ibid.*

24 *Ibid. See* Sharona Hoffman, *Responders' Responsibility: Liability and Immunity in Public Health Emergencies*, 96 GEO. L. J. 1913 (2008) (analyzing the weaknesses of the present theories of liability and sources of immunity for health emergency responders to public health emergencies and proposing a comprehensive immunity provision be incorporated into both federal and state laws which would, in turn, seek to codify a balancing point between the needs of disaster victims with those needs of emergency responders as well as those interests which promote and safeguard the common good).

25 POSNER, *supra* note 2 at 32.

26 Terminiello v. Chicago, 337 U.S. 1, 37 (1949) (Jackson, J., dissenting).

27 *See generally* RICHARD A. EPSTEIN, PRINCIPLES FOR A FREE SOCIETY: RECONCILING INDIVIDUAL LIBERTY WITH THE COMMON GOOD (1998); Robert J. Lipken, *The Quest for The Common Good: Neutrality and Deliberative Democracy in Sunstein's Conception of American Constitutionalism*, 26 CONN. L. REV. 1039 (1994).

28 POSNER, *supra* note 2; Posner & Vermeule, *supra* note 2.

29 *See* George P. Smith, II, *Triage: Endgame Realities*, 1 J. CONTEMP. HEALTH L. & POL'Y 143 (1985).

   The counterpoint to medical *triage*—legal *triage*—has been defined as efforts, during emergencies, to prioritize the vast array of unscripted, developing legal issues (*e.g.*, isolation, quarantine, and forced immunization) which arise and demand an expeditious and legitimate response to the immediate emergency. James G. Hodge, Jr., *Legal Triage During Public Health Emergencies and Disasters*, 58 AD. L. REV. 627, 630–31 (2006).

30 NATIONAL STRATEGY FOR PANDEMIC INFLUENZA, HOMELAND SECURITY COUNCIL 1 (2005), www.whitehouse.gov/homeland/nspic.pdf.

31 U.S. DEP'T. OF HEALTH SERVS., PANDEMIC INFLUENZA PLAN, pt. 1 available at www.hhs.gov/pandemicflu/plan/pdf/HHSPandemicInfluenzaPlan.pdf [hereinafter HHS PLAN].

32 *See generally* NANCY L. ROSENBLUM, BENTHAM's THEORY OF THE MODERN STATE (1978).

33 THE MODEL STATE EMERGENCY HEALTH POWERS ACT (Ctr. for Law & the Pub.'s Health at Georgetown & Johns Hopkins Univs., Proposed Official Draft 2001), available at www.publichealthlaw.net/MSEHPA/MSEHPA2.pdf [hereinafter MSEHPA].

34 THE TURNING POINT MODEL STATE PUBLIC HEALTH ACT (Public Health Statute Modernization Nat'l Excellence Collaborative 2003), available at www.hss.state.ak.us/dph/improving/turningpoint/PDFs/MSPHAweb.pdf [hereinafter TURNING POINT ACT].

35 *See generally* Daniel S. Reich, *Modernizing Local Responses to Public Health Emergencies: Bioterrorism, Epidemics, and the Model State Emergency Health Powers Act*, 19 J. CONTEMP. HEALTH L. & POL'Y 379 (2003).

36 George P. Smith, II, *Distributive Justice and Health Care*, 18 J. CONTEMP. HEALTH L. & POL'Y 421 (2002).

37 *See generally* THE CLASSICAL UTILITARIANS: BENTHAM AND MILL (John Troyer ed. 2003); Gerald J. Postermore, BENTHAM AND THE COMMON LAW TRADITION (1986).

38 Glen N. Schram, *Pluralism and The Common Good*, 36 AM. J. JURIS. 19, 119 (1990–91) (analyzing, principally, the works of Jacque Maritain). *See generally* V. Bradley Lewis,

The Common Good against The Modern State? 16 JOSEPHINUM J. THEOLOGY 357 (2009).

39 *See* Daniel P. Sulmasy, *Four Basic Notions of The Common Good*, 75 ST. JOHN'S L. REV. 303 at 307 (2001).

40 V. Bradley Lewis, *The Common Good in Classical Political Philosophy*, 25 CURRENT ISSUES IN CATHOLIC HIGHER ED. 24, 26 (Winter 2006).

41 *Ibid.* at 25. Common sense helps define the applicable borders of the common good. *See generally* Gary Lawson, *Ordinary Powers in Extraordinary Times: Common Sense in Times of Crisis*, 87 B.U.L. REV. 289 (2007).

42 A. S. Walton, *Hegel, Utilitarianism, and The Common Good*, 93 ETHICS 753, 766 (1983).

43 *Ibid.*

44 *Ibid.*

45 *Ibid.* at 767.

46 *Ibid.*

47 *Ibid.* at 768.

48 *Ibid.* at 771.

49 James F. Childress, *Triage in Response to a Bioterrorist Attack*, in THE WAKE OF TERROR, *supra* note 13 at 77.

50 *Ibid.* at 78.

51 Childress, *supra* note 49 at 78.

52 *Ibid.*

53 Smith, *supra* note 29 at 144. *See* STEDMAN'S MEDICAL DICTIONARY 2025 (28th ed. 2006).

54 JAMES P. ORLOWSKI, ETHICS IN CRITICAL CARE MEDICINE 34 (1999).

55 *Ibid.*

56 *Ibid.*

57 Smith, *supra* note 29 at 144.

58 *Ibid.*

59 *Ibid.*

60 ALBERT R. JONSEN, THE NEW MEDICINE AND THE OLD ETHIC 45 (1990).

61 David E. Hogan & Julio Raphael Laieret, ch. 2 at 19 in DISASTER MEDICINE (David E. Hogan & Jonathan L. Bustein, eds. 2007).

62 Childress, *supra* note 49 at 78.

63 Childress, *ibid.*

64 MILTON D. HEIFETZ, ETHICS IN MEDICINE 197 (1996).

65 *Ibid.*

66 *Ibid.*

67 *Ibid.*

68 ORLOWSKI, *supra* note 54 at 34.

69 Childress, *supra* note 49 at 79 (quoting, Douglas S. Rund & Tondra S. Rausch, TRIAGE at 9 (1981)).

70 *Ibid.*

71 Childress, *supra* note 49 at 79; *See also* ORLOWSKI, *supra* note 54 at 35. ("The severity of an individual's illness or need, is generally tempered by survivability or chance of a successful outcome.")

72 Childress, *supra* note 49 at 79.

73 Smith, *supra* note 29 at 146.

74 *Ibid.* at 147.

75 DUBBER, *supra* note 21.

76 Hogan & Laieret, *supra* note 61 at 27.

77 *Ibid.* at 26.

78 JONSEN, *supra* note 60. *See generally* Mark D. Christian, *et al.*, *Definitive Care for The Critically Ill During a Disaster: Current Capabilities and Limitations*, 133 CHEST J. 8S (May 6, 2008).

79 Hogan & Laieret *supra* note 61 at 17, 19.

80 *Ibid.* at 24.

81 *Ibid.* at 25.

82 *Ibid.* at 26. *See* Lewis Rubinsen, *et al., Definitive Care for The Critically Ill During a Disaster: A Framework for Optimizing Critical Care Surge Capacity*, 133 CHEST J. 18S (May 6, 2008).

83 *Ibid.* Another set of recommendations for patient treatment during a flu pandemic or other incidents of mass casualties was issued in January 2007. The Task Force for Mass Critical Care—a multidisciplinary and governmental group working under the Critical Care Collaborative Initiative—has offered proposals which resemble a battlefield *triage* approach in which, essentially, scarce health care resources are reserved for those most likely to service *triage* teams in hospitals would determine those at high risk of death and very diminished chances of long-term survival. Asha Devereaux, *et al., Summary of Suggestions from The Task Force for Mass Critical Care Summit*, January 26–27, 2007, 133 CHEST J. 8S (May 6, 2008, Supplement).

84 JONSEN, *supra* note 60 at 46.

85 Tamer El-Ghobasky, *Homeless and Haunted: Triage Center Full of Mercy*, N.Y. DAILY NEWS, Aug. 31, 2005, at 7. *See also* Felicity Barringer & Donald G. McNeil, Jr., *Grim Triage for Ailing and Dying at a Makeshift Airport Hospital*, N.Y. TIMES, Sept. 3, 2005, at 13.

86 Tyler J. Curiel, *Murder or Mercy? Hurricane Katrina and The Need for Disaster Training*, 355 N. ENGL. J. MED. 2067 (Nov. 16, 2006). *See* George P. Smith, II, *Refractory Pain, Existential Suffering, and Palliative Care: Releasing an Unbearable Lightness of Being*, 20 CORNELL J. L & PUB. POL'Y 469, 507 (2011).

87 Curiel, *ibid.*

88 *Ibid.*

89 Mary Foster, *Prosecutor Drops Case Against 2 Nurses in Four Post-Katrina Deaths*, WASH. POST, Jul. 4, 2007, at A7.

90 Adam Nossiter, *Grand Jury Won't Indict Doctor in Hurricane Death*, N.Y. TIMES, Jul. 25, 2007, at 10. *See generally* Elizabeth A. Weeks, *Lessons from Katrina: Response, Recovery and The Public Health Infrastructure*, 10 DePAUL J. HEALTH CARE L. 251 (2007).

91 GOSTIN, *supra* note 10 at 97.

92 FURROW *et al., supra* note 9 at 8.

93 *Ibid.*

94 *Ibid.* at 11.

95 Smith, *supra* note 29 at 149.

96 Smith, *supra* note 36.

97 GEORGE P. SMITH, II, BIOETHICS AND THE LAW 47 (1993).

98 Smith, *supra* note 29 at 147.

99 *Ibid.*

100 *Ibid.*

101 Childress, *supra* note 49 at 77. *See* Devereaux *et al., supra* note 83.
       Under the recommendations of The Task Force for Mass Critical Care, which most probably violate federal laws prohibiting age and disability discrimination, those excluded from treatment include people 85 years of age or older; those individuals suffering from severe trauma—including critical injuries from car crashes or shootings; severely burned patients older than 60; those with severe mental impairment, which could include advanced Alzheimer's; and those with severe chronic diseases such as advanced heart failure, lung disease or poorly controlled diabetes. Devereaux *et al., ibid.*

102 Edmund D. Pellegrino, *Rationing Health Care: The Ethics of Medical Gatekeeping*, 2 J. CONTEMP. HEALTH L. & POL'Y 23, 38 (1986).

103 *Ibid.* at 38–39 ("[M]orally valid criteria can be established both for allocation and rationing of national resources dedicated to health and medical care"). *See generally* Kenneth Kipnis, *Overwhelming Casualties: Medical Ethics in a Time of Terror* ch. 6 IN THE WAKE OF TERROR: MEDICINE AND MORALITY IN TIME OF CRISIS (Jonathan Moreno ed. 2003).

104 Childress *supra* note 49 at 78.

105 JOHN F. KILNER, WHO LIVES? WHO DIES? ETHICAL CRITERIA IN PATIENT SELECTION at xi (1990).

106 ORLOWSKI, *supra* note 54 at 34.

107 Michelle A. Daubert, *Pandemic Fears and Contemporary Quarantine: Protecting Liberty Through a Continuum of Due Process Rights*, 54 BUFF. L. REV. 1299, 1300 n. 2 (2006–7).

108 Andrew Singer, Miles A. Nunn, *et al.*, *Potential Risks Associated with the Proposed Widespread Use of Tamiflu*, 115 ENVT'L HEALTH PERSPECTIVES 102 (Jan. 2007).

109 *Ibid.* See N. Pieter O' Leary, *Combating Nature's Insurgency: Tamiflu and Vaccination in The Fight against Avian Influenza*, 10 J. MED. & L. 469 (2006) (reporting on the fact that there are a very limited number of vaccine manufacturers today and only one in the United States).

110 Singer *et al.*, *supra* note 108.

111 *Ibid.* The United States and WHO have an additional 5–6 million courses of Tamiflu for blanketing in specific regions once a confirmed outbreak occurs. *Ibid.*

112 *See* http://www.census.gov/main/www/popclockus.html (last visited Jan. 1, 2012).
There is one birth every 7 seconds. *Ibid.*
The 2010 Census found the American population had grown to 308,745,638. *See* Carol Morello, *U.S. Population up 30 Million, Plus or Minus Several Million, Somewhere between 306 and 313 Million*, WASH. POST, Dec. 22, 2010, at A1.

113 Christopher J. L. Murray, Alan D. Lopez, Brian Chin *et al.*, *Estimation of Potential Global Pandemic Influenza Mortality on The Basis of Vital Registry Data from the 1918–20 Pandemic: A Qualitative Analysis*, 368 THE LANCET 2211 (Dec. 23/30, 2006).

114 *Ibid.*

115 Senator William Frist, Speech, *Pandemic: The Economy's Silent Killer*, National Press Club, Washington, D.C., December 8, 2005, at www.volpac.org/index.cfm?FuseAction=News. Speeches&id=21 (quoting statistics from the Centers for Disease Control). *See* HHS PLAN, *supra* note 31. *See also* Singer *et al.*, *supra* note 108; Marilyn Weber Serafini *infra* note 127, *The Big One?* (reporting that the economic impact of a pandemic to the Nation would be in a range from $87 billion to $203 billion).

116 NATIONAL STRATEGY FOR PANDEMIC INFLUENZA, HOMELAND SECURITY COUNCIL 1 (2005) www.whitehouse.gov/homeland/nspi.pdf (hereinafter National Strategy). *See generally*, Symposium, *Pandemic Preparedness: Lessons Learned and Future Challenges*, 4 ST. LOUIS J. HEALTH LAW & POL'Y 1 (2010); Alfred J. Sciarrino, *The Grapes of Wrath and The Speckled Monster, Part III: Epidemics, Natural Disasters and Biological Terrorism—The Federal Response*, 10 J. MED. & L. 429 (2006).

117 NATIONAL STRATEGY, *ibid.* at 5.

118 *Ibid.*

119 *Ibid.* at 6.

120 *Ibid.* See Christopher Lee, *U.S. Flu Outbreak Plan Criticized*, WASH. POST, Feb. 2, 2008, at A3 (reporting on how anticipated consequences of a mild or serious flu outbreak will not only probably overwhelm medical centers and cause delays in emergency and routine care, but impede the distribution of antiviral vaccines and concluding an infusion of billing must be made by Congress if a disease containment strategy is to be viable).

121 Press Release, Dept. of Health and Human Services, HHS Releases Pandemic Influenza Plan: Plan Provides Guidance to Prepare Nation's Health Care System for a Pandemic, (Nov. 2, 2005) (available at www.hhs.gov/news/press/2005;res/20051102.html).

122 Department of Health and Human Services, What We Do, www.hhs.gov/about/whatwedo. html/ (last visited July 30, 2010).

123 *See supra* notes 121, 122.
The entire 396-page flu plan prepared by HHS is available online. A one-stop access to all U.S. government information on the avian and pandemic flu, which in turn provides access to Homeland Security Council issues, WHO releases, and ongoing updates to the National Strategy for the Pandemic Influenza Implementation Plan One Year Summary, may be found at PandemicFlu.gov.

The American Public Health Association also has a comprehensive listing and discussion of health work force issues. *See* www.apha.org/advocacy/policy/APHA+Prescription+for+Pandemic+flu.htm.

The WHO Guidelines on The Use of Vaccines and Antivirals during Influenza Pandemic are found at WHO/CDS/CSR/RMD/2004.8. In addition, the revised International Health Regulations (IHR) adopted by the WHO in 2007 impose obligations on WHO member states in relation to the notification and containment of infectious disease. BELINDA BENNETT, HEALTH LAW'S KALEIDOSCOPE: HEALTH LAW RIGHTS IN A GLOBAL AGE ch. 6 at 87 (2008).

124 *Supra* note 121. *See* David Brown, *If Bioterrorists Strike, Letter Carriers Might Deliver Antibiotics*, WASH. POST, Oct. 2, 2008, at A2 (detailing a plan being developed by the U.S. Department of Health and Human Services which would build upon the federally funded Cities Readiness Initiative designed to assist some 72 major urban areas in developing strategies to distribute drugs to these target populations within 48 hours of bioterrorists attacks, by providing for the delivery of antibiotics necessary to combat an exposure to anthrax by volunteer letter carriers who might be accompanied by city police officers and who, themselves, would be screened medically, fitted with N95 face masks as well as being issued an appropriate antibiotic for their own family households).

125 HHS PLAN, *supra* note 31, pt. 1, app. D at D-10.

126 Benjamin E. Buckman, *Mitigating Pandemic Influenza: The Ethics of Implementing a School Closure Policy*, 14 J. PUB. HEALTH MGMT. & POL'Y 372 (2008).

127 Marilyn Werber Serafini, *The Big One?* 37 NAT'L JOURNAL 3258, 3260 (Oct. 25, 2005), *Short on Supplies and Nurses*, 37 NAT'L JOURNAL 3264 (Oct. 22, 2005).

A recent study confirmed that non-pharmaceutical interventions used by 43 cities during the 1918 Spanish flu pandemic had a salutary effect on the management of the emergency. The cities that followed these interventions by closing schools, banning public gatherings, isolating flu patients, and placing in quarantine people exposed to them, suffered less than the cities that chose not to enforce these measures. Howard Markel, *et al.*, *Nonpharmaceutical Interventions Implemented by U.S. Cities During the 1918–1919 Influenza Pandemic*, 298 JAMA 644 (Aug. 8, 2007).

128 HHS PLAN, *supra* note 31, pt. 1, app. D, at D-11. *See* James C. Thomas *et al.*, *Ethics in a Pandemic: A Survey of The State Pandemic Influenza Plans*, 97 AM. J. PUB. HEALTH S26 (2007); Christopher Lee, *supra* note 120.

129 *See* Community Strategy for Pandemic Influenza Mitigation, *www.pandemicflu.gov/plan/community/commitigation.html#I.*

In February 2007, the Dept. of HHS and its Center for Disease Control, released a new guidance on community planning strategies which focus on self-quarantine of ill persons at their homes and away from work environments from seven to ten days; home confinement for household members of ill patients for seven days; a cessation of schools and child care programs for upwards of three months and social distancing of adults in the community and at work. *See* www.pandemicflu. gov/plan/community/community_mitigation.pdf.

130 Shane Harris, *Every Community for Itself*, 37 NAT'L JOURNAL 3265 (Oct. 22, 2005). *See also* HHS PLAN, *supra* note 31, at pt. 1.

A Report by The Commission on The National Guard and Reserves on the readiness of these two branches of service to respond to assaults on the homeland from domestic attacks, incidents by bioterrorism and catastrophes, was issued February 1, 2008. Earlier in 2007, the Commission found 88 percent of the Army and National Guard was not ready and fully operational for national emergencies. Greater funding to train and equip the military's 836,000 selected reserves in order to assure that they can operate interchangeably with active duty personnel is, the Commission concluded, needed immediately. It was also recommended by the Commission, that the Pentagon be charged with providing the bulk of support to civilian authorities in the likely event local responders are overwhelmed by a major catastrophe. And, furthermore, it was suggested that state governors be allowed to command federal troops during times of national emergencies.

Ann Scott Tyson, *'Appalling Gap' Found in Homeland Defense Readiness*, WASH. POST, Feb. 1, 2008, at A4.

131 *See* JOHN M. BARRY, THE GREAT INFLUENZA: THE EPIC OF THE 1918 PAN-DEMIC 4 (2004). In the 1918 pandemic, most deaths, surprisingly, occurred in young adults. In the 1957 and 1968 pandemics, as well as the annual flu, infants, the elderly, and the unhealthy are the most at risk. *Ibid. See* HHS PLAN, *supra* note 31, pt. 1, app. D, at D-12.

132 The CDC estimates that the demand for hospitalization will increase 25% even in a moderate pandemic. HHS PLAN, *ibid.*; Serafini, *supra* note 127; Lee, *supra* note 120. *See* Spencer S. Hsu & Mary Beth Sheridan, *Democrats Warn about Hospital Capacity: House Panel Criticizes Medicaid Moves, Cites Cities Inability to Handle Attack*, WASH. POST, May 6, 2008, at A4.

133 It is estimated by the CDC that 10% of the work force will be absent during a pandemic. *Ibid.*

134 HHS PLAN, *supra* note 131 at D-12.

135 The HHS has assumed that the United States can produce 3 to 5 million doses per week of the vaccine; however, it will take 3 to 6 months before the first dose can be produced once the virus is detected. Also, two doses per person are required to protect against the H5N1 virus. *Ibid. See* Neil Munro, *Don't Count on a Vaccine*, 37 NAT'L JOURNAL 3261 (Oct. 22, 2005).

136 HHS PLAN, *supra* note 131 at D-13. *See* ETHICS AND THE PHARMACEUTICAL INDUSTRY, ch. 20 (Michael A. Santoro, Thomas Gorrie eds. 2005).

137 *Ibid. See* Carl H. Coleman, *Beyond the Call of Duty: Compelling Health Care Professionals to Work during an Influenza Pandemic*, 94 IOWA L. REV. 1 (2008).

138 Smith, *supra* note 29 at 146. *See* Devereaux *et al., supra* note 83 which presents a con-temporary adaptation of *triage* to incidents of mass critical care caused by pandemic flu or other health care dissenters.

139 *Ibid. See also* Lea Ann Fracasso, *Developing Immunity: The Challenges in Mandating Vaccinations in the Wake of Biological Terrorist Attack*, 13 DePAUL J. HEALTH CARE L. 1 (2010). Benjamin E. Buckman, *Incorporating Explicit Ethical Reasoning into Pandemic Influenza Poli-cies*, 26 J. CONTEMP. HEALTH L. & POL'Y 1 (2009) (suggesting that the decision by the U.S. government to share its H1N1 vaccine supply with developing countries should have been grounded on explicit ethical reasoning tied to principles of equity rather than justified on purely scientific and utilitarian policies).

140 HHS PLAN, *supra* note 131 at D-13.

141 Smith, *supra* note 29 at 146.

142 HHS PLAN, *supra* note 131 at D-13.

143 Smith, *supra* note 29 at 146.

144 HHS PLAN, *supra* note 131 at D-13.

145 *Ibid.*

146 Smith, *supra* note 29 at 146.

147 The social worth of their works to society and in promotion of the common good, during a pandemic is potentially great—thus they have been listed on the priority list. HHS PLAN, *supra* note 131 at D-13. *See* Wendy E. Parmet, *Pandemic Vaccines—The Legal Landscape*, 362 N. ENGL. J. MED. 1949 (2010).

148 HHS PLAN, *supra* note 31 at D-14.

149 KILNER, *supra* note 105 at 11.

150 HHS PLAN, *supra* note 31 at D-14.

151 *Ibid. See* Parmet, *supra* note 147.

152 Childress, *supra* note 49 at 89.

153 *Ibid.* at 88–89. *See* Spencer S. Hsu & Ann Tyson, *Pentagon to Detail Troops to Bolster Domestic Security*, WASH. POST, Dec. 1, 2008 at A1 (reporting the plans of the U.S. military to have in place, by 2011, some 20,000 troops inside the United States to assist state and local officials to respond to bioterrorist attack or other domestic catastrophes).

154 Thomas A. Glass & Monica Schoch-Spana, *Bioterrorism and the People: How to Vaccinate a City against Panic*, 34 CLINICAL INFECTIOUS DISEASES 217 (2002) ("Failure to involve the public as a key partner in the medical and public-health response could hamper effective management of an epidemic and increase the likelihood of social disruption").

155 Childress, *supra* note 49 at 89.

156 *Ibid.* at 91.

157 HHS PLAN, *supra* note 31 at D-14. *See* Singer, *et al.*, *supra* note 115; Serafini, *supra* note 127.

158 BARRY, *supra* note 131 at 223.

159 *Ibid.* at 223–24.

160 HHS PLAN, *supra* note 31 at D-14.

161 GINA KOLATA, FLU: THE STORY OF THE GREAT INFLUENZA PANDEMIC 5 (1999).

162 *Ibid.* at 4–5.

163 HHS PLAN, *supra* note 31 at D-21.

164 ORLOWSKI, *supra* note 54 at 159.

165 HHS PLAN, *supra* note 31 at D-21.

166 *Ibid.*

167 HHS PLAN, *supra* note 31 at D-21.

168 *Ibid.*

169 *Ibid.*

170 BARRY, *supra* note 131 at 247.

171 *See generally* George P. Smith, II, *Utility and The Principle of Medical Futility*, 12 J. CONTEMP. HEALTH L. & POL'Y 1 (1995).

172 *See* www.whitehouse.gov/homeland/pandemic_influenza-oneear.html; Gardiner Harris, *Limited Capacity is Seen in Flu Defenses*, N.Y. TIMES, Jul. 18, 2006, at 14.

On September 11, 2007, the Federal government released a draft National Response Framework (NRF) designed to establish a national approach to catastrophic incidents and, as such, serve as a blueprint for dealing with terrorist attacks and other disasters. Initial criticism of the document has been that it provides insufficient detail for guidance by local officials charged with managing specific incidents, and—furthermore—is unclear as to levels of accountability and supervision in the chain of command. For the present, the NRF will seek—through 15 federally designated disaster scenarios—to develop separate strategic plans for disaster relief. Spencer S. Hsu, *Proposed Disaster Response Plan Faulted*, WASH. POST, Sep. 12, 2007, at A4. *See* NATURAL RESPONSE FRAMEWORK, Sept. 10, 2007, DRAFT, U.S. Dept. Homeland Security. *See also infra*, note 176, commenting on the finalization of the draft framework.

173 *See* HHS PLAN, *supra* note 31.

174 *Supra* note 172.

175 *Supra* note 172.

176 *Ibid. See* Spencer S. Hsu, *States Feel Left Out of Disaster Planning*, WASH. POST, Aug. 8, 2007, at A1 (reporting, as to the Nation's overall response to disaster planning, that state and local officials charged with emergency management are concerned that the Federal government is acting unilaterally and emphasizing responses to terrorism at the cost of neglecting safeguards against natural disasters). *See also* Eileen Sullivan, *Disaster Response Coordination Positions Bypass FEMA*, Congressional Quarterly, Jul. 23, 2007, *http://public.cq. com/docs/hs/*hsnews110–000002556714. html (commenting on how the National Protection and Programs Directorate, within the Department of Homeland Security, is now the state's contact for disaster preparedness—not FEMA).

On January 22, 2008, the Department of Homeland Security announced a new, final framework for managing domestic incidents which exceed or are anticipated to exceed state resources or when an incident is managed by Federal departments directly and declared to be Incidents of National Significance. *See generally* Spencer S. Hsu, *DHS to Unveil New Disaster Response Plan*, WASH. POST, Jan. 19, 2008, at A3.

This National Response Framework is seen as a direct response to the previous concerns of state and local units of government regarding the level of their participation in disasters which required a unified "all-hazards response." The power of FEMA is, consequently, restored and this Agency has the delegated responsibility to clarify and coordinate heretofore diffuse any confusing levels of responsibility among the states and their municipalities. This Framework document is required by, and integrates under, the larger National Strategy for Homeland Security. It supersedes the corresponding sections of the National Response Plan (2004, with 2006 revisions) and is available at www.fema.gov/NRF. Updates and amendments to the Framework and its various specific indexes are to be posted at this internet connection as made available.

177 *Supra* note 172.

178 *Ibid.*

179 Donald G. McNeil, Jr. & Denise Grady, *To Flu Experts, 'Pandemic' Label Confirms the Obvious,* WASH. POST, Jun. 12, 2009, at A12.

180 Donald G. McNeil, Jr., *Avian Flu Fears Said to Help U.S. Prepare for Swine Flu,* WASH. POST, Jun. 5, 2009, at A14.

181 ALAN SIPRESS, THE FATAL STRAIN: ON THE TRAIL OF AVIAN FLU AND THE COMING PANDEMIC (2009).

182 Donald G. McNeil, Jr., *Avian Flu Fear Said to Help U.S. Prepare for Swine Flu,* WASH. POST, Jun. 5, 2009, at A14.

183 *Ibid.*

184 *Ibid.*

185 David Brown & Spencer S. Hsu, *Students 1st in Line for Flu Vaccine,* WASH. POST, Jul. 10, 2009, at A1.

186 *Ibid.*

187 Denise Grady, *Swine Flu Plan Would Put Some at Head of Line for Vaccine,* N.Y. TIMES, Jul. 30, 2009, at A18.

188 Richard P. Wenzel, *What We Learned from H1N1's First Year,* N.Y. TIMES, April 13, 2010, at A25; Donald G. McNeil, Jr., *Most Americans Think Swine Flu Pandemic is Over, a Harvard Poll Finds,* N.Y. TIMES, Feb. 6, 2010, at A12.

189 David Brown, *We May Not be Through with the Flu,* WASH. POST, Feb. 23, 2010, at HE1.

190 *Ibid.*

191 Wenzel, *supra* note 188.

192 *Ibid.*

193 *Ibid.*

194 Joby Warrick & Anne E. Kornblut, *U.S. is Unprepared to Handle Major Bioterrorism Attack, Commission Finds,* WASH. POST, Jan. 27, 2010, at A7. *See generally* COMM'N ON THE PREVENTION OF WEAPONS OF MASS DESTRUCTION PROLIFERATION & TERRORISM, WORLD AT RISK: THE REPORT OF THE COMMISSION ON THE PREVENTION OF WMD PROLIFERATION AND TERRORISM (2008), available at http://documents.scribd.com/docs/15bq1nr19aerfu0yu9qd.pdf.

195 *Ibid. See* Sheri Fink, *U.S. Healthcare System said to be Unprepared for Nuclear Disaster,* WASH. POST, Apr. 8, 2011, at A3 (reporting on a similar conclusion made by a new study of the issue by the Department of Homeland Security).

196 Wendy K. Mariner, George J. Annas & Wendy E. Parmet, *Pandemic Preparedness: A Return to the Rule of Law,* 1 DREXEL L. REV. 341 (2009).

197 *Ibid.*

198 *Ibid.* "Community engagement" is the watch word. *Ibid.* at 345.
    Presently, the American public remains distrustful of governmental advice regarding national health emergencies and—thus—is uninformed. Fink, *supra* note 195.

199 George P. Smith, II, *Human Rights and Bioethics: Formulating a Universal Right to Health, Health Care, or Health Protection?* 38 VANDERBILT J. TRANSNAT'L LAW 1295, 1319 (2005).

200 BENNETT, *supra* note 123 at 85.

201 *Ibid.* at 125.
202 *Ibid.* at 87. In addition, these regulations lack an effective enforcement mechanism to ensure compliance. There are no mandatory requirements. In fact, the only "incentive" for participating by the WHO member states is peer pressure and public knowledge of their actions. *See* Eric Mack, *The World Health Organization: New International Health Regulations: Incursion on State Sovereignty and Ill-Fated Response to Global Health Issues*, 7 CHI. J. INT'L L. 365 (2006). *See generally* GEORGE J. ANNAS, WORST CASE BIOETHICS: DEATH, DISASTER, AND PUBLIC HEALTH at chs. 13, 25 (2010).
203 BENNETT, *supra* note 123 at 118.
204 *See* Lawrence O. Gostin, *Influenza A (H1N1) and Pandemic Preparedness Under the Rule of International Law*, 301 JAMA 2376 (Jun. 10, 2009).
205 World Health Organization, pmbl., para. 3, Jul. 22, 1946. *See* Lawrence O. Gostin, *Influenza A (H1N1) and Pandemic Preparedness Under the Rule of International Law*, 301 JAMA 2376 (Jun. 10, 2009).
206 Daubert, *supra* note 107 at 1338.
207 *Ibid.*
208 MSEHPA, *supra* note 33.
209 TURNING POINT, *supra* note 34.
210 Daubert, *supra* note 107 at 1338. *See generally* Robert M. Pestronk, *et al.*, *Improving Laws and Legal Authorities for Public Health Emergency Legal Preparedness*, 36 J. L. MED. & ETHICS 47 (2008).
211 *Ibid.*
212 *Ibid.*
213 Lawrence O. Gostin, *The Model State Emergency Health Powers Act: Public Health and Civil Liberties in Time of Terrorism*, 13 HEALTH MATRIX 3 (2003); Lawrence O. Gostin, Jason W. Sapsin, Stephen P. Teret *et al.*, *The Model State Emergency Health Powers Act: Planning for and Response to Bioterrorism and Naturally Occurring Infectious Disease*, 288 JAMA 622 (Aug. 7, 2002).
214 Daubert, *supra* note 107 at 1337. *See also* for current updates and comparisons of the state enactments with the Model Act at the web page address for the Georgetown Center for Law and the Public Health at www.publichealthlaw.net/. (Accessed August 25, 2010 with no additional state listings.)
215 *Ibid.* at 1337.
216 *See* Brody *et al.*, *How States Are Using the Turning Point Model State Health Act*, 33 J. L. MED. & ETHICS 97 (2004).
217 *See supra* note 33, Georgetown Center for Law and the Public Health web page, for current updates and comparisons of the various state enactments with the Model Turning Point Act. Available at www.publichealthlaw.net/Resources/Modellaws.htm.
218 Daubert, *supra* note 107 at 1341.
219 *Ibid.*
220 *Ibid.*
221 *Ibid.*
222 *Ibid.* at 1342.
223 *Ibid.* at 1299. *See generally* Lawrence O. Gostin & Benjamin E. Beckman, *Pandemic Influenza: Ethics, Law and The Public Health*, 59 AD. L. REV. 121, 171–74 (2007).
224 Daubert, *supra* note 107 at 1301.
225 *Ibid.*
226 *Ibid.* at 1328, 1329.
    For a recent application of isolation and quarantine, *see* David Brown, *Man with Rare TB Detained, Isolated: He Ignored Orders, Traveled Extensively*, WASH. POST, May 30, 2007, at A3.
227 Lorena Matei, *Quarantine Revision and The Model State Emergency Health Powers Act: 'Laws for the Common Good,'* 18 SANTA CLARA COMPUTER & HIGH TECH. L. J. 433, 438 *passim* (2001–2). *See also* Annas, NEW ENG. J. MED., *supra* note 13 (expressing concerns over the misuse of public health emergency measures); Mariner *et al.*, *supra* note 196 at

381–82 for a listing and discussion of Pandemic Preparedness Principles for Laws Governing Individual Conduct.

228 *See* Sue Blevins, *The Model State Emergency Health Powers Act: An Assault on Civil Liberties in The Name of Homeland Security*, *www.heritage.org*/Research/HomelandSecurity/H748.cfm; The Institute for Health Freedom's analysis of the Act at www.forhealthfreedom.org/ Publications/Informed/RevisedModelState.html.

229 Matei, *supra* note 227 at 439. *See* Fidler, *supra* note 12, for a discussion of the balancing components necessary to validate health law governance measures.

230 Gostin *et al.*, JAMA, *supra* note 213 at 627.

231 *Ibid.*

232 *Ibid.* at 626–28 (for a discussion of civil liberty protections).

233 *Ibid.* at 622.

234 *See supra e.g.*, notes 9–13, 20–26, 93–97, 206–7.

235 HHS PLAN, *supra* note 31.

236 MSEHPA, *supra* note 33.

237 TURNING POINT, *supra* note 34.

238 POSNER, *supra* note 2 at 149.

239 *Ibid.*

240 *Ibid.* at 34.

241 *Ibid.* at 35.

242 *Ibid.* at 34. *See* Fidler, *supra* note 12.

243 POSNER, *supra* note 2 at 33–34. *See generally* Nancy E. Kass, *An Ethics Framework for Public Health and Avian Influenza Pandemic Preparedness*, 78 YALE J. BIOLOGY & MED. 235 (2005).

244 POSNER, *supra* note 2 at 149.

245 *Ibid.* at 147.

246 *Ibid.*

247 *See generally* MARK A. LUTZ, ECONOMICS FOR THE COMMON GOOD: TWO CENTURIES OF SOCIAL ECONOMIC THOUGHT IN THE HUMANISTIC TRADITION (1999); Hoffman, *supra* note 24.

248 Sulmasy, *supra* note 39.

249 *See generally* Lawson, *supra* note 41.

250 Terminiello v. Chicago, *supra* note 26. *See generally* POSNER, *supra* note 2.

7   Autonomy, decisional capacity and informed consent

Introduction and overview

Within the phrase, informed consent, is to be found both manipulative and coercive vectors of force. First, the health care provider:

> must gain the 'consent' of the patient to prove that she was not physically or psychologically forced into a procedure. We then insist that this consent be 'informed,' recognizing that if a patient readily agrees to one thing about which she understands, little or about which she has a false understanding, we have somehow or other abrogated or sidestepped her autonomous decision-making rights.[1]

The patient–physician relationship is central to the foundations of medical morality. From it emerges normative guidelines that effectuate ideally the end of medicine—namely, to render "a right and good healing action in the interests of a particular patient."[2] Technical competence, then, is shaped by this goal and—indeed—the very act of medical profession is to be considered as unauthentic if it neglects to fulfill the real expectation of technical competence.[3] It is upon both the patient–physician relationship and acknowledged technical competence that a "participatory moral agency" builds that forces a disclosure of all those levels of information necessary for the patient to make a valid choice and genuine consent to surgically invasive or non-invasive medical treatments.[4]

While the desire for obtaining information may be seen as stronger than the one for actually making the determinative health care decision, itself, not every patient wants information.[5] Indeed, realizing the fact that most individuals make decisions rather badly, forces many to choose to delegate medical decision-making to others.[6] It is, quite simply, for those declining to make their own decisions "psychologically attractive to pass responsibility for hard choices to others."[7] When these delegations occur, it might be wise to consider developing a "full social impact calculus" which in turn considers the complete number of persons affected by them[8]—for example, the immediate family members, close friends, social workers as well as spiritual and health care providers. This calculus could, as well, be taken when the initial decision for sustaining treatments or accessing them are made—with some cases even arising where the sum of the social, economic and medical consequences "on others may outweigh the impact on the person most affected."[9]

Patient information deficits must be remedied by the physician to the fullest extent possible.[10] The information disclosed must be complete, clear and understandable in the patient's own language which allows knowledge not only of nature of the illness, its prognosis and the alternative modes of treatment together with their cost and probable effectiveness, but the levels of discomfort and side effects on the ultimate quality of life. This duty of disclosure cannot be exercised by the physician on the grounds of patient ignorance or harm. To do so would underscore the inequality in information between patient and doctor and obstruct the goal of a morally valid consent that in turn is the memorialization of the patient's individual moral agency.[11]

The physician must always guard against manipulating patient choice and consent in order simply to accommodate his own personal or social philosophy. Setting valid limits on the degree to which manipulated consent is morally permissible is difficult. Two major situations are recognized commonly where a physician can—and indeed should—exert moral agency for patients and make the value choice on their behalf. The most common case is where the patient and/or family request the physician to act accordingly—this, because of their emotional unwillingness or intellectual instability to deal with the immediate situation. In cases of this nature, it would be a failure of the authenticity of his act of profession for the physician not to assume moral agency and decide what course of action should be undertaken. When dealing with surrogate decision-makers, it is doubly important for the physician to ascertain with certainty that the surrogate is being guided by the best interests of the patient.[12]

The second situation where a physician should exert moral agency for the patient is to be found in those emergency cases—in an intensive care or coronary care unit or in an operating or emergency room—where, because of the urgency of the situation, it is impossible for the physician to consult the patient, the immediate family or designated surrogate decision-maker. In both of these situations, the physician's Golden Rule should be to act in such a manner as to "accord the patient the same opportunity to express or actualize his own view of what he considers worthwhile" as would be desired by the physician.[13] This Rule, then, re-enforces the mandate to bring compassion to not only the patient's illness, but exhibit it as a "conscious advertence" in the act of profession and the act of medicine as well.[14]

The other side in the equation of informed decision-making is obviously the patient. Thus, the ethics of the good patient require that one be truthful in the information that one gives to the physician; avoid manipulating him or her; follow faithfully mutually agreed upon recommendations; educate oneself so that he or she may comprehend the facts disclosed by the physician and realize a partial obligation to participate in those reasonable therapeutic experiments designed to promote a healing of the patient's own disease or those directed toward the discovery of possible cures for that disease for others (non-therapeutic).[15] What is seen in totality, then, between the patient and the physician, is a set of mutually binding obligations which—if met—assure informed decision-making in health care services.[16]

Complex elements of human behavior are at play in testing the extent to which an informed choice has been given. Social research has shown that patients—to a large extent—make health care decisions based on the "framing effect."[17] In other words, a patient's reaction to choices depends, significantly, on the manner in which the alternatives are framed—as for example, the numerical or statistical way risks are presented. It has been shown, accordingly, that when treatment options are presented in terms of the number of people who might die rather than survive, such options become considerably less attractive.[18]

The fact that informed consent requires a fair presentation of benefits as well as risks,[19] leads to the conclusion that consent procedures should be evaluated and tested in terms of both their costs and their benefits or, in other words, utilitarian terms.[20] Indeed, the common-place analysis of consent in terms of autonomy and competence is often consistent with the very maximization of utility.[21] Generally, autonomy maximizes utility simply because individual values (or utilities) determine what an individual chooses to be best.[22]

The ongoing debate regarding the efficacy and integrity of the doctrine of informed consent and its application has been termed "oblique and inconclusive,"[23] and—indeed—little more than a "fairy tale."[24] The reason for this state of affairs is laid to a structural weakness reflecting, as such, not only a rapacious health care delivery system that is increasingly cost-conscious,[25] complex and sophisticated[26] but—as well—by constraints imposed by the tort law system, human psychology, and the physician–patient relationship,[27] all of which are largely intractable.[28] Coupled with these foundational issues is recognition that the level of both empirical research and analysis, together with comparative risk evaluation necessary to resolve the uncertainties, is not being pursued.[29]

Yet, for all of the weaknesses, the doctrine of informed consent—and its offspring, negotiated consent[30] in elder care situations—serves a significant purpose in contemporary society: namely, as both a construct and often a template for establishing an interdependent relationship, if not therapeutic partnership, between the patient and his physician where truth-telling becomes the crux of the doctrine and a true moral relationship between both parties is recognized.[31]

The purpose of this Chapter, then, is to probe the foundations and applications of informed consent in a variety of situations and thereby test its validity. The conclusion to be drawn from this analysis is that while the doctrine has yet to become an integral part of the ethos of medicine,[32] it still provides an important mechanism for maintaining a purposeful discourse between physician and patient and, as such, nurturing and preserving their essential partnership of healing and of trust.[33]

Malpractice and informed consent

Professional or lay standards

A claim for malpractice is recognized essentially when a patient, as a direct result of a physician's failure to render that level of care consistent with what would have been given by other practicing physicians in the community in question, is injured.[34] Thus it is seen that the standard of conduct against which the defending physician's conduct is measured is tied to the conduct that other similar situated professionals in the field would have followed under the same or similar circumstances—with the end result being that the objective standard of reasonableness is thereby excluded totally from the evaluation.[35]

As to the elements of a cause of action for failure to obtain informed consent to either a medical treatment or procedure, there is less uniformity of view.[36] Indeed, under older case law, the duty to obtain an informed consent to a medical intervention was inherent in the essential idea that non-consensual touching was (and is) a legal battery.[37] Modern case law, however, now takes one of two approaches to the duty to obtain informed consent,[38] yet treats the central issue as one of negligence.[39]

Some states require a professional standard to be followed that in turn imposes a duty upon all physicians to inform their patients of not only the same risks[40]—but the alternatives to any proposed medical treatment in the same manner as other physicians would practicing in the community. Accordingly, it was held in a 1981 case in Illinois,[41] that applying the reasonable medical practitioner standard of informed consent meant that there must indeed by specific expert medical testimony "of the necessity to inform patients of possible alternatives."[42] Consequently, even though a separate cause of action may well arise in a case of this nature for failure to obtain informed consent apart from one in malpractice as well, with regard to the defending doctor's behavior *vis-à-vis* the specific prosecuting patient, the *same* standard of conduct will apply—namely, adherence to that level of care given in the relevant community by other practitioners.[43]

Other states choose to apply what is regarded as a "lay" or "prudent patient" standard of informed consent—thereby requiring a physician to inform the patient of all sources and degree of information which an average, ordinary reasonable patient should and would require in order to make an informed decision regarding the need to submit to a proposed treatment therapy.[44] Under this standard of informed consent:

> ... a physician is liable to his or her patient if (1) the physician fails to disclose any risk in the recommended treatment, or the existence of any alternative methods of treatment, that a reasonable person would deem material in deciding whether to undergo the recommended treatment; (2) the patient would have forgone the recommended treatment had he or she known of the undisclosed information; and (3) as a result of the

recommended treatment, the patient actually suffers an injury the risk of which was disclosed, or the patient actually suffers an injury that would not have occurred had the patient opted for one of the undisclosed methods of treatment.[45]

Decisional capacity

In order to test whether a patient is adequately informed, or in other words, has decisional capacity to make a choice to either undergo—or forgo—medical care and treatment, the courts must resolve any and all issues relevant to the patient's competency.[46] Rather than articulate one unequivocal standard to determine capacity, the courts have almost always sought testimony—especially from psychiatrists and other care providers—of a patient's mental state.[47] Traditionally, a patient was found, by physicians, to have decisional capacity for health care decision-making "whenever that patient agreed with the physician."[48]

The President's Commission for The Study of Ethical Problems in Medicine and Biomedical and Behavioral Research determined in 1980 that there are three components to decisional capacity: possession of a set of values and goals; ability to both communicate and to understand information; and an ability to reason as well as to deliberate about one's options.[49] In addition, the scholarly community has endeavored to bring clarity to the issues by developing five tests for determining decisional capacity: evidencing choice; reasonable outcome of choice; choice based on "rational" reasons; ability to understand; and actual understanding.[50]

The first test—evidencing choice—is the one most respectful of patient autonomy and focuses not on assessing the quality of patient decision making but, rather, the presence or the absence of a decision.[51] The second test seeks to determine whether a patient decision is essentially congruent with one that the proverbial "reasonable" person would make under similar circumstances. This test is—generally—the most frequently used one by physicians and courts alike.[52] The third test attempts to discern where patient decision-making is due to, or as a consequence of, mental illness.[53] Although appealing from the clinical viewpoint, it poses conceptual issues as a legal test which, in turn, makes it essentially defective.[54]

The third test raises issues of establishing methods to distinguish rational from irrational reasons[55] and to prove causation—or, in other words, that an actual decision made by a patient is a product of irrationality.[56] Even though a patient's reasons seem irrational, it remains impossible to proceed to prove the actual decision made by the patient is a product of irrationality. The fourth test would appear to be the most consistent one with the law of informed consent—for, here, what is measured is the ability of the patient to not only understand the risks and the benefits as well as the alternative to treatment, but the consequence of no treatment.[57] Unwise decisions are allowed as the actual decision-making need neither be rational in either the process or the outcome.[58]

In attempting to evaluate the level of actual understanding that a patient has, it remains for the physician to accept an obligation to—first—educate the patient, and then directly determine whether the patient understands what has been explained.[59] Autonomous health care decisions simply cannot be made without a sufficient level of comprehension which in turn allows for understanding.[60] Yet, interestingly, there is no legal duty imposed upon a physician to "try to ensure understanding"[61]—this, simply because such a requirement would be impossible to enforce.[62] The degree to which adequate understanding has been reached is not only vague but difficult to evaluate because a "deficient understanding may be attributable in whole or in part to physician behavior as well as to the patient's behavior or character."[63] While patients may expect fully that, in their relationships with their physicians, their interests and needs will be the central focus of attention, when issues are presented over what standards must be used to ascertain whether a patient has received reasonable and necessary information in order to make self-determining decisions, the individual patient "becomes the reasonable patient"[64]; and, consequently, the objective standard of proof prevails over the individual or subjective standard of autonomy.[65]

As a direct consequence of the weaknesses seen in these five tests for decisional capacity, some hold to the conclusion that there simply will never be one clear test for competence[66]—this, because of two reasons: patients lack a level of intellectual ability or understanding of medical information relevant to decisions concerning their care[67] and competency judgments are mired in a vortex of semantic and legal rules and, thus, "reflect social considerations and societal biases as much as they reflect matters of law and medicine."[68]

The foundational paradigm

The 1972 case of Canterbury v. Spence[69] presents a modern, comprehensive or focal paradigm of the legal concept of informed consent in application. There, a young boy complaining of back pain submitted to a myelogram which revealed a filling defect. The boy's mother was contacted after the test and an operation was recommended by Dr. William T. Spence—the attending physician—stating that such an operation was "not anymore [serious] than any other operation."[70] The boy submitted to the operation without being informed that the risk carried with it was one of paralysis. Mrs. Canterbury arrived at the hospital *after* the operation and signed a consent form. The boy fell from his bed a day after the operation while, without assistance, he attempted to void. He thereupon became paralyzed and required to undergo surgery yet another time. This time, Mrs. Canterbury signed a consent form *before* the operation. Years later, the youth hobbled about on crutches, " ... a victim of paralysis of the bowels and urinary incontinence."[71] At trial, Dr. Spence testified that paralysis is to be expected in the neighborhood of one percent of the cases of operations of the type performed here. The central issue of the case was the scope and application of the doctrine of informed consent.

Because there is a duty to disclose, the scope of that duty should be known. Any standard set in terms of what is done in the profession will be at odds with the patient's prerogative to decide on prospective therapy. This right of self-decision shapes the boundary of the duty to reveal.[72] In order that the patient's interest in achieving individual determination of treatment is fulfilled, it is the law which must set the standard for adequate disclosure.[73] The test enunciated in Canterbury, then, is " ... [a] risk is thus material when a reasonable person, in what the physician knows or should know to be the patient's position, would be likely to attach significances to the risks or clusters of risk in deciding whether or not to forgo the proposed therapy."[74] This includes a discussion of the inherent and potential dangers of the proposed treatment, the alternatives to that treatment and the results likely if the patient remains untreated.

The courts have noted two exceptions to the general rule of disclosure. The first is where the person is unconscious or otherwise incapable of consenting and there is imminent harm which would result from failure to treat which in turn outweighs any harm threatened by the proposed treatment.[75] If possible, consent of relatives should then be obtained. The second exception arises when the disclosure threatens the patient so as to become infeasible from a medical point of view. The critical inquiry, then, would be whether the physician was guided by sound medical judgment.[76] This privilege does not carry with it the paternalistic notion that the physician may remain silent simply because diligence might prompt the patient to forgo therapy the physician maintains the patient needs.[77]

There is always a danger in this area of consideration that a subjective, hindsight test might be employed. Canterbury speaks to this concern and resolves it by requiring a determination of whether a prudent person in the patient's position would have decided to undergo treatment if informed of all perils bearing significance.[78] This affords opportunity for medical testimony regarding the relevance of certain risks as will other testimony by anyone having sufficient knowledge and capacity to testify. The courts thus assume a determinative role in assessing liability.[79]

In the pre-Canterbury period, courts sought to enforce a narrower objective test for materiality (reasonable doctor) and a broad-based test for causation (subjective patient). With Canterbury, a broad test for materiality is advanced (reasonable patient) and a narrower objective test for causation (what a reasonable patient would have chosen) preferred.[80] Although criticism has been maintained that with Canterbury the courts are incorrectly treating informed consent as but another branch of negligent medical practice instead of recognizing the patient's interest in autonomy and the right to make an informed choice about medical care as the key interest protected by the informed consent doctrine, these criticisms are muted when hard questions are raised regarding how to value the protected interest and determine damages for interference thereto.[81]

Alternative treatment

Utilizing either the professional standard or the lay standard to informed consent, a physician is under a duty to inform the patient of not only appropriate alternative treatments—in addition to the alternative of no treatment at all—but to describe and evaluate the benefits and the risks of those treatments to his at-risk patient.[82] Not every conceivable alternative to every detail of treatment need be provided, however.[83] Setting the limits of a physician's duty to inform of alternative treatments continues to be a struggle for the courts. If a professional standard of informed consent is adhered to, much difficulty in application is alleviated, since a jury panel will seek to decide the issue in conflict by comparing the testimony of competing medical experts.[84] If, however, the lay standard is followed, the jury determination is more complex—this, owing to the fact that an evaluation must be made of what an average, ordinary reasonable patient would both want and need to know under similar circumstances.[85] Obviously, a decision reached according to this standard requires considerable and complex analysis of the credibility of opinions of opposing experts on varying community standards. Of additional complexity is the court's need to comprehensively instruct a jury on the elements of a medically acceptable alternative before the jury can then be allowed to decide whether the average reasonable patient would, indeed, have wanted to know of the alternative.[86]

Medical acceptability is the criterion by which a determination of whether an alternative treatment is to be disclosed.[87] The obvious difficulty here is in coming to grips with those components or elements of a particular treatment—especially a new one—that thereby qualify it as acceptable; and, furthermore, determining to whom it must be found acceptable.[88]

> In terms of a doctor's duty to disclose, this issue can be broken down into two parts. First, what criteria, objective or subjective, make a particular treatment acceptable? Second, are there additional factors which create (or excuse) the particular physician's duty to know about the treatment?[89]

The etiology of every new medical treatment—whether it be surgery, drug, therapy, or an exotic technique—shows an initial evaluation or classification of it as experimental.[90]

In those cases where a "lay" approach to informed consent is followed, it must be recognized straight away that it cannot be extended effectively in order to determine what specific alternative treatments are medically acceptable although it may well indeed be used as a mechanism through which acceptable treatments are revealed.[91] The consequence of applying the "lay" standard or approach in order to enable a jury to determine whether a reasonable patient would have given due consideration to the treatment and accepted it as medically valid would lead to an interesting quandary for the concerned physician who would never be in a position to know actually what alternatives should be described. This in turn could drive the physician to even describe "quack" treatments for fear that some future jury could find that some reasonable patient might have wished to be informed of such treatments.[92]

The wiser approach to develop here would be to acknowledge the standard for medical acceptability as being based solely on the perception of the reasonable practitioner.[93] In this way, the pivotal inquiry would not necessarily be whether a reasonable practitioner would inform a patient of the particular alternative. Rather, the question to be raised would be simply whether an average, ordinary reasonable practitioner would believe the treatment was a viable "medically acceptable" alternative; or stated otherwise, whether it was recognized as an appropriate modality of treatment by a significant number of acknowledged experts in the field.[94] The role of expert testimony, then, would be to essentially explore both the number and the respectability of those accepting the treatment.[95] Developing and following this standard would allow a physician to "avoid the danger of having to describe the theories of quacks or to explain treatments too new to have a track record, but could still be held to have a duty to keep up with the relevant literature and other sources of information, and to inform of new treatments as they met the criteria of acceptance."[96]

Future treatment

It is often maintained that if a particular medical treatment were to be classified as futile, an attending physician is under no obligation to provide it to the patient. Indeed, the assertion goes even further: namely, that the physician need not even advise his patient of the existence of such treatment.[97] Judging the futility of any treatment is, arguably and correctly, a medical matter. No input from the patient is thus required. Since a futile treatment offers no benefit to the patient, it can be argued that a physician has neither obligation to render treatment of a non-beneficent nature nor—for that matter—does a patient have a right to demand it.[98]

Without knowledge of medical or surgical alternative and without having access to information regarding the pros and cons of each, a patient obviously has few if any tools with which to form a therapeutic alliance with his physician or even enter into a meaningful treatment dialogue with him.[99] While the doctor avoids conflicts with his patient, this veil of silence often robs the patient of his right of self-determination—all under the guise of medical paternalism.[100] Whenever a treatment is labeled futile, it is exempted from the requirement of discussion. Thus, the label itself "becomes a very powerful tool for relieving physicians of the requirement to talk with their patient. The label marks off a realm in which it is argued that the requirement does not apply."[101]

Uninsurable treatment options

One ethical *rationale* for not offering to patients useful uncovered medical services is physician discomfort over patient requests to "game the system," or—in other words—manipulate and deceive third party payers in their health plans.[102] Inasmuch as the vast majority of physicians believe such patient requests are unethical, some might wish—in the first instance—to avoid such tense encounters by electing not to offer useful but uncovered services.[103] Other reasons proffered for refusing health care information include—rather paternistically—the compassionate desire not to raise levels of expectation, especially for Medicaid or other economically impoverished patients who have medical coverage restrictions. In other words, "why offer a useful medical service to someone who cannot afford it?"[104]

Financial pressures on physicians are also seen as a significant determinant in decisions to withhold treatment information. For physicians with "more than 25 percent of income at risk" for patient care costs, a trend has been shown for neglecting to offer patients optimal but uncovered services.[105] This approach—in turn—revives earlier institutional concerns over "gag clauses" in managed care programs. In the late 1990s, these provisions were thought of as prohibiting physicians, by contract, from discussing with their patients medical services options which were not covered in their health plans.[106] Today, "gagging" continues—not by contract, necessarily, but for other reasons as noted, all of which have the ultimate effect of compromising the very doctrine of informed consent.[107] The pivotal ethical concern, then, is: "to what degree is it possible, and a professional obligation, for physicians to try to explain to their patients why some useful services are not covered?"[108]

Informed decision-making and negotiated consent

Although it is seen that the foundation of informed consent is now well embedded in both the legal and medical arenas, negotiated consent is far from being as widely accepted. In fact, the ideal of negotiated consent is only beginning to emerge as a viable alternative to the traditional informed consent standard, particularly with application to health care for the elderly.

The informed consent standard, which is based upon autonomy, emerged from the acute care environment and from a narrowly conceived view of the relationship between professional caregivers (physicians) and those dependent upon them (patients).[109] Historically, the "right" to make one's own decisions regarding treatment or, alternatively, non-treatment, no doubt can be traced back to America's early history—and more particularly the law of the Massachusetts Bay Colony in 1649 which forbade treatment of patients without their consent.[110] This position was, over the years, fortified by the Common Law which held, consistently, that—without informed consent—a competent adult could not be treated medically.[111] In 1990, the United States Supreme Court acknowledged this individual decision-making capacity to be grounded in a liberty interest protected and validated by the 14th Amendment to the Constitution.[112]

The concept of negotiated consent recognizes the ideal of autonomy, yet in a more limited fashion.[113] It recognizes the need for some version of "autonomy respecting paternalism" in the environment of long-term care, particularly involving elderly patients.[114] Fundamentally, paternalistic interventions that serve to enhance autonomy and allow the patients to decide and act in keeping with their own values compose the underpinnings of negotiated consent.[115]

Working principles

In light of the unique issues and moral dilemmas involved in long-term care for the elderly, the interactions between patients and practitioners are primarily acute transactions.[116] As such, enhancing the autonomy among patients of long-term care facilities is an extraordinarily difficult task.[117] The conditions at hand are very different from those encountered outside of residential care facilities, where informed consent is the prevalent model.[118] Recognizing these differences, negotiated consent attempts to address the various concerns involved and balance the involved parties' competing interests.[119] Under the negotiated consent standard, many legitimate views must be considered involving the patient, family, and institution.[120] The result is a shared or dispersed authority for decision-making in which no single party has the exclusive power of decision[121] and a non-algorithmic process whereby negotiation is not governed by strict deductive rules.[122] Instead, negotiation is more "heuristic in its cognitive style, implying less reliance on codes of ethics and more attention to opportunities for discussion."[123] Even in those instances in which the idea outcome is not attainable, a common situation among the frail elderly, negotiation serves to "make the best of a bad situation."[124]

In order to implement effectively negotiated consent, there must be active participation by the patient or the patient's surrogate and consultation with all parties holding an interest in the decision.[125] Furthermore, the patient must have at least a cursory knowledge of legal and ethical rights and the opportunity for scrutiny and enforcement of those rights by an outside higher authority.[126] In addition, the element of power in the deliberative process plays an integral part of the negotiated consent formula. Obviously, little chance for negotiation exists if one party has such superior power as to leave the other party with no chance for deliberation.[127] By the same token, negotiated consent does not insist on absolute equality between the parties, either.[128] Instead, the doctrine essentially supports the concept of "shared decision making" between the physician and patient in those situations in which it is possible.[129]

Although the ideals of virtue and compassion called for in negotiated consent may be sophistic, they are by no means quixotical. The introduction of negotiated consent in health care for the elderly is designed primarily to urge a different set of ideals and emphasize that practitioners must demonstrate virtues alongside the purported rights a patient is supposed to possess.[130]

New directions

In American society, individuals who reach the age of majority are permitted a broad range of choice.[131] They may choose their jobs, their relationships, and the patterns by which they live.[132] These rights of choice, however, are often denied elderly persons because they are unable to effectuate preference without assistance.[133] The need for assistance will become more critical when it is realized that by 2027, it is predicted that a majority of hospital services, 51% of in-patient admissions and 59% of beds will be given order to the elderly.[134] This very group will top seventy million people by 2030 which will, in turn, mean approximately one out of every five Americans will be included within it.[135]

As the population of aging citizens grows, so does the need for them to make pivotal decisions regarding their medical treatment.[136] Reality dictates that the capacity of elderly patients to make such decisions is often impaired by a higher incidence and prevalence of chronic brain disease,[137] coupled with the burden of coping with numerous other medical afflictions. Moreover, the risk for elderly patients may be compounded because they are more likely to be excluded from the medical decision-making process as a result of reduced physician contact, ageism, and paternalism.[138]

Even for the elderly patient, informed consent for medical decision-making has been the standard consent practice in the medical community for a number of years.[139] Particularly for the elderly, however, this process has failed in a number of areas, one of which is the issue of a patient's competence to consent to treatment.[140] Thus, with the doctrine of negotiated consent as an alternative to the traditional model of informed consent, the needs and desires of elderly patients ideally have a greater chance of being addressed adequately and equitably.

Health care surrogate decision-makers have been required—legally—to anchor their decisions to withhold medical treatment either using a substituted judgment template or a best interests model.[141] Under substituted judgment, the surrogate seeks to establish—by clear and convincing evidence—that the incompetent at-risk patient, based on his system of values, would want medical treatment withdrawn.[142] Contrariwise, using the best interests model, requires an assessment to be made of the benefits and burdens (or costs) of treatment—this, in order to determine what is medically efficacious for the patient.[143]

Dependent elderly persons pose a special problem for health care professionals in that their decisions often require the involvement of helpers and facilitators.[144] Such involvement may result in differing standards of judgment and measures of worth being applied to an elder's individual choice.[145] The results are conflicting value systems that often reflect the competing concerns of institutional and individual self-protection and convenience.[146] In the end, the elderly person is at a great risk of losing the right to decide about the course and conduct of his or her life.[147]

In such a scenario, the model of negotiated consent provides a realistic and viable means by which the interests of all parties involved may be represented. Negotiated consent allows for the interaction of all affected parties, including the patient, family, clergy, and physicians.[148] This process assures the presentation of a multitude of differing views while, ideally, preserving the values of the patient.

The process of negotiated consent also combats another ill of the traditional informed consent doctrine. Commonly, informed consent can provoke anxiety and evoke previous experiences, fantasies, and associations for a patient, triggering an occasional primitive defense response.[149] With negotiated consent, the interaction of the parties and the commitment to shared dialogue should reduce the likelihood of such a response, if not completely eliminate it.

A further deficiency of the informed consent model, as applied to older patients, is their inability to comprehend the specific elements of informed consent information.[150] Thus, as a group, geriatric patients may have some impairment in providing their informed consent with regard to medical procedures.[151] Because the process of negotiated consent involves, among other things, the friends and family of the patient, it is likely that there is a greater sense of trust among the parties, particularly if the patient needs assistance to comprehend fully the intricacies of the specific consent.

The doctrine of negotiated consent is certainly not without its shortcomings. First of all, self-determination for long-term care residents is a valid ideal; however, it requires opportunity, capacity, and motivation on their part.[152] Although the opportunity and capacity factors receive a majority of the attention within the medical community, the motivational factor must be addressed seriously, particularly with elderly persons.[153] If elderly patients are not sufficiently motivated to exercise the rights being secured for them, the doctrine of negotiated consent serves no additional benefit for the patients. Moreover, entertaining the multitude of opinions necessary for negotiated consent may require an overly burdensome and time-consuming recording process, and could even result in an invitation to litigation should the parties to the negotiation decide later that they are dissatisfied with the outcome.[154] Although perhaps a valid criticism, nevertheless, recording the outcome of the negotiation is obligatory for the process of negotiated consent to remain valid.[155]

Conclusions

Toward the end of achieving clarification of the doctrine of informed consent and thus making it more practical and relevant in contemporary society, suggestions have been made to re-conceptualize the very principle of autonomy itself.[156] Accordingly, by recalibrating the individualistic model of interpretation—which is embedded in the notion that autonomy is satisfying wishes or desires[157]—to a more liberal, relational mode which "stresses interactions through relationships with parents, teachers, friends and agents of the state,"[158] as well as considers other values such as happiness, security, justice or public order, a more balanced template for making informed health care decisions could then be used.[159] This new construct would, perforce, allow for a fuller and more vibrant conception of autonomy "that strikes a balance between the individual and community, between rights and obligations."[160]

Even though acceptance of the proposed re-conceptualization of patient autonomy may be fraught with administrative complications, and even be "ultimately unachievable" as a practical construct for ensuring autonomous decisions,[161] this process of re-evaluation should have a salutary effect in that "it may have a positive influence on the doctor–patient relationship itself by symbolizing respect and enhancing trust."[162]

Perhaps it is a correct assessment that no meaningful collaboration or hoped-for therapeutic alliance can be achieved between doctor and patient until physicians, themselves, treat patients as adults and not children; learn that there is a real distinction between their ideas of best treatment and those which are seen as *best* by their patients; learn how to acknowledge their own ignorance in diagnosis, as well as treatment and prognosis and thereby explain to their patients the inherent uncertainties in both the art and science of medicine which, in turn, give rise to valid differences of belief based upon clinical experience.[163] Sadly, all too often, the quest for diagnosis and cure or, what has been termed, "The Riddle," seduces many physicians and forces them to ignore the realities of pathological processes.[164]

In projecting the future of health care for the elderly, in particular, the standard of negotiated consent is undoubtedly a more desirable standard to implement for all parties involved than the traditional informed consent. Despite the assault on its viability, the imperative of negotiated consent focuses ultimately on the concept of "keep listening" as opposed to "keep talking."[165] This goal, even though it is oftentimes difficult to achieve, may provide the elderly patient with a stronger sense of participation in the direction of his medical treatment and, hopefully, with a greater sense of trust and confidence and allow the "ethics of intimacy rather than the ethics of strangers [to] take root and flourish."[166]

Seen as a normative value rather than an empirical constant,[167] perhaps—in reality—the consequences of the doctrine of informed consent are of less importance than the values it seeks to promote.[168] To be sure, the doctrine needs to be contextualized both procedurally and substantively in legal doctrine.[169] Setting new dialogic responsibilities for physicians, however, may not succeed in strengthening the process.[170] Indeed, in the present cost-conscious health care environment, such an imposition may only serve to further complicate its simple and direct mandate: namely, to provide a knowledgeable atmosphere for a therapeutic partnership or moral agency between physician and patient to occur.[171] In addition, without the doctrine of informed consent, then, there would be little opportunity to create an atmosphere in which—in health care delivery systems—both interdependence and interrelationship are acknowledged, professionally and legally, as practical normative values.[172]

Although the doctrine of informed consent will always remain a relative term, then, "with the degree of completeness resting on so many variables including of course the nature and reliability of the source," it should be seen as more than an aspirational goal.[173] Viewed accordingly, it should serve as a useful construct for embedding the doctrine as an integral part of the ethos of

medicine[174]—an ethos tied to a recognition of patient trust and partnership
with the physician as the cornerstone of the healing enterprise[175] which must
always seek to provide "a right and good healing action in the interests of a
particular patient."[176] In the final analysis, however, it remains for the profession of medicine, not the legal profession, to formulate and then effect a
truly contemporary doctrine of informed consent—one, to be sure, that is
responsive to the "proddings of the law," but, more importantly, one that is
cognizant of the very complex and nuanced interactions between patients and
their physicians.[177]

Notes

1 WILLARD GAYLIN & BRUCE JENNINGS, THE PERVERSION OF AUTONOMY
   55 (1996). *See also* GEORGE J. ANNAS, THE RIGHTS OF PATIENTS 116–17 (3d ed.
   2004). *See generally* Edmund D. Pellegrino, *The Human Person, the Physician and the Physician's
   Ethics*, 62 LINACRE Q. 74 (1995); *Patient-Physician Autonomy: Conflicting Rights and Obligations
   in the Physician-Patient Relationship*, 10 J. CONTEMP. HEALTH L. & POL'Y 47 (1994).

2 Edmund D. Pellegrino, *Toward a Reconstruction of Medical Morality: The Primacy of The Act
   of Profession and the Fact of Illness*, 4 J. MED. & PHIL. 32, 47 (1979).

3 *Ibid.* at 49.

4 *Ibid. See generally* DANIEL P. SULMASY, THE HEALER'S CHOICE (1997); THOMAS
   SZASZ, THE THEOLOGY OF MEDICINE ch. 1 (1977).

5 CARL E. SCHNEIDER, THE PRACTICE OF AUTONOMY, PATIENTS, DOCTORS
   & MEDICAL DECISIONS 110 (1998). *See* TERRANCE McCONNELL, INALIENABLE
   RIGHTS: THE LIMITS OF CONSENT IN MEDICINE AND THE LAW 77, 78 (2000)
   (maintaining the position that physicians are *not* obligated to comply with such patient
   wishes because such a waiver is valid only if it is both voluntary and informed).

6 SCHNEIDER, *ibid.* at 99. *See also* MARK A. HALL, *ET AL.*, HEALTH CARE LAW
   AND ETHICS 208 (6th ed. 2003).

7 SCHNEIDER, *ibid.* at 175.

8 Roger B. Dworkin, *Medical Law and Ethics in The Post-Autonomy Age*, 68 IND. L. J. 727,
   737 (1993).

9 *Ibid. See generally* ROGER B. DWORKIN, LIMITS: THE ROLE OF THE LAW IN
   BIOETHICAL DECISION MAKING ch. 7 (1996).

10 Pellegrino, *supra* note 2 at 50. *But see*, ROBERT M. VEATCH, *infra* note 76 (discussing
    the therapeutic privilege to withhold information); Karen M. Coulson, *Informed Consent:
    Issues for Providers*, 16 HEMATOL. ONCOL. CLINS. NORTH. AM., 1365, 1374 (2002).

11 Pellegrino, *supra* note 2 at 50. *See* Patrick Guinan, *Autonomy Has Not Killed Hippocrates*, 9
    NAT'L CATH. BIOETHICS Q. 681 (2009) (maintaining autonomy should not displace
    the doctor–patient relationship).

12 Pellegrino, *supra* note 2 at 51.

13 *Ibid.*

14 *Ibid. See* EDMUND D. PELLEGRINO & DAVID C. THOMASMA, THE RESTORA-
    TION OF BENEFICENCE IN HEALTH CARE (1988).

15 Pellegrino, *supra* note 2 at 52, 54–55. *See* Len Doyal, *The Moral Importance of Informed
    Consent in Medical Research: Concluding Reflections* in INFORMED CONSENT IN MEDICAL
    RESEARCH at 313 (Len Doyal & Jeffrey S. Tobias, eds. 2001) (arguing that certain types
    of medical research—epidemiological, for example—should be exempted from the
    informed consent requirement and, further, that in certain other cases where the research
    subject is incompetent, as with children having the consent of their parents, or in trauma
    cases where there is an acceptable risk–benefit ratio). *See* DANIEL CALLAHAN, WHAT

PRICE BETTER HEALTH? (2003) (arguing that the therapeutic/non-therapeutic distinction gives rise to "therapeutic misconception" which arises when "a clinician researcher carries out research of no expected or intended benefit to a patient but which the patient believes will offer a chance of benefit"). *See also* Guido Calabresi, *Reflections on Medical Experimentations in Humans*, 98 DAEDALUS 387, 401 (1964) (advocating some form of consent should always be required which seeks to strike a balance between present and future lives). *See generally* Jonathan Montgomery, *Informed Consent in Clinical Research with Children*, in INFORMED CONSENT IN MEDICAL RESEARCH, *ibid.* at 173; ANNAS, *supra* note 1 at ch. IX.

16 *See* Dan W. Brock, *The Ideal of Shared Decision Making between Physicians and Patients*, 1 KENNEDY INST. ETHICS J. 28 (1991); Arthur L. Caplan, *Informed Consent and Provider-Patient Relationships in Rehabilitation*, 69 ARCH. PHYS. REHABIL. 312 (1988).

17 MARSHALL S. SHAPO, PRINCIPLES OF TORT LAW, 133–34 (2003).

18 *Ibid.*

19 *Ibid.*

20 JONATHAN BARON, AGAINST BIOETHICS 129 (2006).

21 *Ibid. See also* LAW AND BIOETHICS 134–35 (Michael Freeman, ed. 2008).

22 BARON, *supra* note 20 at 97.

23 Peter R. Schuck, *Rethinking Informed Consent*, 103 YALE L. J. 900, 904–5 (1994).

24 Jay Katz, *Informed Consent—Must It Remain a Fairy Tale?* 10 J. CONTEMP. HEALTH L. & POL'Y 69 (1994).

There are significant deficiencies in the regulation of informed consent in human subject research. *See infra* note 90, THE ETHICS AND REGULATION WITH HUMAN SUBJECTS at 355–70.

25 *See generally* TIMOTHY S. JOST, DISENTITLEMENT? THE THREATS FACING OUR PUBLIC HEALTHCARE PROGRAMS AND RIGHTS-BASED RESPONSE (2003); George P. Smith, II, *Distributive Justice and Health Care*, 18 J. CONTEMP. HEALTH L. & POL'Y 421 (2002), *Social Justice and Health Care Management: An Elusive Quest*, 9 HOUSTON J. HEALTH L. & POL'Y 1 (2008).

26 *See generally* SCHNEIDER, *supra* note 5.

27 Pellegrino, *supra* note 1; SCHNEIDER, *ibid.* at 205.

28 Schuck, *supra* note 23.

29 *Ibid.*

30 *See generally* Harry R. Moody, *From Informed Consent to Negotiated Consent*, 28 THE GERONTOLOGIST 64 (Supp. 1988).

31 GAYLIN & JENNINGS, *supra* note 1 at 55.

32 Katz, *supra* note 24 at 91.

33 *See generally* Pellegrino, *supra* note 1; Edmund D. Pellegrino, *Rationing Health Care: The Ethics of Medical Gatekeeping*, 2 J. CONTEMP. HEALTH L. & POL'Y 23 (1986). *See also* ALBERT R. JONSEN, THE NEW MEDICINE AND THE OLD ETHICS (1990); Mark A. Hall, *Law, Medicine and Trust*, 55 STAN. L. REV. 463, 478 (2002) (maintaining that without a minimal level of trust, patients will neither disclose information to the physician nor follow medical recommendations made to him).

34 Laura H. Dietz, Annotation, *Physicians, Surgeons and Other Healers*, 61 AM. JUR. 2d §202 (1981). *See also* HALL, ET AL., *supra* note 6 at 201, 203, 210.

35 Dietz Annotation, *ibid.*

36 *Ibid. See* Aaron D. Twerski & Neil B. Cohen, *Informed Decision Making and The Law of Torts: The Myth of Justiciable Causation*, 1988 ILL. L. F. 607.

37 Dietz, *supra* note 34 at §§150–52. *See* FOWLER V. HARPER, FLEMING JAMES & OSCAR S. GREY, 1 THE LAW OF TORTS §3.2 at 268 (1986).

38 Hunter L. Prillaman, *A Physician's Duty to Inform of Newly Developed Therapy*, 6 J. CONTEMP. HEALTH L. J. & POL'Y 43, 44 (1990).

39 Dworkin, *supra* note 8 at 729.

Since the decision in Salgo v. Leland Stanford Jr. University Board of Trustees in 1957, the courts have been emphasizing and developing a negligence of "failure to use due care" theory of liability. 154 Cal. App. 560, 578, 317 P. 2d 170, 181 (1959). This theory in turn places the physician in default for failing to educate adequately his patient to the *collateral* risks involved in the treatment. Indeed, *Salgo* provided the groundwork for the explosion of cases dealing with informed consent. There, as now, the physician is confronted with a perplexing problem: namely, how to balance the patient's need to know the risks and alternatives to treatment in order to give an informed consent with the individual patient's mental and emotional condition to accept and understand the medical information. *Ibid. See also* David Thomasma & Edmund D. Pellegrino, *Medicine, Science, Self-Interest: Value Sets in Conflict in Human Experimentation*, in RESEARCH ON HUMAN SUBJECTS: ETHICS, LAW AND SOCIAL POLICY at xvii *passim* (David N. Weisstub, ed. 1998).

Under *Salgo*, then, a physician owes a duty to his patient to disclose facts necessary to the formation of an intelligent consent and, further, subjects himself to liability for violation of that duty. *Salgo, ibid.* At best confusing, the Salgo Rule allows plaintiff's counsel to argue that there must be full disclosure since there is an established duty to disclose. Yet, a court may use *Salgo* as justification for holding for the defendant on the issue of the adequacy of disclosure—sustaining the proposition that the amount of information the physician gave the patient was sufficient for him to understand the risks and alternatives of the proposed treatment. Michael J. Myers, *infra*, note 73 at 1339. The discretion allowed to physicians has tended to subject them to liability in cases involving high risk and to exonerate them when a court considers the risk to be light. *Ibid.*

40 Hondroulis v. Schuhmacher, 553 So. 2d 398 (La. 1989, Hondroulis II).

41 *See, e.g.*, Ziegert v. South Chicago Community Hospital, 99 Ill. App. 3d 83, 425 N.E. 2d 450 (1981).

42 Prillaman, *supra* note 38 at 45.

43 *Ibid.*

44 *Ibid. See also* David Thomasma & Edmund D. Pellegrino, *Medicine, Science, Self-Interest: Value Sets In Conflict in Human Experimentation*, in RESEARCH ON HUMAN SUBJECTS: ETHICS, LAW AND SOCIAL POLICY at xvii *passim* (David N. Weisstub, ed. 1998); *infra* note 90, THE ETHICS AND REGULATION OF RESEARCH WITH HUMAN SUBJECTS, chs. 3, 4, 7, 13–16; GEORGE P. SMITH, II, DISTRIBUTIVE JUSTICE AND THE NEW MEDICINE 113–14 (2008). *See generally* RESPONSIBLE RESEARCH: A SYSTEMS APPROACH TO PROTECTING RESEARCH PATIENTS (Daniel D. Federman, *et al.*, eds. 2003); KENNETH GETZ & DEBORAH BORFITZ, INFORMED CONSENT: A GUIDE TO THE RISKS AND BENEFITS OF VOLUNTEERING FOR CLINICAL TRIALS (2002); 45 CFR §46.01 (2009), Federal Policy for the Protection of Human Subjects; FURROW *et al.*, *infra* note 46 at 411 *passim*.

On July 22, 2011, the federal government proposed extensive revisions to the Common Rule which has governed nearly all human-subject researched and financed by the government through 15 agencies for the past 20 years. 76 FED. REG. 44339–40 (July 25, 2011) (pertinent to 45 CFR Parts 46, 160, 164).

45 Neal v. Lee, 365 Pa. Super. 464, 478, 530 A.2d 103, 111 (1987).

46 BARRY R. FURROW, *ET AL.*, BIOETHICS: HEALTH CARE LAW AND ETHICS 280 (6th ed. 2008). *See generally* JONATHAN HERRING, OLDER PEOPLE IN LAW AND SOCIETY ch. 3 (2009); ETHICS AND LAW FOR THE HEALTH PROFESSIONS chs. 13, 14 (Ian Kerridge, *et al.*, eds., 3rd ed. 2009).

47 FURROW *et al.*, *supra* note 46.

48 *Ibid.*

49 *Ibid.* at 283.

50 *Ibid.* at 281 (analyzing and referencing the work of Loren Roth, Alan Meisel and Charles W. Lidz).

51 *Ibid.* at 281.

52 *Ibid.*

53 *Ibid.* at 282.

54 *Ibid.*
55 *Ibid.*
56 *Ibid.*
57 *Ibid.*
58 *Ibid.*
59 *Ibid.* at 283.
60 SHEILA A. M. McLEAN, AUTONOMY, CONSENT AND THE LAW 47 (2009).
61 *Ibid.* at 91.
62 *Ibid.*
63 FURROW *et al.*, *supra* note 46 at 283.
64 McLEAN, *supra* note 60 at 215.
65 *Ibid.*
66 FURROW, *et al.*, *supra* note 46 at 285.
67 *Ibid.* at 284.
68 *Ibid.* at 285. *But see* Carl H. Coleman, *Research with Decisionally Incapacitated Human Subjects: An Argument for a Systematic Approach to Risk-Benefit Assessment*, 83 IND. L. J. 743 (2008).
69 464 F.2d 772 (D.C. Cir. 1972), *cert. denied*, 409 U.S. 1064 (1972). *Accord*, Wilkinson v. Vesey, 295 A.2d 676 (R.I. 1972). *See also* Cobbs v. Grant, 8 Cal. 3d 229, 502 P.2d 1, 104 Cal. Rptr. 505 (1972); Nathanson v. Kline, 186 Kan. 393, 350 P.2d 1093, clarified, 187 Kan. 186, 354 P.2d 670 (1960); Schloendorff v. Society of New York Hospital, 211 N.Y. 125, 105 N.E. 92 (1914), overruled on other grounds by Bing v. Thunig, 2 N.Y.2d 656, 143 N.E.2d 3, 163 N.Y.S.2d 1 (1957).
70 Canterbury v. Spence, *ibid.* at 777. *See* ANNAS, *supra* note 1 at 116–17.
71 Canterbury v. Spence, *ibid.* at 776.
72 Canterbury v. Spence, *ibid.* at 786.
73 *See* Michael J. Myers, Comment, *Informed Consent in Medical Malpractice*, 55 CAL. L. REV. 1396, 1407–10 (1967).
74 Canterbury v. Spence, 464 F.2d 722 at 787.
75 *See* Dunham v. Wright, 423 F.2d 940, 941–42 (3rd Cir. 1970).
76 *See* Roberts v. Wood, 206 F. Supp. 579, 583 (S.D. Ala. 1962). *See also* THOMAS BEAUCHAMP & JAMES CHILDRESS, PRINCIPLES OF BIOMEDICAL ETHICS ch. 4 (6th ed. 2009).
   There is a therapeutic privilege to withhold information from a patient if it is either considered potentially harmful or it would cause any counter-therapeutic deterioration— no matter how slight—in either the patient's physical, psychological or emotional well being. ROBERT M. VEATCH, MEDICAL ETHICS 203, 204 (2d ed. 1997). The "urgency of the situation" justifies this exception to the doctrine of informed consent. JAY KATZ, EXPERIMENTATION WITH HUMAN BEINGS 37, 84 (1972). *See also* Kathleen M. Boozang, *The Therapeutic Placebo: The Case for Patient Deception*, 54 FLA. L. REV. 687 (2002) (arguing, for example, that if viewed as effective treatment, with a therapeutic effect being achieved by its prescription and use, the representation that placebo use is therapy or medicine is neither untrue nor unethical); HALL, *ET AL.*, *supra* note 6 at 207; George J. Annas, *Questing for Goals: Duplicity Betrayal and Self-Deception in Postmodern Medical Research*, 12 J. CONTEMP. HEALTH LAW & POL'Y 297, 300, 314 (1996) (asserting that the very concept of therapeutic research should be eliminated altogether since it confuses the ideology of medicine with the ideology of science).
77 Myers, *supra* note 73 at 1409–10. *See generally* Allan Meisel, *The 'Exceptions' to the Informed Consent Doctrine: Striking a Balance between Competing Values in Medical Decisionmaking*, 1979 WIS. L. REV. 413.
78 Canterbury v. Spence, 464 F.2d 722 at 791. *See* Schuck, *supra* note 23 at 936 (where the author states that there is a judicial reluctance "to presume that a properly informed patient would have acted differently in making a treatment decision than he did—much less that a better medical outcome would have been achieved by such a hypothetical decision").

79 Landmark examples of the way in which courts have treated the application of informed consent include: Corn v. French, 71 N.W. 280 289 P.2d 173 (1955) (physician held liable where mastectomy was performed with a signed consent form, but patient had told physician that she did not want anything removed); DiRosse v. Wein, 261 N.Y.S. 2d 623, 24 App. Div. 2d 510 (1965) (failure to tell of the danger of exfoliative dermatitis from "gold" treatment for rheumatoid arthritis, resulting in exfoliative dermatitis, imposed liability on the physician); Darrah v. Kite, 301 N.Y.S. 2d 286, 32 App. Div. 2d 208 (1969) (failure to give adequate and timely explanation of the risks of ventricolograms, imposed liability on a neurologist).

80 Twerski & Cohen, *supra* note 36 at 615, n. 30.

81 *Ibid.* at 620, n. 47.

82 Prillaman, *supra* note 38 at 47.

83 *Ibid. See* Coulson, *supra* note 10 at 1371.

84 Prillaman, *ibid.* at 48.

85 *Ibid.*

86 *Ibid.*

87 *Ibid.* at 52.

88 *Ibid.*

89 *Ibid. See* ANNAS, *supra* note 1 at 127–28.

90 Prillaman, *supra* note 38 at 52.

In a landmark case in California, in 1990, it was determined that an individual patient must first give an informed consent to a surgical procedure that would in turn yield tissues which would be transformed, subsequently, through genetic engineering, into commercial products of considerable value. John Moore v. The Regents of The University of California *et al.*, 51 Cal. 3d 120, 793 P.2d 749, 271 Cal. Rptr. 146 (1990). *See* Washington University v. Catalona, 490 F. 3d (8th Cir. 2007) (where Missouri law was affirmed by recognizing biological materials are considered donated by research participants for research purposes as an *inter vivos* gift—with the University being accepted as donee). *See also* Greenberg v. Miami Children's Hospital Research Institute, 264 F. Supp. 2d 1064 (S.D. Fla. 2003) (where donations by a party of body tissue and blood samples for medical research which were subsequently sources for commercialization precluded the donor from a claim for recovery under a theory of conversion but did merit a claim under the theory of unjust enrichment). *See generally* OONAGH CORRIGAN, *ET AL.*, THE LIMITS OF CONSENT: A SOCIO-ETHICAL APPROACH TO HUMAN SUBJECT RESEARCH IN MEDICINE (2009); CARL H. COLEMAN, *ET AL.*, THE ETHICS AND REGULATION OF RESEARCH WITH HUMAN SUBJECTS chs. 3, 7 (2005); ANNAS, *supra* note 1 at ch. IX.

91 Prillaman, *supra* note 38 at 57.

92 *Ibid.*

93 *Ibid.*

94 *Ibid.*

95 *Ibid.* at 58.

96 *Ibid. See* ANNAS, *supra* note 1 at ch. IX.

97 Susan M. Wolf, *Conflict between Doctor and Patient*, 16 L. MED. & HEALTH CARE 197, 198 (1988).

98 *Ibid. See* Patrick A. Tully, *Morally Objectionable Options: Informed Consent and Physician Integrity*, 8 NAT'L CATH. BIOETHICS Q. 491 (2008) (arguing that all treatment options should be disclosed while discussing any serious moral concerns that either the physician or the patient has about any of those options).

99 Wolf, *supra* note 97 at 198. *See generally* JOSEPH M. JACOB, DOCTORS AND RULES (1988).

100 *See generally* ALLEN E. BUCHANAN & DAN W. BROCK, DECIDING FOR OTHERS: THE ETHICS OF SURROGATE DECISIONMAKING (1989); Guinan, *supra* note 11.

For a discussion of state interests in protecting competent patients who reject life sustaining treatment, *see* FURROW *et al.*, *supra* note 46 at 269 *passim*. In addition, *see* Washington v. Glucksberg, 521 U.S. 702 (1997).

101 Wolf, *supra* note 97 at 199. *See generally* George P. Smith, II, *Utility and The Principle of Medical Futility*, 12 J. CONTEMP. HEALTH L. & POL'Y 1 (1996).

102 Matthew K. Wynia, Jonathan B. VanGeest *et al.*, *Do Physicians Not Offer Useful Services Because of Coverage Restrictions?* 22 HEALTH AFFAIRS 190, 194 (Jul./Aug. 2003).

103 *Ibid.*

104 *Ibid.* at 194, 195. *See* HALL, *ET AL.*, *supra* note 6 at 191.

105 *Ibid.* at 195. *See* ANNAS, *supra* note 1 at 113.

106 *Ibid.* at 196.

107 *Ibid.*

108 *Ibid.* *See generally* Douglas A. Grimm, *Informed Consent for All: No Exceptions*, 37 NEW MEXICO L. REV. 39 (2007).

109 Moody, *supra* note 30 at 64. *See* Brian F. Holland, *Autonomy in Long Term Care: Background Issues and a Programmatic Response*, 28 THE GERONTOLOGIST 3 (Supp. 1988) (where the observation is made that patient autonomy is not a value indigenous to medical contexts, but one imported into medicine from extrinsic social agendas such as that of constitutional law and the evolution of individual rights). *Ibid.* at 4. *See also* Dworkin, *supra* note 8, challenging the view that autonomy should be the dominant value in medical law and ethics.

110 GEORGE J. ANNAS, THE RIGHTS OF PATIENTS 113 (3rd ed. 2004). *See generally* RUTH R. FADEN & TOM BEAUCHAMP, A HISTORY AND THEORY OF INFORMED CONSENT (1986).

111 *See e.g.*, Canterbury v. Spence, *supra* note 69. *See generally* Jennifer Rosato, *Using Bioethics Discourse to Determine When Patients Should Make Health Care Decisions for Their Children: Is Deference Judgment?* 73 TEMPLE L. REV. 1 (2000).

112 Cruzan v. Dir. Mo. Dep't of Health, 497 U.S. 261, 276–80 (1990). *See generally* Joseph T. Monahan & Elizabeth A. Lawhorn, *Life-Sustaining Treatment and the Law: The Evolution of Informed Consent, Advance Directives and Surrogate Decision Making*, 19 ANNALS HEALTH L. 107 (2010).

113 Moody, *supra* note 30 at 64.

114 *Ibid.* *See generally* Donald Vandeveer, PATERNALISTIC INTERVENTION: THE MORAL BOUNDS OF BENEVOLENCE (1986).

115 Moody, *supra* note 30 at 64; Guinan, *supra* note 11.

116 Moody, *ibid.*

117 *See* Harry R. Moody, *Ethical Dilemmas of Nursing Home Placement*, 11 GENERATIONS 16–23 (1987). The difficulties are heightened by professional interventions that verge on being more social than medical (*e.g.*, eating, bathing, exercise), the patients' need for a degree of regimentation in their lifestyles, and the continuous fluctuation in competency or decisional capacity of the patients. *See* Moody, *supra* note 30, at 64–65.

118 Moody, *supra* note 30 at 65.

119 *Ibid.*

120 *Ibid.* at 67.

121 *Ibid.* Instead, negotiated consent proposes the structure of a team decision-making process, allowing for greater influence and more effective communication. *Ibid.*

122 Moody, *supra* note 30 at 67.

123 *Ibid.*

124 *Ibid.*

125 *Ibid.* at 67. The notion exists, particularly with elderly patients, that a patient ought to be aware that negotiations are underway. Furthermore, the patient should know which parties are active participants in the negotiation process and ultimately, any decision derived at should be presented in such a manner as to be publicly defensible on a wide-scale basis. *Ibid.*

126 *Ibid.*

127 *Ibid.* at 68.

128 *Ibid.*

Although the physician base of experience endows them greater facilities to reason more accurately about medical issues than can their patients, the patient has the option of non-compliance and thereby retains an element of power for himself. SCHNEIDER, *supra* note 5 at 68.

129 *See* Moody, *supra* note 30 at 68, citing President's Commission for the Study of Ethical Problems in Medicine and Biomedical and Behavioral Research, MAKING HEALTH CARE DECISIONS: A REPORT ON THE ETHICAL AND LEGAL IMPLICATIONS OF INFORMED CONSENT IN THE PATIENT-PRACTITIONER RELATIONSHIP (1982).

130 Moody, *ibid.* at 69. *See* HERRING, *supra* note 46 at 92.

131 Nancy N. Dubler, *The Dependent Elderly: Legal Rights and Responsibilities in Agent Custody*, in ETHICAL DIMENSIONS OF GERIATRIC CARE, 137 (Stuart F. Spicker, *et al.*, eds. 1987).

132 *Ibid.*

133 *Ibid.*

134 Laura B. Benko, *Boomer Bust?* MODERN HEALTHCARE, Jul. 28, 2003, at 24. *See also* L. Jaime Fitten & Martha S. Waite, *Impact of Medical Hospitalization on Treatment Decision-Making in the Elderly*, 150 ARCHIVES INTERNAL MED. 1717 (1990). *See generally* James Lubitz *et al.*, *Health, Life Expectancy, and Health Care Spending among the Elderly*, 349 N. ENGL. J. MED. 1048 (2003).

135 Betty Booker, *Nursing-Home Costs Soar; Local Prices Average $64,000 Annually*, RICH. TIMES DISPATCH, Aug. 7, 2003, at A1.

136 Fitten & Waite, *supra* note 134.

137 *See ibid. See also* E. Kokmen, *et al.*, *Epidemiologic Patterns and Clinical Features of Dementia in a Defined U.S. Population*, 105 TRANS. AM. NEUROLOGICAL ASS'N. 334–36 (1980); W.A. Rocco, *et al.*, *The Epidemiology of Dementia*, 19 ANN. NEUROLOGY 415–24 (1986).

138 Fitten & Waite, *supra* note 134 at 1717.

139 *See ibid.*

140 *See* Fitten & Waite, *supra* note 134 at 1717; Joseph T. Monahan & Elizabeth A. Lawhorn, *Life-Sustaining Treatment and The Law: The Evolution of Informed Consent, Advance Directives and Surrogate Decision Making*, 19 ANNALS HEALTH L. 107 (2010).

141 JANET L. DOLGIN & LOIS L. SHEPHERD, BIOETHICS AND THE LAW 745–49 (2005).

142 *Ibid.*

In assessing an incompetent patient's system of values, a surrogate decision-maker (often, ultimately, a court) is admittedly probing—subjectively—what a majority of similarly situated patients would do in like circumstances. This investigative process is, thus, linked inextricably to a "reasonable person" inquiry. *See* Superintendent of Belchertown State School v. Saikewicz, 370 N.E. 2d 417 (Mass. 1977); DOLGIN & SHEPHERD, *supra* note 141. *See also* HERRING, *supra* note 46 at 91–92.

143 DOLGIN & SHEPHERD, *supra* note 141.

Interestingly, for both seriously ill newborns and critically ill adults lacking decisional capacity, there is a shared commonality of factors used under the best interests test, among them being: the chance of therapeutic success from continued life sustaining treatments; the risks involved with either treatment or non-treatment; the extent to which, if successful, a particular therapy will extend life together with the pain and discomfort that such a treatment will bring to the patient and—finally—an assessment of the quality of life which a patient of this type will experience either with or without treatment. *Ibid. See* HERRING, *supra* note 46 at 64 *passim*.

144 Nancy N. Dubler, *supra* note 131 at 137. *See generally* L. Jaime Fitten, *et al.*, *Assessing Treatment Decision-Making Capacity in Elderly Nursing Home Residents*, 38 J. AM. GERIATRICS SOC. 1097 (1990).

145 Dubler, *supra* note 131 at 137.

146 *Ibid.*

147 *Ibid.*

148 Harry R. Moody, *supra* note 30 at 67. *See also* Dworkin, *supra* note 8 (arguing for a "full social impact calculus" in the decision-making process).

149 J. P. Hes, *et al.*, *Some Psychological and Legal Considerations in the Determination of Incompetence in the Elderly*, 7 MED. LAW 151, 153 (1988).

150 Barbara Stanley, *et al.*, *The Elderly Patient and Informed Consent*, 252 JAMA 1302, 1305 (1984).

151 *Ibid.* The study revealed that, in comparison to their younger counterparts, older patients did show poorer comprehension, yet generally also seemed to make equally reasonable decisions. Thus, the quality of decision-making was not noted to be significantly affected adversely until comprehension ability was deemed to be severely impaired, as in severe senile dementia. *Ibid.*

152 Moody, *supra* note 30 at 69.

153 *Ibid.* Moody points out that, especially with elder patients, it is possible to provide opportunities and to safeguard rights, but without motivation, they will derive no benefits from these acts. It is essentially their own liberty that they must exercise in order to take advantage of the opportunities being made available to them. *Ibid.*

154 Moody, *supra* note 30 at 68.

155 *See ibid.* A basic example of what should be recorded is as follows: "Family talked it over and decided in favor of trying the new treatment. Patient agreed it was best." *Ibid.*

156 McLEAN, *supra* note 60 at 23.

157 *Ibid.* at 15–20.

158 *Ibid.* at 22.

159 *Ibid.* at 24, citing Isaiah Berlin, *Two Concepts of Liberty* in ISAIAH BERLIN, FOUR ESSAYS ON LIBERTY 170 (1961).

160 McLEAN, *supra* note 60 at 24.

161 *Ibid.* at 56.

162 *Ibid.*

163 JAY KATZ, THE SILENT WORLD OF DOCTOR AND PATIENT xi (1986).

164 SHERWIN B. NULAND, HOW WE DIE 249, 265 (1994).

165 Moody, *supra* note 30 at 70; Guinan, *supra* note 11.

166 Moody, *ibid.* at 69. *See generally* HENRY R. MOODY, ETHICS IN AN AGING SOCIETY (1992).

167 Schuck, *supra* note 23 at 956.

168 *Ibid.* at 937.

169 *Ibid.* at 951.

170 *Ibid.* at 935.

171 Pellegrino, *supra* notes 1, 2. As more and more physicians leave the private practice and associate themselves with hospitals, doctor–patient relationships are eroded and corporate profit incentives are strengthened. Hal Scherz, *Obamacare Undermines Doctor–Patient Relationships*, WASH. EXAMINER, Apr. 13, 2011, at 24.

172 GAYLIN & JENNINGS, *supra* note 1 at 243.

173 Jeffrey S. Tobias, *Contemporary Challenges in Clinical Research: Paying Lip Service to Informed Consent, or a Genuine Shift of Gear?* in INFORMED CONSENT IN MEDICAL RESEARCH, *supra* note 15 at 318, 319. *See supra* notes 17–22 and accompanying text; *supra* notes 54–68 and accompanying text for discussion of the present weaknesses of the doctrine of informed consent.

174 Katz, *supra* note 24 at 91 (arguing that until the doctrine becomes an integral aspect of the ethos of medicine, it is condemned to remain a fairy tale); Schuck, *supra* note 23 at 937 (asserting the consequences of the doctrine are of less importance than those values it instantiates and promotes).

175 *See generally* Edmund D. Pellegrino & John L. Harvey, *Whom Should the Patient Trust?* AMERICA, Oct. 1, 2001, at 19.

176 Pellegrino, *supra* note 2 at 47; PELLEGRINO & THOMASMA, *supra* note 14. *But see* William M. Sage, *Should the Patient Conquer?* 45 WAKE FOREST L. REV. 1505 (2010) (assessing the inefficiencies and inequities of patient-centered health care systems).

   In the final analysis, a patient must be able, realistically, to expect "honesty and competence" from his physician and a modicum of kindness and caring in treatment. ANNAS, *supra* note 1 at 123.

177 Katz, *supra* note 24 at 71. *See generally* KATZ, *supra* note 163.

8   An easeful or troubling death

Introduction

A Gallup poll of 1,003 adults taken in May, 2007, found 49 percent of Americans subscribe to the view that doctor-assisted suicide is acceptable morally, while 44 percent found it to be morally wrong.[1] When one has a disease which cannot be cured and results in a life with severe pain, 56 percent of those polled expressed the opinion that physicians should be allowed, legally, to assist such a patient, upon request, to commit suicide.[2] Always more popular than physician-assisted suicide in contemporary culture, the poll found 71 percent favored euthanasia—with 27 percent of those polled opposing it.[3] Interestingly, since 1970, the range of support for euthanasia has been from 65 percent to 75 percent.[4]

A similar survey of 1,500 adults conducted by the Pew Research Center in 2005 found 60 percent of Americans believe that there is an inherent moral right which allows them to end their lives if they are in great pain with no hope of improvement.[5] Some 53 percent believe one has the same moral right to end his life if found to be suffering from an incurable disease.[6] Deeply divided over the issue of legalizing physician-assisted suicide, 46 percent of those polled approved of laws permitting doctors to assist patients to end their lives, while 45 percent opposed.[7]

These two surveys illustrate, dramatically, one of the dominating issues in health care management: end-of-life care. Since everyone dies, death is but an inevitable aspect of the human condition—dying badly in a troubling manner is not. As a social problem, dying badly, then, requires a social solution.[8] Through hospice care and palliative management, bold—yet compassionate—steps may be taken to resolve this problem by the advancement of epidemiologically well-grounded approaches to end-of-life care systems.[9] These systems seek to balance the "new epidemiology of dying"[10] which demands virtually automatic heroic procedures to be followed with oftentimes confused family responsibilities to essentially "micro-manage recurring series of life-threatening complications within a progressively degenerative and incurable chronic disease."[11] What is needed at the end of life is a level of confidence that professional care will be provided by care givers who are competent and kind and bring comfort and show respect through the entire dying process.[12]

Palliative management

The first element of palliative treatment in hospice care is symptom control, pharmacological and psychological, in the dying patient. Palliative care, then, seeks to relieve the experience of total pain—physical, mental, social, and spiritual—for patients when rehabilitative care or prolongation of life are no longer attainable goals.[13] Once physical pain is controlled or managed, attention is given over to psychological, social, and spiritual care.[14] By palliating the whole person, then, the phenomenon of existential pain is addressed and the core value of palliative care—quality of life—is revealed.[15]

Mercy, charity, compassion and dignity

Mercy is seen as a complex cluster of phenomena—formulated obscurely and imposed imperfectly.[16] Among the ten modes of mercy which have been classified,[17] compassionate mercy, for purposes of this chapter, is the cornerstone for justifying end-of-life assistance in terminal illness. It becomes, as well, a fortifying template when the Principle of Continuing Adjusted Care to medical needs is recognized as controlling. When, for example, a terminally ill patient is incapable physically of taking his or her own life or, where the process of dying has gone awry, the physician must be allowed to intercede; and ethics justification is validated when compassionate mercy is read into the principle of adjusted care.[18] Assistance in ending a terminal medical condition is seen, rightly then, as but a supplement to this principle and not as an extension of it.[19]

Care is considered as adjusted when its use is calibrated to the progression of a specific medical condition. Thus, palliative care is usually given at the end-stage of a terminal illness while curative and rehabilitative care is seen as primary care given at the onset of illness.[20] It is essential to a compassionate and common-sense approach to the management of pain and suffering often encountered in the dying process that care be adjusted continually to the burdens of disease. The noble goal of care of this quality, then, is to simply manage refractory pain even though a very real potential exists for hastening death rather than merely prolonging life at its end-stage.[21]

Defined as an acknowledgment of another's suffering which prompts a response to assist in alleviating the suffering, compassion is often regarded as the motivation for subsequent merciful acts.[22] Mercy is oftentimes used synonymously with compassion or benevolence.[23] Indeed, acts of this nature have been termed "responsible benevolence."[24] For others, charity is seen as the ultimate value in caring for the dying[25]; and they suggest beneficence and benevolence may combine, properly, to become "loving charity."[26] When there is suffering, its elimination or management is central and can well be seen as trumping the biomedical principle of autonomy.[27]

Acknowledging every person's intrinsic human dignity might also be seen as grounds which prompt a response to suffering.[28] Although human dignity should properly be seen as intrinsic—conferred, as such, by God—and neither capable of being "lost" nor "gained" by human judgments,[29] its loss is, nevertheless, one of some 19 conditions of discomfort and distress which haunt individuals as they approach death.[30] While no universal conception of dignity is to be found, it is better understood and applied within specific contexts and built, as such, upon two notions of basic dignity and personal dignity.[31] The tenets of basic dignity are grounded in the Kantian idea that there is an intrinsic universal worth found in all human beings deserving of respect.[32] Personal dignity references particular notions of dignity within a social and individual context.[33]

Rather than grapple with taxonomical subtleties, contemporary palliative care practitioners refrain from attempting to define dignity altogether and, instead, subsume concerns about it under quality of life issues which in turn conduce—essentially—to determining, and then executing, patient wishes and desires for a dignified death.[34] Stated otherwise, the search in palliative management is for validation of a human right to a "mercifully easy death."[35] The alleviation of existential pain or profound psychological distress at the end-state of a terminal illness is nothing more, for many, than but recognition of a basic human right to a merciful death. Accordingly, in those cases where medical treatment is deemed futile, terminal sedation should be recognized as an integral part of symptom control in palliative care.

At its core, the principle of mercy directs that one not only refrain from causing pain or suffering and—when ethically appropriate as a complement to the principle of adjusted medical care—act to relieve it.[36] Under this view of mercy as an operative principle or normative standard of conduct, the bioethical principles of non-malfeasance and beneficence are synthesized and morph into mercy.[37] Under both principles, the paramount consideration is to promote and safeguard the well-being of the patient by assuring comfort and dignity.

Shaping the issue of medical futility

When medical treatment is deemed to be "futile," it frees the physician from the moral, medical, and legal duty to provide it.[38] While most reasonable persons agree with this proposition, much disagreement exists as to the definition of futile treatment and who decides whether a given treatment is futile.

The Council on Ethical and Judicial Affairs of the American Medical Association determined in June, 1994, that "physicians are not ethically obliged to deliver care that, in their professional judgment, will not have a reasonable chance of benefitting their patients. Patients should not be given treatments simply because they demand them. Denials of treatment should be justified by reliance on openly stated ethical principles and acceptable standards of care"[39] " ... not on the concept of 'futility' which cannot be meaningfully defined."[40] This position can be seen either as definitive, or merely as a mechanism to validate the transfer of authority to make ethically charged decisions from patients to physicians.[41] Is the doctrine of medical futility inexplicable as the AMA Council has determined, or, can it provide a framework for principled medical decisions? The conclusion to be drawn is that medical futility defines the bounds of good practice and humane medical conduct. It therefore serves as an indispensable construct for sound medical judgments.

Physicians often make end-of-life decisions without informing the patient or family. As a result, extraneous factors such as race, wealth, gender, and age of the patient, as well as judgments on the quality of the patient's life and concerns with cost containment, may cloud a physician's determination to withhold or withdraw treatment. A clear working definition of futility is needed to ensure that physicians not only inform patients and their families about the decision to withdraw or withhold treatment, but also to provide the patients, their families, and the courts with objective criteria against which they may judge the medical decision.[42]

The issue of futility sparks the most discussion when a patient is in a persistent vegetative state (PVS) and the physician directs a do not resuscitate (DNR) order.[43] A patient diagnosed as being in such a state has no chance of regaining consciousness or returning to a sapient existence.[44] Similarly, when a patient suffers from severe and irreversible dementia[45]—meaning that he is unable to initiate any purposeful activity and only accepts nourishment and bodily care in a helpless, passive state—his condition could be classified as futile. The definitional scope of futility could also include treatment for those in a deep, irreversible coma for an extended period of time (*i.e.*, six months to a year), as well as those who are permanently vegetative.[46] The central point to any determination that medical treatment is futile should be an understanding, if not a realization, that terminal illness should not be the sole and necessary criterion for withholding treatment. For example, many comatose or barely conscious patients are not terminally ill yet are in such an irrevocable state of mental and physical deterioration—with no realistic hope of a qualitative restoration of health—that they should be properly classified as outside the bounds of treatment.[47]

A DNR is ordered when a physician concludes that it is not worth the effort to effect cardiopulmonary resuscitation (CPR) in the event of cardiac or respiratory arrest. While the law does not prevent a physician from ordering a DNR, problems arise due to the absence of clear guidelines for making the DNR decision and the fact that patients and their families are often unaware whether and why such a decision is made.[48]

Medical futility v. patient autonomy: a true battle?

With the expansion of patient autonomy, the debate over medical futility has increased over time. Thirty-five years ago, there was no need for this debate because technology had not given physicians the tools to provide many treatments that are available today and because, furthermore, few patients questioned their doctors' orders. As the role of the patient increases in choosing care, so does the debate surrounding futile care. It might be suggested that futility is the point at which to draw the line on the advancement of patient autonomy. This is not necessary, however, because the goals of patient autonomy and cessation of futile treatment are not inconsistent. Patient autonomy does not convey the right to demand futile treatment. In effect, offering or administering futile treatment undermines patient autonomy by raising false expectations of recovery.[49] Patient autonomy includes the right to be a fully informed participant in every aspect of the medical decision-making process, as well as the right to refuse medically prescribed lifesaving treatment.[50]

In 1990, in a concurring opinion in the case of Cruzan et ux. v. Dir. Missouri Dept. of Health et al., Justice Sandra Day O'Connor of the U.S. Supreme Court observed that the artificial delivery of food and water should be viewed properly as medical treatment and—as such—may be rejected under the principle of liberty found within the Due Process Clause of the Constitution.[51]

English Law is unequivocal in allowing a competent person the right to refuse medical treatment altogether even though such a refusal results in death.[52] Accordingly, patient rights of autonomy or self-determination are abridged, not when there is a denial of opportunities to make *any* medical decision, but rather when there is a denial of an opportunity to make "a *rightful* medical decision."[53] Patient autonomy does not give the patient the right to demand futile treatment because this is not a rightful medical decision. The patient does not have a right to the treatment because it has been determined that the treatment is not warranted for persons in his condition. The patient does not have a right to opt out of the class to which his medical condition relegates him.

Patient autonomy gives rise to a negative right rather than a positive right—for, the patient has a right to refuse a given treatment but *not* a corresponding right to demand a given treatment.[54] Once it has been determined what is futile, a patient's autonomy is not invaded or sacrificed if the physician does not honor the request for such treatment because patients are simply not entitled to futile treatment. The physician, by virtue of his training and expertise, is given the right to determine what treatment alternatives are available to the patient. "No ethical principle or law has ever required physicians to offer or accede to demands for treatments that are futile."[55] Even civil malpractice standards in America do not require a physician to render useless interventions. Moreover, a physician does not have a legal duty to act contrary to his conscience. Therefore, because patient autonomy does not give the patient the right to demand futile treatment, autonomy is not invaded when the physician withholds treatment on these grounds.[56]

On the contrary, withholding or withdrawing futile treatment furthers the goals of the patient autonomy movement because administering futile treatment, in fact, undermines patient autonomy. Offering treatments known medically to be futile, erode, if not destroy, the principle of autonomy or self-determination because use of such intervention invites, as seen, a level of hope and raises false expectations of recovery. Indeed, "[s]uch offers send a mixed message, implying a real choice when none exists."[57] Deception of this sort distorts the patient's perspective and deprives him of the opportunity to make informed decisions. Thus, the doctrines of futility and patient autonomy share the *same* goals of giving the patient reasonable control over his treatment. A patient will have the right to refuse any treatment offered, but—as observed—that right does not extend so far as to require the physician to yield to demands for treatments that are futile. By withholding futile treatment, the physician is showing respect for the patient by simply being honest about the chances of recovery and the futility of providing a given treatment.

Some may contend that a patient or his family has a greater right to demand that treatment be continued once the physician has begun to treat. The mere fact that a physician has begun treatment, however, does not obligate him to continue to administer that treatment once it becomes apparent that it is futile.[58] Patients and their families alike cannot successfully argue for the continuation of such assistance.[59] Even if a patient and his family could justify such a demand on a reliance theory, physicians would simply find other reasons for not administering the treatment in the first place.[60] This would frustrate, rather than further, the goals of patient autonomy because physicians would be depriving patients of care to which they are rightly entitled.

The duty *not* to administer futile treatment

Three reasons why physicians should have a duty *not* to provide futile treatment may be advanced.[61] It has been argued that if it were an option, rather than a duty, physicians could use the term "as a subterfuge for rationing, cost containment, or refusals to treat vulnerable patients."[62] If each physician was given the discretion to provide treatment deemed to be futile, patients with the means—either independent wealth or superior insurance—could bypass the doctrine of futility by merely changing physicians. This would limit drastically its effect by relegating it to a device for depriving treatment for those who cannot afford it.

It is next argued that since the public looks to the medical profession to set medical standards, making *ad hoc* assessments of futility by individual physicians rather than enforcing objective criteria developed by the medical profession would be an abdication of professional responsibility.[63] A substantial burden must be placed on the medical profession to take action in order to preserve its stature and credibility by mandating uniform treatment for all patients in a given condition.

Lastly, it is maintained that offering futile care exploits the public's fear of death and exaggerates the results that medicine and science can achieve. This leads to false expectations and inevitable disappointment, which in turn, undermines the public's confidence. While these arguments support the proposition that physicians should have an affirmative duty *not* to administer futile treatment, more compelling arguments can be found.

Scientific and ethical futility

In America, it is accepted generally that scientifically futile treatment need neither be offered nor provided to a patient who requests it. Put directly, when the medical result expected by either the patient or his family cannot be achieved, it is termed scientifically futile.[64] For example, even if a request by a seriously ill patient is made for use of laetrile drug therapy, it need not be honored by the attending physician—this, simply because this drug is useless under this particular circumstance. Similarly, antibiotics need not be prescribed to a child with a viral illness—this, again, even though the child's parents request it. The reason for this position is that, as a matter of science, the antibiotic will be ineffective in treating that illness. Finally, even though a patient with a cold may request a CAT scan, the physician may refuse to issue the order. Since there is no reason to believe that there will be any efficacious connection between what can be discovered on the scan and the appropriate treatment of the cold, the CAT scan is inconsequential or futile.[65]

The question becomes more complicated when a patient's request for treatment, though not scientifically futile, is—in the opinion of the health care provider—*ethically futile*. Care is deemed ethically futile if it will not serve the underlying interests of the patient. One example will suffice. To keep a patient's body aerated and nourished when that patient is in a persistent vegetative state, is thought by some providers to be ethically futile. Under these circumstances, health care providers maintain that it is beyond the scope of medicine to sustain corporeal existence if nothing qualitatively can be achieved beyond that level of mere existence. And, if conditions arose where CPR became an option, these same conservative health care providers would deem it ethically futile to perform this procedure when the object of the intervention would be but to prolong the patient's life by a few hours.[66]

When conflicts arise in cases of this nature which test the standards for determining ethical or even scientific futility, the best route to follow in order to keep issues out of the courts, is to refer such cases to Hospital Ethics Committees where non-binding recommendations can be made and which, in turn, can assure the certainty of fair, objective judgment that patients and their families need in critical end-of-life care.[67]

Futility disputes are inevitably about optimizing end-of-life care.[68] The transition from curative to palliative measures requires good lines of communication between the clinician, patient, and family; and ethics committees can be a tool for effecting these lines. Ideally, this transition becomes simply the exchange of curative goals of care for comfort measures.[69] Simply stated, then, the shared goal is "to reach a mutual understanding about disease trajectory and what goals of care might be appropriate given the changing medical facts and patient/family preferences."[70]

Pain management or patient preference

The argument that efforts should always be undertaken to eliminate pain or other symptoms of human suffering, rather than the person exhibiting them,[71] ignores completely the principle of autonomy or self-determination. Pain management, from a communitarian standpoint, may salve the conscience of the health care provider by forestalling, or perhaps, dispelling the need to even consider euthanasia—instead, allowing time to take its course passively. From the competent patient's standpoint, however, pain management ignores his moral and legal right—acting for whatever purposes are clear to him—to end his life with a semblance of dignity.

While patient pain may be managed effectively today, what occurs when this is merely palliative and the disease that gave rise to the pain continues its malignant progression toward terminality? What if, as a consequence of the reduction in pain, an individual becomes exceedingly debilitated and his overall quality of functional existence becomes low or even worthless because of the consequent restrictions or reductions in lifestyle and the utter dependence upon others for daily life assistance? Are individual patient preferences, recognized as futile by all reasonably objective medical standards, to be subsumed under a contrived medical mandate of sanctified purposefulness?[72] Sadly, today there are no well-established strategies for evaluating and managing refractory existential distress.[73] Whose values and preferences, then, should be given priority—the individual patient's or those of the medical community?

In a 1997 United States Supreme Court case, Washington v. Glucksberg, the Court held that a statutory prohibition in the state of Washington against "causing" or "aiding" a suicide does not offend the Fourteenth Amendment to the Federal Constitution either on its face or "as applied to competent, terminally ill adults who wish to hasten their deaths by obtaining medication prescribed by their doctors."[74] As significant as this holding is, the concurring opinion by Justice Day O'Connor has more direct relevance here. In this opinion, she states—unequivocally—that "a patient who is suffering from a terminal illness and who is experiencing great pain has no legal barriers to obtaining medication, from qualified physicians, to alleviate that suffering (by palliative care), even to the point of causing unconsciousness and hastening death."[75]

In England, while it is recognized as unlawful for a physician to administer analgesics to bring about a patient's death—even if such action is prompted by the goal of relieving his suffering—it is also recognized that if, in accordance with proper medical practice, a physician prescribes drugs to relieve pain not to end life, no actionable offense will arise. Interestingly, in cases where high qualities of pain-relieving drugs have been given with the result of death, there have been few prosecutions. And, in those prosecutions, it is rare for a conviction to be obtained.[76]

There is a global effort being undertaken presently to advance the notion that pain relief should be—indeed—recognized as a human right.[77] Defining chronic pain as persisting or recurring for more than three months, the representatives from the World Health Organization, the International Association for the Study of Pain and the European Federation of the International Study of Pain, found over a third of households in Europe (36 percent) have chronic pain sufferers and in the United States, some 43% of all households surveyed report chronic pain.[78] Chronic non-cancer related pain and pain in at-risks groups is of particular concern.[79]

Seen as a basic human right, pain relief—of whatever character or modality—must be extended logically and with compassion to those with existential pain when it becomes refractory and cannot be controlled. In such cases when this extreme type of psychological distress is encountered in the case of terminal patients, and—despite aggressive efforts to identify a tolerable therapy which does not compromise consciousness—terminal or deep sedation should be deemed appropriate as consistent with the principle of adjusted care.

Some physicians maintain improvements in hospice and palliative care now result in allowing even the most stricken patients to be helped effectively through their final days.[80] Others maintain between three percent and ten percent of the terminally ill cannot be helped by pain killers.[81] Even though palliative or terminal sedation is uncommon,[82] it must remain as a medically sound and compassionate response to refractory pain—be it physical or psychological. The question is thus framed: Why should an individual within this group be denied the freedom to die with carefully supervised assistance?[83]

Should the fear of a proverbial "slippery slope" toward public approval of active euthanasia be allowed to trump a standard of common dignity and mercy at the end-stage of life for the terminally ill? In truth, "the slippery slope is the human condition." And, thus, "we are already on it and unable to escape."[84] "It is our destiny to struggle along in life, upwards or downwards, with very uncertain footing. There is no safe plateau of moral security; we are constantly faced with painful dilemmas ... (with the goal of human moral effort) but to keep seeing and drawing the line, and struggling to stay above it."[85]

Double effect—traditional and contemporary perspectives

The principle of double effect—sometimes also stated to be either a doctrine or rule—is grounded in Roman Catholic philosophy and moral theology.[86] It proposes to structure specific guidelines to aid in determining when, ethically, it is permissible to pursue a course of action to achieve a good end—notwithstanding appreciation of the fact that negative or bad results will, as well, flow from the initiating conduct.[87] The coverage and application of the principle has, over time, been embraced by philosophers and ethicists as having a profound relevance to assessing complex cases of health care ethics either in its classical application or by implication.[88] Indeed, it is contended that the principle has "improved care of the dying, and forms a common ground for competing notions of good care for the dying."[89]

For the conduct of the actor to be acknowledged as ethically permissible, four conditions must be met: 1. The nature of the action must be good or morally neutral and, thus, not prohibited; 2. A good effect or consequence must be intended to flow from the action, and not a bad or evil one; 3. The good or positive result must not be used as a direct causal consequence of the evil result; and 4. The good or positive result must be proportionate to any evil result.[90] When all four conditions are met, the personal conduct of the agent being evaluated is held to be ethically permissible—this, even though an undesirable or "bad" result occurs.[91]

Moral distinctions or subtleties

In palliative care management, a moral distinction has all too often been recognized by some between an act of withdrawing treatment and withholding treatment—an omission.[92] Accordingly, because of this ambiguous viewpoint, it is asserted that a greater degree of accountability or responsibility must be assumed—legally—for the consequences of an individual's actions rather than his omissions.[93]

Subtle complexities infuse this "distinction" because in the event a decision which leads to either an act or an omission is made does not necessarily, *ipso facto*, mean that its efficacy is grounded on a moral justification.[94] Rather, any such justification for treatment should be based primarily "on whether the care given or not given is appropriate to the patient's wishes [and] physical condition. ..." together with "certainty of [medical] progress."[95] Yet, the fact remains in palliative management, society imposes moral and legal responsibility on care givers for both omissions as well as actions.[96]

In cases of artificial hydration—when a moral distinction is drawn between the withholding of treatment and the withdrawal of it[97]—greater blame may be given to the act of withdrawing treatment than withholding it.[98] When cases of this type are present, physicians become reluctant—if not unwilling—to commence treatment, even though medically appropriate, in order to avoid stopping it when it becomes subsequently inappropriate. The effect of this action may well result in undertreating at-risk patients.[99]

Another defensive response by physicians to the effort to chart a moral distinction between the withholding and withdrawal of treatment—which makes this putative moral distinction, itself, neither logical nor helpful—is seen in physician conduct which manifests itself in an unwillingness "to stop life-prolonging treatment when it is no longer appropriate because this constitutes a withdrawal of treatment which is seen as potentially blameworthy particularly as it may contribute to the patient's death."[100] The end result when physician conduct of this nature occurs is that overtreatment may be the norm.[101]

Competing intentions

Inasmuch as the doctrine of double effect analyzes two consequences flowing from an action and seeks to place a "substantive moral judgment" on the content of the intention of one action (and its consequences) as opposed to the other action,[102] the doctrine presents itself as a muddled template bereft of objective certainty for decision-making.[103]

There is no moral principle which advances or recognizes a presumption of evil intent before an action is taken. Accordingly, it is improper to argue or to assume that the withdrawal of treatment equates with an intentional taking of another's life. To do such would be a distortion of moral reasoning and show a misguided "understanding" of the foundations of health care and the professional ethics of its care givers. Differences in prudential judgment are, to be sure, a given in many critical care cases. What should guide the decision-making process is making final judgments which are humane, compassionate, merciful, and beneficent which, in turn, advance the goal of a death with dignity.[104]

Proportionality

Rather than continue to be mired in obfuscation as a consequence of being tethered to the doctrine of double effect in medical decision-making, a far more realistic, operative standard for evaluating the morality of end-of-life medical actions, is found in the principle of proportionality, standing on its own merit, without being seen as an integral component of the doctrine of double effect.

The principle of proportionality is closely related to the principle of medical futility. Essentially, proportionality recognizes that overuse, as well as underuse, of medical treatment and advanced life-extending technologies, may create an unreasonable burden where the harm and suffering inflicted by such a modality of treatment may be disproportionate to any realistic benefit to be derived from it. When this happens, it is recognized that there is no obligation to provide specific treatment.

Proportionality is relatively easy to state and visualize as a cost-benefit theory where costs are balanced against benefits. In practice, however, seeking to quantify both factors in a balancing equation is quite difficult. It is generally thought that this principle can be actualized or structured with considerably less difficulty and more precision through the use of advanced medical directives. Sadly, experience has shown popular and widespread use of such directives to be wanting.[105]

British accommodations

This very issue of proportionality was resolved in August, 2006, by the Court of European Human Rights in Strasbourg when it heard an appeal by a

46-year-old British citizen suffering from Friedreich's ataxia—a rare and progressive neurological condition. The appeal was from a judgment by the British Appeal Court which held physicians have a right to withdraw food and water, as medical treatments, from an incapacitated patient if, in their judgment, it is in the patient's best interest.[106] Leslie Burke, the plaintiff, had argued that he had the right to receive artificial nourishment and hydration when the progress of his illness prevents his communication of this wish.[107] While acknowledging that the British law shows a clear preference for prolonging life wherever possible, the Strasbourg court ruled that since nutrition and hydration were properly seen as medical treatment, the National Health Service could not guarantee that treatment when physicians, to the contrary, held the opinion that such was not in a patient's best interests.[108]

Interestingly, as this case unfolded in the British judicial system, in May, 2005, the British government—through its Health Secretary—stated that it would be unfair for the courts to require the General Medical Council (GMC) to expend £1,500 a day (approximately $3,000.00) for any life insured with the National Health Service (NHS).[109] A spokesman for the Health Secretary said judicial interference and oversight in health care management, especially when requirements for life-prolonging treatment are contraindicated in cases of futility, would create serious consequences for the functioning of the NHS.[110] While, under current GMC guidelines, a competent patient may decide between treatment options offered by a physician, the patient cannot require his physician to offer treatments which are clinically inappropriate "or which cannot be offered for other reasons—having regard to the efficient allocation of resources."[111]

Prosecutorial guidelines

On February 25, 2010, the British Crown Prosecution Service issued a document entitled, *Policy for Prosecutors in Respect of Cases of Encouraging Assisting Suicide*.[112] Attempting to resolve moral ambiguities in cases of assisted suicide and mercy killings, the guidelines nonetheless fail to address not only the condition or degree of suffering the person requesting the suicide is experiencing, nor do they address the situation in which a patient is neither terminally ill nor disabled but is suffering from severe depression or psychological distress. The guidelines do not change the law prohibiting assisted suicide. Rather, they provide guidance on which cases are *likely* to be prosecuted. They attempt to distinguish between "compassionate support" for which there would be a less likelihood of prosecution, from cases of "malicious encouragement" which would be prosecuted.[113]

An ethical tribunal

In an eloquent Richard Dimbleby Lecture given by the British author, Terry Pratchett, entitled, *Shaking Hands with Death*, broadcast on the BBC, on

February 1, 2010, a proposal was put forward to have a national euthanasia tribunal which would assist in establishing the facts of each case brought forward for assistance in death well before the death is to occur.[114] Such a process would ensure that a "litigant" (applicant) would thereby know whether a request for assistance would result in a legal prosecution if pursued or be allowed without being sanctioned. Patterned in part, no doubt, after ethics committees utilized in many hospitals,[115] such a tribunal would, however, be a formal governmental body. Ideally, the composition of the tribunal, "acting for the good society" would include a Family Law lawyer, and a physician "experienced in dealing with the complexities of serious long-term illnesses."[116]

The members of the tribunal would be required to be over 45 and, thus, have "acquired the rare gift of wisdom."[117] Mr. Pratchett maintained that wisdom and compassion should—for purposes of decision-making in this tribunal—be equal to the law.[118] In assessing the merits of an application for assistance, attention would be required to testing the decisional capacity of the applicant, as well as the nature of the life-threatening or incurable disease from which he is suffering.[119] Assurances would be sought that the applicant is not seeking assistance in dying as a consequence of pressure or influence from a third party. The reasonableness of the request for aid in dying would be assessed or evaluated based solely upon the facts of each medical case heard.[120]

Roman Catholic viewpoints

In 1957, His Holiness Pope Pius XII addressed the issue of care at the end-of-life and laid a foundation for Catholic teaching by stating that under certain circumstances—when, that is, treatments are deemed "extraordinary" and excessively burdensome—they may, licitly, be withdrawn.[121]

Building upon this foundation, in 1980, the Sacred Congregation for The Doctrine of the Faith issued its Declaration on Euthanasia which provides a useful construct for Catholics. In discussing the terms, "proportionate" and "disproportionate" in the context of medical treatment, the Congregation declares " ... it will be possible to make a correct judgment as to means by studying the type of treatment to be used, its degree of complexity and comparing these elements with the result that can be expected taking into account the state of the sick person and his or her physician and moral resources."[122] Dr. Edmund D. Pellegrino, former Chairman of the President's Council on Bioethics, and a pre-eminent Catholic ethicist, suggests a "disproportionate" means would, in fact, be a futile means.[123]

The Catechism

The second edition of THE CATECHISM OF THE CATHOLIC CHURCH published in 1997 has two important and relevant paragraphs to the present inquiry.

Paragraph 2278 states:

> Discontinuing medical procedures that are burdensome, dangerous, extraordinary, or disproportionate to the expected outcome can be legitimate; it is the refusal of "over-zealous" treatment. Here one does not will to cause death; one's inability to impede it is merely accepted. The decisions should be made by the patient, whose reasonable will and legitimate interests must always be respected.

Paragraph 2279 states further that:

> Even if death is thought imminent, the ordinary care owed to a sick person cannot be legitimately interrupted. The use of painkillers to alleviate the sufferings of the dying, even at the risk of shortening their days, can be morally in conformity with human dignity if death is not willed as either an end or a means, but only foreseen and tolerated as inevitable palliative care is a special form of disinterested charity. As such it should be encouraged.

Magisterial directives

There is broad acknowledgment that for many people at the end-stage of life, the natural process of dying suppresses appetite and, thus, makes nutrition unduly burdensome. Forced feeding by tube or hand is not only inappropriate but lacking in compassion in circumstances of this nature.[124] When an individual is brain dead or in such a condition where medical treatment would be ineffective or, indeed, futile, there is both an ethical and legal consensus that life-sustaining efforts should not be undertaken.[125]

Catholic theologians and the *magisterium* are consistent in their conclusions that the use of some form of life support is not always an absolute necessity.[126] Individual clinical evaluations are determinative of medical courses of action.[127] Accordingly, even though—for example—a decision to use life support has been made, it may be re-evaluated depending upon ongoing patient assessments of the present efforts of therapy[128] and the principle of adjusted care.[129]

In 2001, the United States Conference of Catholic Bishops issued a set of Ethical and Religious Directives for Health Care Services to guide the administration of artificial nutrition and hydration. Directive 58 states specifically:

> There should be a presumption in favor of providing nutrition and hydration to all patients including patients who require medically assisted nutrition and hydration as long as this is of sufficient benefit to outweigh the burdens to the patient.[130]

Interpretations of this directive acknowledge, uniformly, that where the burdens associated directly with artificial nutrition and hydration outweigh the benefits it provides or, where continued use of such procedures would be futile simply because the patient is no longer able to metabolize nutrients, such courses of medical action need not be undertaken.[131] Construed and applied as such in developing policies for the administration of Catholic hospitals, Directive 58 should not be seen as an impediment to medical judgments regarding end-of-life care. Indeed, this Directive endeavors to codify a humane and practical common-sense template which is used, routinely, in medical decision-making.[132]

Pontifical ambiguities: euthanasia by omission?

In a March 20, 2004, address to the International Congress on Life-Sustaining Treatments and The Vegetative State held in Rome, His Holiness Pope John Paul II declared that artificial hydration and nutrition must be seen as ordinary care—with any cessation and/or removal of artificial feeding tubes recognized as "euthanasia by omission."[133] Even though not an official encyclical, this statement has clouded the direction the Catholic Hospital Association (CHA)—whose membership is comprised of over five hundred American hospitals—should take on this issue.[134]

Presently, hospitals with the Association may not offer medical services forbidden by church doctrine to Catholic and non-Catholic patients alike.[135] The extent to which this pontifical statement is either accepted or implemented as doctrinal by the U.S. Conference of Catholic Bishops, has ongoing ramifications regarding the legal validity of advance health care directives within Catholic hospitals. More specifically, the effect of such directives made by individuals having decisional capacity to forgo—under specified conditions—extraordinary medical treatment designed to prolong life, becomes exceedingly problematic.[136] For the present, the CHA guidelines remain in place and allow for the termination of medical treatment in cases of hopelessness.[137]

An ethical construct for decision-making

When does treatment become futile? Stated otherwise, when does the medical futility of existence become so obvious that sustaining it becomes useless or, indeed, of no socio-legal, philosophical, ethical, or religious "value"?

The concepts of ordinary versus extraordinary lifesaving treatment must be recognized as highly relative or situational—not only as to time and locale, but also in their application to individual cases. Indeed, both of these concepts have the ultimate effect of serving as value judgments which determine whether a given modality of treatment poses an undue hardship on the patient or provides positive hope for a direct and positive benefit. Accordingly, if a particular mode of either medical or surgical intervention imposes either too great a burden on the patient, or offers no reasonable hope of beneficial recovery, such treatment could be classified as extraordinary, and thus, non-obligatory. This determination is essentially a quality of life statement. In reaching it, either knowingly or unknowingly, a substituted judgment is made that if the proxy decision-maker were in a similar situation to the patient, he would (or would not) wish to survive in such a state of impairment. Alternatively, a best interests standard could be utilized with the central question being: what course of action is in the patient's best interests?[138]

The basic ethical goals of man should be to respect, safeguard, and advance individual autonomy, seek equity and justice in dealing with one another, and undertake beneficent actions which minimize human suffering and seek to actualize the social utility of the purposes of life. From a Judeo-Christian perspective, the meaning of life is tied to two inextricable components of love: love of God and love of neighbor—for it is through love of others that God is, in turn, recognized and loved.[139] Under this interpretation, the very meaning of life is to be found in human relationships and the qualities of respect, concern, compassion, and justice that support these associations or relationships.[140]

Social justice

Under the theory of social justice, each individual is recognized as having an equal opportunity to maximize his potential. A point may be reached, however, where maintenance of an individual defies the very concepts of humanitarianism and justice. Accordingly, when an individual's medical condition reaches a level where it represents a complete negation of those qualities associated with being a human and maintaining a "relational-potential"[141] with others, the best and most reasonably prudent decision regarding treatment would be that it not be undertaken or that it be withdrawn and only palliative care be administered.[142] When maintenance of life means the prolongation of pain, with little or no chance of a real or sustainable level of qualitative recovery, there is no opportunity to grasp or seek the overall meaning of life or "relational-potential," or to seek "growth in love of God and neighbor" through continued human relationships. At this point, such actions should be recognized as being futile and cease.[143]

In attempting to structure an ethical construct for decision-making in critical at-risk cases, a balancing test should be utilized that weighs the gravity of the harm in allowing lifesaving actions versus the utility of the benefits stemming from the actions. Accordingly, the gravity of the harm would be assessed in terms of not only social and economic costs that might induce serious financial hardships to all members of the primary or afflicted interest group (*e.g.*, the family), but the religious, philosophical, and ethical "costs" (or compromises) as well. The utility of the benefits would be measured in terms of an evaluation of the positive consequences that flow to the threatened individual and to society. In truth, then, this balancing test seeks to arrive at a cost-effective decision through a cost-benefit analysis.[144]

In order to strengthen and add substance to the balancing test, a number of specific factors may be considered or utilized. Indeed, the late Dr. Joseph Fletcher, an Anglican priest, posited a number of such factors that he termed, alternatively, as qualities or indicators of humanhood.[145] The central most factor to be considered in any balancing equation is whether the at-risk patient has a functioning cerebral cortex—for, without it, one is "nonexistent and an object rather than subject." Minimal intelligence combines with rationality to build self-awareness and self-control, as well as an ability to be emotive and intuitive. Other factors of importance include: time consciousness, a sense of futurity tied to a theological assertion, a sense of the past, the ability to display curiosity instead of indifference, changeability, a capability to relate to others, compassion or an ability to express concern for others, an ability to communicate, the ability to be idiomorphous or distinctive, and the ability to assert control in life-directing situations and not display utter helplessness.[146]

Taken together, the Fletcher indicators present a test of humanhood which is shaped by the exigencies of each clinical situation. As such, these factors are shaped or even controlled by a situational ethic which adapts flexibly to each individual problem instead of being directed uniformly by a rigid and unyielding *a priori* ethical standard. Driven by a case-by-case methodology, the boundaries of the situation ethic are incapable of absolute determination. Yet, the basic norm used in decision-making will be love, human compassion, common dignity or simply mercy.[147]

Some of the indicators of humanhood may have greater or lesser significance depending upon the diagnosis and prognosis of each case and the balance sought to struck. For example, some patients and their families might well make trade-offs, desiring to place greater value and emphasis on self-control over a sense of the past and an ability to be emotive and intuitive. Other patients and families may value an ability to communicate over compassion and the ability to express concern for others. In employing the standard of reasonableness as the linchpin in any ultimate medical decision regarding the continuation of medical treatment or the recognition that such would be medically futile, two primary questions under the ethical construct for decision-making are proposed: (1) whether the medically at-risk individual possesses a real likelihood of sustaining a "relational-potential" with others; and (2) whether the present or proposed course of medical treatment not only minimizes suffering, but also seeks to maximize the potential utility of a life that functions at qualitative levels of cognition.[148]

Cases in point

Three paradigmatic examples may now be presented which show the scope, the complexity, and the need for basic common sense together with a sense of compassion or mercy in palliative care management.

The Switzerland decision

It was announced in February, 2007, Switzerland's high court, the Bundesgericht, or Supreme Court, held that—under appropriate conditions—

people with serious mental illnesses could receive assistance to die—this, in a country where physician-assisted suicide for a terminally ill patient is, under certain circumstances, allowed. The effect of this decision is to place mental illness on the same level as physical ones.[149]

In this case, a 53-year-old Swiss national suffering from a bipolar disorder, who had attempted suicide on several previous occasions, joined an association called "Dignitas" from which he learned how to end his life. In order to take this step, he was advised to obtain 15 grams of sodium phenobarbital which he could in fact obtain without a prescription. He followed the procedure necessary to make application for the drug and stated, voluntarily, his intention to obtain this chemical through Dignitas. His application was denied by the Health Directorate for Zurich on the grounds that that drug was an addictive, psychotropic chemical which could be obtained properly only with a doctor's prescription.

The High Court found that severe psychic illness can—as with physical illness—rob a patient of his will to live. In some cases of this nature, the use of sodium phenobarbital is not contraindicated or foreclosed as a violation of a physician's ethical duties. An important distinction should be drawn, however, between someone wishing to die because of a curable psychic illness and someone who wishes to undertake the same act, is competent, and resolves this course of action after a medical evaluation.

A medical evaluation, in situations of this nature, needs to be supported through expert psychological opinion. The responsibility for the proper administration of sodium phenobarbital cannot be delegated to a suicide assistance organization such as Dignitas or Exit, for example. Indeed, in order to validate the genuineness of the suicide desire and test the competence of the individual requesting assistance in ending his life, examination and determination must be made by medical specialists and not by organizations who seek to accommodate, on demand, suicide assistance.

Professor Arthur Caplan of the Bioethics Center at the University of Pennsylvania, cautioned that if this policy were to be implemented widely in Switzerland or, for that matter, elsewhere, it would place physicians in a most difficult position: namely, "distinguishing 'competent' requests from persons with mental illness from 'incompetent' or 'temporarily desperate' persons with mental illness—something psychiatry and psychology are not always adept at doing."[150] Dr. Caplan continued by observing that this High Court ruling allows anyone alleging that they are suffering unbearable psychological or emotional pain, to request assistance in dying—pain, as such, for example, from burns disfigurement, or emotional trauma occasioned by the loss of a child or spouse or even from career setbacks or failure.[151]

The Netherlands legalized euthanasia in 2001 and Belgium followed suit in 2002.[152] Interestingly, in 2006, the University of Lausanne announced that it would allow terminally ill mentally stable patients to undertake assisted suicide within the hospital, itself. As such, it became the first hospital in Europe to allow this.[153]

The Katrina tragedy

In the aftermath of Hurricane Katrina in Louisiana, on July 19, 2006, the Attorney General of the State ordered charges of "Mercy Killing" filed against a physician and two nurses in New Orleans who injected four patients with a combination of morphine and midazolam. As many as 14 bodies showed indications that lethal doses of drugs had been administered. In combination, these drugs are administered routinely to relieve pain or anxiety.[154]

The patients who died, ranging from 61 to 90 years of age, were literally stranded on the seventh floor of Memorial Medical Center in a long-term care unit. In all, some 250 patients were unable to leave the hospital because of high flood waters. The four patients at the center of the controversy were among 24 who died on the seventh floor. Because of their chronic medical needs, the seventh floor patients were non-ambulatory and in need of supportive care. None were considered in imminent danger of dying, however, prior to the onset of the hurricane.[155] Inside the hospital, itself, the temperature rose to 100 degrees, there was no electricity and no waste disposal system. In a word, the hospital was in a crisis, yet none of the patients had asked for assistance in euthanizing themselves.[156]

The stranded patients were *triaged* or rated according to their potential for survival.[157] "Red" was the color used to denote critical care; "black" meant moribund with only comfort care administered. The salvageable were, over time, put on helicopters and transferred to a local airport where the airport personnel re-evaluated them again before routing them to other health care facilities outside of New Orleans. Some of these patients rated red and needing critical care, were classified as moribund or black and not given heroic treatments. Different levels of care were given according to the availability of medical resources at specific locations.[158]

Should the physician and her two nurses been seen as murderers or, as humane physicians acting in a manner justified medically under the circumstances? Is this not a direct case in point for application of the principle of ethical futility? Rather than being vilified as criminals, the physician and her nurses acted with humaneness, compassion, and mercy in sedating their moribund patients trapped on the seventh floor of Memorial Hospital. Common sense and decency prevailed, ultimately, and the physician and the nurses were exonerated—this, as a consequence of a New Orleans Grand Jury's refusal to indict them.[159]

Emilio's case

On December 28, 2006, Emilio Gonzales was born in Children's Hospital in Austin, Texas. He was placed in a pediatric intensive care unit where he slept most of his days—a sleep induced by pharmacological agents. Emilio was tethered to a respirator so that he could breathe. In March, 2007, Emilio's case was declared to be futile and, thus, within the provisions of the Texas Futile-Care

Law, allowed the hospital to request Emilio's mother to find—within ten days—another facility to accept and care for him. This case was complicated by the fact that although the baby did not meet the criteria to be declared brain dead, he was diagnosed with a terminal neurometabolic disorder termed Leigh's disease. In order to sustain Emilio, a transferring hospital would have been required to perform a tracheotomy and insert and maintain a feeding tube. Continuing treatment of this nature is not only potentially painful but purely palliative and has no curative value. Thirty-one health care facilities were contacted regarding transfer care for Emilio—with none of them agreeing to accept him as a patient.[160]

Texas is one of four states,[161] in addition to Colorado,[162] Florida,[163] and Virginia,[164] which has enacted futile care legislation. Under the Texas law, a hospital ethics committee is empowered to declare the care of a terminally ill patient to be of no medical benefit and to discontinue care, accordingly, as seen, within a ten-day time frame. Within that limit, the family is required to find a medical facility willing to accept their terminal relative. If no transfer can be arranged, the hospital may proceed to withdraw life support.[165] Colorado allows transfer care for patients in a terminal condition or persistent vegetative state but does not set a specific time frame to effect such a transfer.[166] Florida allows a health care provider to transfer a patient, within seven days, if it is unable—for moral or ethical reasons—to comply with a patient's advance directive or treatment decision made by a surrogate decision-maker.[167] In Virginia, the transfer period is 14 days after a futile care determination is made.[168]

In a 2005 report by the National Right to Life Committee, 11 states were found to have legislation requiring patient care (consisting of life-sustaining treatment)—with no interruption—until a transfer is completed. Seventeen other states, together with the District of Columbia, have laws which mandate treatment pending a patient's transfer yet, interestingly, do not define the type of treatment required. Twenty-two other states have laws addressing the issue but are complex and even ambiguous regarding whether treatment pending a transfer need be provided.[169]

Led by the group, Texas Right to Life, and others, Texas legislators were lobbied to change the present futile care law so that no deadline could be imposed until an actual patient transfer was made. The lead attorney in the Emilio Gonzales case framed the issue thusly: "The benefit of treatment for this child is continued life. Yes, he will never be a normal little boy, but there are plenty of people out there who are not normal but continue life and enjoy it to the level they are capable of."[170]

In mid May, 2007, the Texas Senate approved an amendment to the futility law by extending the period of medical evaluation from ten days to twenty-one, thus barring any transfer until this period of time had elapsed.[171] A hospital ethics committee would, ultimately, be responsible for making the prognosis and the legislation would demand nutrition and hydration be continued regardless of a patient's classification of medical futility. Even more disconcerting, for some, was the provision within the proposed legislation which allowed for appeals by relatives to the judicial process in order to extend the life of such patients even longer.[172]

While this Senate Bill 439 was defeated subsequently, the Texas Hospital Association agreed to lengthen the time frame before life support could be withdrawn and to prepare uniform guidelines for futile care.[173] Sadly, on May 30th, the very day the Senate Bill died, so also did Emilio.[174]

Conclusion

Dying is, "[b]y and large, a messy business."[175] It is both "ugly and dirty" in a world that is intolerant of such qualities.[176] Perhaps the only true dignity found within the occurrence of death is a full appreciation of the life that precedes it.[177]

The management of death can surely be both more humane and more efficient when the principle of medical utility is harmonized with patient autonomy. By defining medical utility as the maximization of the welfare of patients in need of treatment, it is clear that criteria are essential in determining, in a fair and equitable manner, who will receive and benefit from an initial use of continuation of scarce medical resources, and conversely, who will not. Social utility is, of necessity, an integral force in framing a required balancing question which, in turn, reveals a vexatious problem: namely, finding a process or designing a template for determining how the needs and prognosis of a particular patient are weighed and evaluated against the *macro* needs of society. Stated otherwise, how can physicians serve two masters—society and patients—in determining the type and amount of medical care?

The principle of medical futility, delineated and tested in the manner proposed herein, can serve as a catalyst for public action, acceptance, or both. Furthermore, medical futility can serve as the dominant vector of force in validating the very essence of utility, and thus, resolve the inherent conflict between patient needs and greater societal goals. The fact that there is a pressing national and international need for a clear, objective, and practical definition of futility is without doubt. Yet, the reality of the situation dictates that regardless of the definition settled upon, a debate between and among the medical professionals and social policy makers will arise inevitably. The public, because of its inherent lack of sophistication in this area, will depend upon both groups to educate them and win their acceptance. To fail in this mission means, simply, an increase in suits for medical malpractice by uninformed patients and their families or proxy decision-makers.

Once defined criteria for medical futility are accepted by health care providers and the public which they serve, this restructured principle affords the ideal construct for determining the utilitarian balance between patient and majoritarian preferences, wants, or needs. It achieves this by institutionalizing a balancing point that distinguishes the medical actions agreed upon as useful, reasonable, or promotive of restorative quality with those actions not beneficial to patients or economically feasible for society to undertake. By setting forth various medical and surgical interventions not regarded as reasonable or efficacious for use by certain patients with profiles which show that there is no assurance of a sustained level of qualitative rehabilitation or salvageability, these criteria—in a real way—act as a socio-legal-medico-economic *triage*.[178]

Dr. Pellegrino suggests that the primary goal in dealing with cases of futility is achieving for the patient a level of "total good." This, in turn, is realized when a carefully calibrated balance is struck between three criteria—effectiveness, benefit, and burden—reached co-operatively within an "alliance" between the treating physician, the patient, or his surrogate decision-maker.[179] Futility is not an isolated, empirical yes/no test. Rather, each judgment of futility takes all aspects of a patient's total life experience into account—physical, mental, spiritual, and life goals. Consequently, each judgment "demands prudential assessments for a particular person in a particular experience of illness and within a particular metaphysical and theological context."[180]

Physicians must always be leery of being forced to practice "irrational medicine"—demanded by those patients, who expect "everything be done" even though treatments may be judged medically futile.[181] To attempt to demand or to order treatment when a medical condition is diagnosed as futile "violates the first principle of traditional medical ethics—beneficence"—which mandates that actions taken by a physician always be for the patient's good.[182]

Upon the acceptance or adoption of guidelines for determining futility, a three-tiered decisional structure is proposed as a mechanism for determining whether a given treatment for a given patient falls within the scope of these guidelines. Accordingly, the treating physician would be given the primary responsibility for making the decision to withdraw or withhold treatment on the grounds of futility. Although he would be under a duty not to prescribe treatment deemed futile by him, he would be obliged to inform the patient, and if necessary, the family, of this decision and its rationale. This would provide the patient and family with a basis for an "appeal" to a hospital ethics committee, if such course were elected.[183] Any further appeal from an adverse finding by the committee would be to the courts, where a limited review of the reasonableness of the decision to withdraw or withhold treatment would be undertaken.

Absent both a redefinition of death to include a PVS and a failure to achieve a broad consensus to establish criteria for treatment based upon the extent and duration of neurologic damage, perhaps a less contentious approach to the effort of redefining the principle of medical futility would be the acceptance of a presumption that those existing permanently in a vegetative state would not want to be kept alive for an indefinite period of time. Accepting this presumption would, in turn, allow a standard of adjusted care to be established which would include, routinely, cessation of treatment after a reasonable time. Although the standard of reasonableness would perforce vary with clinical conditions, it would be tied with sufficient clarity to a recognition of irreversibility. Consistent with this new medico-legal presumption, would be a shift in the burden to those wishing maintenance of a vegetative state to show that they are acting in accordance with what they know, from clear and convincing evidence, to be the wishes of the patient.[184]

Since administering futile medical treatment is tantamount to inflicting cruel and unusual punishment on patients and an abridgement of their rights of self-determination, it is incumbent upon physicians to recognize that they should accept the imposition of an affirmative legal, professional, moral, and ethical duty *not* to prescribe a modality of treatment that falls clearly within the scope of being considered futile, freakish, or torturous. The utilitarian value of a revalidated and operative principle of futility is all too apparent. Let it be used in a reasonable and compassionate manner to end the cruel punishment of terminal and hopeless cases of "human" existence and, at the same time, hopefully, give rise to an ethic of palliative care and less to a relentless pursuit of technologies that extend "life" to the point of indecency and inhumaneness.[185] Inasmuch as physicians have permitted, legally, under the rubric of "forgoing life-sustaining treatment," to end the lives of the terminally ill for over twenty-five years, it becomes "a major hypocrisy" to perpetuate distinctions among the various means used to hasten death. No real difference can be drawn truthfully between "actively hastening death" and "passively hastening death."[186]

Linguistic ambiguity has plagued the role of palliative sedation versus terminal sedation within palliative care management[187] in much the same way as it has when efforts are made to find a clear line of demarcation between physician-assisted suicide and active euthanasia.[188] Taxonomical purities are simply not to be found. Instead, shadow boxing becomes the principal spectator sport—with eyes riveted to efforts which are directed toward discerning a distressed patient's intent as to treatment or non-treatment[189] as well as that of his treating physicians.[190]

While autonomy or self-determination has, heretofore, been the cornerstone of health care management, and especially so in end-stage illness, perhaps more clarity in the whole decision-making process could be obtained if benevolence were to be either substituted for autonomy or merged into it. In this way, instead of challenging intentional acts of professional competence designed to acknowledge cases of medical futility through actions measured by mercy, compassion or charity, emphasis would be placed on a reformulated justification for palliative sedation for end-state refractory pain—either physical or psychological. Accordingly, proportionality would become pivotal in any legal, ethical, or medical inquiry[191]—with mercy, compassion, or charity being integrated with or subsumed under the inquiry as normative, operative standards for actions designed to manage pain and suffering and guided, ultimately, by a situation ethic[192] of humane adjusted care.[193]

Two ethical guidelines are seen in direct conflict when a physician is forced to deal with a patient experiencing refractory symptoms in a terminal illness:

specifically, the ethical mandate to relieve the patient's suffering and, at the same time, not cause his death.[194] While not considered absolute, these principles may not be overridden unless for compelling reasons.[195]

The balance necessary to address these conflicting guidelines is to be found in the standard of proportionality. Isolated, and indeed unshackled, from the confusing and cumbersome doctrine of double effect,[196] this standard would then become the operative policy for assessing and determining reasonable medical and ethical conduct. Thus, in dealing with the administration of opioids and sedatives intended to have therapeutic effects and unintended "side" effects which are not desired but accepted,[197] compassion, benevolence, or mercy allows a higher priority to be placed by the physician on "relieving refractory symptoms than to prolonging an existence by severe suffering for a few hours or days or even a few months."[198]

Consistent with the application of the standard of proportionality in medical decision-making, if lower doses of opioids or sedation are ineffective in addressing refractory pain, dosing may be increased. Because of varying individual responses to therapy and tolerance to analgesics, a policy setting dosage ceilings should be viewed as not only inappropriate,[199] but one lacking in compassion.

A process, if indeed not a template, for relieving a dying patient's intractable pain and suffering is—in the final analysis—to be found within detailed plans or protocols for the administration of palliative sedation. It is essential that these plans contain a realistic time-line for death and that there is provision made for requiring an understanding by the entire medical team, the patient, and immediate family and friends and, if appropriate, surrogate decision-makers, of the consequences which will flow from applying a protocol of this type.

Consideration should be given to a patient's spiritual values, psychological concerns, together with an appreciation of the parameters of nursing care for end-stage illnesses. Finally, when these factors are not only recognized but charted properly within pertinent medical records which in turn also show clearly not only the levels of monitoring to be undertaken but dosing limits,[200] an easeful death without refractory pain and existential suffering is within the reach of everyone.[201]

Notes

1 Joseph Carroll, *Public Divided Over Moral Acceptability of Doctor-Assisted Suicide*, www.gallup. com/poss/27727/public-divided-over-moral-acceptability-doctorassisted- ... (Mar. 10, 2010).

2 *Ibid.*

3 *Ibid.*

4 *Ibid.*

5 The Pew Research Center For The People and The Press, *More American Discussing—and Planning—End-of-Life Treatment*, STRONG PUBLIC SUPPORT FOR RIGHT TO DIE (Jan. 5, 2006).

6 *Ibid.* at 2.

7 *Ibid.* at 2.

8 Bruce Jennings, *et al.*, *Access to Hospice Care: Expanding Boundaries, Overcoming Barriers*, 33 HASTINGS CENTER RPT. S3 (Special Supp. 2003). See Peter A. Singer, *et al.*, *Quality of End-of-Life Care*, 282 JAMA 163 (Jan. 13, 1999).

9 Thomas H. Murray & Bruce Jennings, *The Quest to Reform End of Life Care: Rethinking Assumptions and Setting New Directions*, 35 HASTINGS CENTER RPT. S52, S54 (2005).

10 *See* JOANNE LYNN, SICK TO DEATH–AND NOT GOING TO TAKE IT ANY-MORE (2004).

11 Murray & Jennings, *supra* note 9 at S54.

12 LYNN, *supra* note 10 at 12.

13 *See* HOSPICE: THE LIVING IDEA (Cicely Saunders, Dorothy H. Summers & Neville Teller eds. 1981); Margaret A. Crowley, *The Hospice Movement: A Renewed View of The Death Process*, 4 J. CONTEMP. HEALTH L. & POL'Y 295 (1988).

14 Cicely Saunders, *Spiritual Pain*, 4 J. PALLIATIVE CARE 29 (1988). *See* also Richard B. Fife, *Are Existential Questions the Norm for Terminally Ill Patients?* 5 J. PALLIATIVE MED. 815, 817 (2002).

15 Stein Kaasa & Jon Loge, *Quality of Life in Palliative Care: Principles and Practice*, 17 PAL-LIATIVE MED. 11 (2003).

16 Steven Tudor, *Modes of Mercy*, 28 AUSTRALIAN J. LEGAL PHIL. 79, 100 (2003). *See also* STEVEN TUDOR, COMPASSION AND REMORSE: ACKNOWLEDGING THE SUFFERING OTHER (2001).

17 Tudor classifies mercy as: magnanimous; stoic; pardoning; exploitative; favoring; compromising; unconfident; reforming; forgiving and compassionate. *Ibid., Modes of Mercy* at 89–100.

18 MARGARET P. BATTIN, ENDING LIFE: ETHICS AND THE WAY WE DIE 66 (2005). *See* George P. Smith, II, Monograph, WHEN MERCY SEASONS JUSTICE (2007).

19 DAVID C. THOMASMA & GLEN C. GRABER, EUTHANASIA: TOWARD AN ETHICAL SOCIAL POLICY 129 (1990).

20 *See* Sidney Wanzer, *et al.*, *The Physicians Responsibility Toward Hopelessly Ill Patients: A Second Look*, 320 N. ENGL. J. MED. 844 (Mar. 30, 1989); Marc Sapir, *The Spectrum of Medical Care: Curative, Rehabilitative and Palliative*, 279 JAMA 20 (1998).

21 THOMASMA & GRABER, *supra* note 19.

22 *Modes of Mercy, supra* note 16, at 95. *See also* Patrick Guinan, *The Christian Origin of Medical Compassion*, 5 NAT'L CATHOLIC BIOETHICS Q. 21 (2005).

23 *Modes of Mercy, ibid.* at 81.

24 L. VAN ZYL, DEATH AND COMPASSION: A VIRTUE BASED APPROACH TO EUTHANASIA 197 (2000).

25 Edmund D. Pellegrino, *Decisions at the End of Life: The Use and Abuse of the Concept of Futility* in THE DIGNITY OF THE DYING PERSON (Proceedings of the Fifth Assembly of the Pontifical Academy of Life, Feb. 1999), at 219–41 (J.V. Correa & E. Sgreccia eds. 2000).

26 *Ibid.* at 225, 241.

27 Lois Shepherd, *Sophie's Choice: Medical and Legal Responses to Suffering*, 72 NOTRE DAME L. REV. 103, 106, 119 (1996).

28 Lois Shepherd, *Dignity and Autonomy after Washington Glucksberg: An Essay about Abortion, Death and Crime*, 7 CORNELL J. L. & PUB. POL'Y 431, 465–66 (1998).

29 Pellegrino, *supra* note 25.

30 DEREK HUMPHRY, FINAL EXISTS 135–36 (1991).

31 Ruth Macklin, *Reflections on the Human Dignity Symposium: Is Dignity a Useless Concept?* 20 PALLIATIVE CARE 212 (2004).

32 *Ibid.* at 212. *See* DIGNITY AND DYING: A CHRISTIAN APPRAISAL (John F. Kilner, *et al.*, eds. 1996).

33 Macklin, *supra* note 31 at 212 *passim.*

34 Annette F. Street, *Constructions of Dignity in End-of-Life Care*, 17 J. PALLIATIVE CARE 93, 95, 99 (2001).

35 BATTIN, *supra* note 18 at 80.

36 *Ibid.* See also Lois Shepherd, *Face to Face: A Call for Radical Responsibility in Place of Compassion*, 77 ST. JOHN'S L. REV. 445 (2003).

37 *See* BATTIN, *supra* note 18 at 90.

38 Lawrence J. Schneiderman & Nancy Jecker, *Futility in Practice*, 153 ARCH. INTERN. MED. 437, 440 (1993) (stating that "overwhelming agreement has been reached in the medical community that physicians are not required to provide futile treatment").
  A physician has no duty to continue treatment, once it has proven to be ineffective. Although there may be a duty to provide life-sustaining machinery in the *immediate* aftermath of a cardio-respiratory arrest, there is no duty to continue its use once it has become futile in the opinion of qualified medical personnel. Barber v. Superior Court, 147 Cal. App. 3d 1006, 1017–18 (1983). "[I]f a treatment is clearly futile ... there is no obligation to provide the treatment." Nancy S. Jecker & Lawrence J. Schneiderman, *Medical Futility: The Duty Not to Treat*, 2 CAMB. Q. HEALTHCARE ETHICS 151, 156 (quoting THE HASTINGS CENTER, GUIDELINES ON THE TERMINATION OF LIFE-SUSTAINING TREATMENT AND THE CARE OF THE DYING 19 (1987)).

39 Council on Ethical and Judicial Affairs, American Medical Association, *Current Opinion*, 2.03, CODE OF MEDICAL ETHICS (1994).

40 *Ibid.*, *Opinion* 2.035 ("Futility").

41 BARRY R. FURROW, *ET AL.*, BIOETHICS: HEALTH CARE LAW AND ETHICS (5th ed. 2004) at 310.

42 *See* George P. Smith, II, *Utility and The Principles of Medical Futility: Safeguarding Autonomy and the Prohibition Against Cruel and Unusual Punishment*, 12 J. CONTEMP. HEALTH L. & POL'Y. 1 (1995). *See* Amir Halevy, *Medical Futility, Patient Autonomy, and Professional Integrity: Finding the Appropriate Balance*, 18 HEALTH MATRIX 261 (2008).

43 Robert D. Truog, *et al.*, *Sounding Board: The Problems with Futility*, 326 N. ENGL. J. MED. 1560 (1992).

44 *See* Marcia Angell, *The Case of Helga Wanglie: A New Kind of 'Right to Die' Case*, 325 N. ENGL. J. MED. 511, 512 (1991).

45 Sidney H. Wanzer, *The Physician's Responsibility Toward Hopelessly Ill Patients*, 310 N. ENGL. J. MED. 955, 958 (1984).

46 *See* DANIEL CALLAHAN, SETTING LIMITS: MEDICAL GOALS IN AN AGING SOCIETY, 181 (1988). *See generally* GEORGE P. SMITH, II, LEGAL AND HEALTH-CARE ETHICS FOR THE ELDERLY (1996).

47 Nancy K. Rhoden, *Litigating Life and Death*, 102 HARV. L. REV. 375, 442–43 (1988).

48 *See* Marni J. Bonnin *et al.*, *District Criteria for Termination of Resuscitation in the Out-of-Hospital Setting*, 270 JAMA 1457 (1993).

49 *See* Kathleen Boozang, *Death Wish: Resuscitating Self-Determination for the Critically Ill*, 35 ARIZ. L. REV. 23 (1993).

50 Lawrence J. Schneiderman *et al.*, *Medical Futility: Its Meaning and Ethical Implications*, 112 ANNALS INTERNAL MED. 949 (1990).
  It has been suggested that the ethical principle of autonomy should be re-shaped and thus redefined as the principle of relational authority. Accordingly, a variety of relationships a patient experiences are obligations he assumes would be factored into health care decisions. Communitarian ideals would, thus, direct ultimate actions rather than individualistic concepts. HERRING, *infra* note 52 at 125–30. *But see* GEORGE J. ANNAS, THE RIGHTS OF PATIENTS 122 (3rd ed. 2004) suggesting rather than emphasizing patient autonomy and access to information, sick people prefer kindness and caring from their health care providers.

51 497 U.S. 261 at 288, 289 (1990). In 1999, the British Medical Association defined medical treatment to include food and water delivered through a tube. It went further and endorsed the withholding and/or withdrawal of tube-delivered food and water not only

186 Law and Bioethics

from patients in persistent vegetative states, but from those suffering from severe dementia or serious stroke. KEOWN, *infra* note 52 at 20.

52 JONATHAN HERRING, MEDICAL LAW AND ETHICS 421, 482 (2006). *See also* JOHN KEOWN, EUTHANASIA, ETHICS AND PUBLIC POLICY: AN ARGUMENT AGAINST LEGISLATION 58 *passim* (2002).

53 Nancy S. Jecker & Robert A. Pearlman, *Medical Futility: Who Decides?* 152 ARCHIVES INTERNAL MED. 1140, 1142 (1992).

54 *See* Lance K. Stell, *Stopping Treatment on the Grounds of Futility: A Role for Institutional Policy,* 11 ST. LOUIS U. PUB. L. REV. 481, 484 (1992).

55 Schneiderman, *supra* note 50 at 950.

56 *See generally* Edmund D. Pellegrino, *Patient and Physician Autonomy: Conflicting Rights and Obligations in the Physician-Patient Relationship,* 10 J. CONTEMP. HEALTH L. & POL'Y 47 (1993).

57 Stuart J. Younger, *Futility in Context,* 264 JAMA 1295 (1990).

58 Schneiderman, *supra* note 50 at 950.

59 *Ibid.* at 953. Under the Uniform Health Care Decisions Act, the health care provider may decline to comply with instructions which would be "medically ineffective" (§13(d)), contrary to generally accepted "health care standards" (§§7(f), 13(d)) or be in violations of "conscience" (§7(c)). 9 UNIF. LAWS ANN. 93 (1993). *See also supra* note 39.

60 Stell, *supra* note 54 at 487–88.

61 Jecker & Schneiderman, *supra* note 38 at 155.

62 *Ibid.* at 155.

63 *Ibid.*

64 BATTIN, *supra* note 18 at 309.

65 *Ibid.*

66 *Ibid.* at 311.
   When used in patients dying of some underlying fatal disease or when the heart muscle is, itself, damaged seriously, cardiopulmonary resuscitation is of dubious, or little—if any—value at all. Pellegrino, *supra* note 25 at 219–41.

67 *See* George P. Smith, II, *The Ethics of Ethics Committees,* 6 J. CONTEMP. HEALTH L. & POL'Y 157 (1990). Iowa allows for substitute medical decision-making boards who are empowered to make health care decisions for any individual who is medically incompetent and who does not have a guardian or family member to assist him. IOWA CODE §§135.28–29 (2009). These boards are not authorized to make decisions which would discontinue life sustaining treatment, however. IOWA ADMIN. CODE §641–85.2(5) (2009). New York has a Surrogate Decision Making Committee Program which makes decisions for persons with mental disability who reside in state-operated or state-licensed facilities. N.Y. COMP. CODES R. & REGS., tit. 14, §710.0 (2009).

68 JOSEPH J. FINS, A PALLIATIVE ETHIC OF CARE 85 (2006).

69 *Ibid.* at 86.

70 *Ibid.*

71 *See* Margaret A. Somerville, *The Song of Death: The Lyrics of Euthanasia,* 9 J. CONTEMP. HEALTH L. & POL'Y 1, 74 (1993).

72 *See* HELGA KUHSE, THE SANCTITY-OF-LIFE DOCTRINE IN MEDICINE (1987).

73 Paul Rousseau, *Existential Suffering and Palliative Sedation: A Brief Commentary with a Proposal for Clinical Guidelines,* 18 AM. J. HOSPICE & PALLIATIVE CARE 151 (May/Jun. 2001). *See* George P. Smith, II, *"Refractory Pain, Existential Suffering and Palliative Care: Releasing The Unbearable Lightness of Being,"* 20 CORNELL J. L. & PUB. POL'Y 469 (2011).

74 Washington v. Glucksberg, 521 U.S. 702 (1997). In a companion case, Vacco v. Quill, a New York state prohibition on assisting suicide was found not violative of the Equal Protection Clause of the 14th Amendment, 531 U.S. 793 (1997). *See generally,* Rob McStay, *Terminal Sedation: Palliative Care for Intractable Pain, Post Glucksberg and Quill,* 29 AM. J. L. & MED. 45 (2003).

75 521 U.S. at 736, 737, O'Connor, J.
76 HERRING, *supra* note 52 at 426, 427. *See also* ch. 8 for an expanded analysis.
77 Arthur G. Lipman, *Pain as a Human Right: The 2004 Global Day against Pain*, 19 J. PAIN & PALLIATIVE CARE PHARMACOTHERAPY 85 (2005).
78 *Ibid.* at 88.
79 *Ibid.* at 90.
80 *Doctors Change Euthanasia Stance*, BBC NEWS, http://news.bbc.co.uk/2/hi/health/51239 74.stm (accessed June 30, 2006).
81 Minette Marrin, *An Acceptable Way to Arrange our Death*, www.timesonline.co.uk /article/ O,2088–2179494,00.html (accessed May 16, 2006).
82 Bernard Lo & Gordon Rubenfeld, *Palliative Sedation in Dying Patients*, 294 JAMA 1810, 1815 (Oct. 12, 2005).
83 Marrin, *supra* note 81.
84 *Ibid.*
85 *Ibid.*
86 Timothy E. Quill, Rebecca Dresser & Dan W. Brock, *The Rule of Double Effect – A Critique of Its Role in End-of-Life Decision Making*, 337 N. ENGL. J. MED. 1768 (1997).
87 *Ibid.*
88 FIONA RANDALL & ROBIN S. DOWNIE, PALLIATIVE CARE ETHICS: A GOOD COMPANION, at 23 (1996).
89 FURROW, *ET AL.*, *supra* note 41 at 10.
90 Quill *et al.*, *supra* note 86.
91 *Ibid.* Standing alone, without being tethered to the second condition, the undergirding policy supporting the principle of double effect is to be seen as validating ethically the use of medication in controlling pain—even when death may result. DAVID C. THOMASMA, HUMAN LIFE IN THE BALANCE 176 (1990).
92 RANDALL & DOWNIE *supra* note 88 at 74. *See also* GEORGE P. SMITH, II, LEGAL AND HEALTHCARE FOR THE ELDERLY 111–19 (1996).
93 RANDALL & DOWNIE, *supra* note 88 at 74.
94 *Ibid.*
95 *Ibid. See generally* James L. Bernat, *Chronic Disorders of Consciousness*, 367 THE LANCET 1181 (Apr. 8, 2006); Christine Laine & Frank Davidoff, *Patient-Centered Medicine: A Professional Evolution*, 275 JAMA 152 (1996).
96 RANDALL & DOWNIE, *supra* note 88 at 74.
97 *Ibid.*
98 *Ibid. See* Daniel Callahan, *Terminal Sedation and The Artefactual Fallacy* in TERMINAL SEDATION: EUTHANASIA IN DISGUISE at ch. 9 (Torbjorn Tannajo ed. 2004).
99 RANDALL & DOWNIE, *supra* note 88 at 74.
100 *Ibid.*
101 *Ibid.*
102 Suzanne Ost, *Euthanasia and The Defense of Necessity: Advocating a More Appropriate Legal Response* in THE CRIMINAL JUSTICE SYSTEM AND HEALTH CARE LAW at 103 (Charles A. Erin & Suzanne Ost, eds. 2007).
103 *Ibid.* at 103–4.
104 John F. Kavanaugh, *S.J., Killing and Letting Die*, AMERICA, Sept. 23, 2000, at 23. *But see* Edmund D. Pellegrino, *The Place of Intention in The Moral Assessment of Assisted Suicide and Active Euthanasia* in INTENDING DEATH: THE ETHICS OF ASSISTED SUICIDE AND EUTHANASIA at 163 (Tom L. Beauchamp ed. 1995) (arguing that both intention and intentionality are "integral elements in the nature of moral acts").
105 *See generally* Ronald B. Miller, *Physician Orders to Supplement Advance Directions: Rescuing Patient Autonomy*, 20 J. CLIN. ETHICS 212 (2009).
106 R (on the application of Burke) v. General Medical Council [2005] EWCA CIV. 1003; [2006] QB 273 [2005] 3 FCR 169, 85 BMLR.
107 *Ibid.*

108 Steve Doughty, *Patient Loses His Last Plea to Stop Doctors from Letting Him Die*, DAILY MAIL, Aug. 9, 2006, at 24.

109 Sam Lister, *Minister Puts a Price on The Right to Life*, www.timesonline.co.uk/article/0,2–1618268,00.html (May 19, 2005).

110 *Ibid.*

111 *Ibid.*

112 The Policy Guidelines may be found at: www.cps.gov.uk/publications/prosecution/assisted_suicide_policy.html (Feb. 25, 2010).

113 *Ibid.*

114 www.guardian.co.uk/society/2010/feb/02/terry-pratchett-assisted-suicide-tribunal (Feb. 2, 2010).

115 *Ibid. See* Smith, *supra* note 67.

116 *Ibid.*

117 *Ibid.*

118 *Ibid.*

119 *Ibid.*

120 *Ibid.*

121 Pellegrino, *supra* note 25 at 219.

122 *Ibid.* at 229.

123 *Ibid.*

124 LOIS SHEPHERD, IF THAT EVER HAPPENS TO ME: MAKING LIFE AND DEATH DECISIONS AFTER TERRI SHIAVO 148–53 (2009).

125 Lois Shepherd, *Asking Too Much: Autonomy and Responsibility in The End of Life*, 26 J. CONTEMP. HEALTH L. & POL'Y 72, 75 (2010).

126 Kevin D. O'Rourke, O.P., *When to Withdraw Life Support?* 8 NAT'L CATH. BIOETHICS Q. 663, 671 (2008).

127 Alan Sanders, *The Clinical Reality of Artificial Nutrition and Hydration for Patients at The End of Life*, 9 NAT'L CATH. BIOETHICS Q. 293, 364 (2009).

128 O'Rourke, *supra* note 126 at 671.
     If the hope of benefit or degree of burden of a medical treatment changes with time, this may serve to validate a withdrawal of life supports. *Ibid.*

129 THOMASMA & GRABER *supra* note 19.

130 Directive 58, U.S. Conf. of Catholic Bishops, ETHICAL & RELIGIOUS DIRECTIVES FOR CATHOLIC HEALTH CARE SERVICES (4th ed. 2001).

131 ARTIFICIAL NUTRITION AND HYDRATION: THE NEW CATHOLIC DEBATE (Christopher Tollefsen ed. 2008); O'Rourke, *supra* note 126 at 671. *See generally* John H. Connery, *Prolonging Life: The Duty and Its Limits*, 47 LINACRE Q. 151 (1980).

132 GEORGE P. SMITH, II, THE CHRISTIAN RELIGION AND BIOTECHNOLOGY: A SEARCH FOR PRINCIPLED DECISION MAKING 215–17 (2005).

133 *Ibid.* at 216.

134 *Ibid.*

135 *Ibid.*

136 *See generally* Miller, *supra* note 105.

137 Smith, *supra* note 132.

138 TOM L. BEAUCHAMP & JAMES F. CHILDRESS, PRINCIPLES OF BIOMEDICAL ETHICS at 171–73 (3rd ed. 1989).

139 Richard A. McCormick, S.J., *To Save or Let Die: The Dilemma of Modern Medicine*, in HOW BRAVE A NEW WORLD? at 346 (Richard A. McCormick ed. 1981).

140 *Ibid.*

141 *Ibid.* at 347.

142 *See* GEORGE P. SMITH, II, FINAL CHOICES: AUTONOMY IN HEALTH CARE DECISIONS ch. 4 (1989).

143 McCormick, *supra* note 139 at 347.

144 George P. Smith, II, *Quality of Life, Sanctity of Creation: Palliative or Apotheosis*, 63 NEB. L. REV. 709, 734 (1984). *See, Is The Sanctity of Life Ethic Terminally Ill?*, in WRITINGS ON AN ETHICAL LIFE at 170–85 (Peter Singer, ed. 2000).

145 Joseph Fletcher, *Indicators of Humanhood: A Tentative Profile of Man*, 2 HASTINGS CENTER RPT. 1 (Nov. 1972).

146 *Ibid.* at 1–3.

147 BATTIN, *supra* note 18 at 8. *See* JOSEPH FLETCHER, SITUATION ETHICS: THE NEW MORALITY (1966); Joseph Fletcher, *Love is The Only Measure*, 83 COMMONWEALTH 427 (1966).

148 Smith, *supra* note 92 at 734–35.

149 X v. Health Directorate of Zurich, Feb., 2006 (Peter B. Rutledge transl.). *See* www.bger. ch/index/jurisdiction/jurisdiction-inherit-template/jurisdiction-recht/jurisdiction-recht-urteile 2000.htm. *See* also www.findlaw.com/12international/countries/ch.html (Swiss Supreme Court). Jacob M. Appel, *A Suicide Right for The Mentally Ill: A Swiss Case Opens The Debate*, 37 HASTINGS CENTER RPT. 21 (May-Jun. 2007).

150 AP, *Mentally Ill in Switzerland Could Win Right to Die*, www.msnbc.msn.com/ud/ 16951542/print/1/displaymode/1098/ (Mar. 8, 2007).

151 *Ibid.*

152 For a discussion of the European approach to patient's rights to self-determination, *see* TIMOTHY S. JOST, READINGS IN COMPARATIVE HEALTH LAW AND BIOETHICS at 278–340 (2nd ed. 2007).

153 *Desperate Battle for Death With Dignity*, YORKSHIRE POST, Feb. 13, 2007, at 1. *See* Greg A. Sachs, *Dying From Dementia*, 361 N. ENGL. J. MED. 1595 (Oct. 15, 2009) (arguing for the need to recognize the terminal nature of advanced dementia and thus treat it as a terminal illness requiring palliative care). *See* R. Sean Morrison & Albert L. Sui, *Survival in End-Stage Dementia Following Acute Illness*, 284 JAMA 47 (Jul. 5, 2000) (finding that when patients with advanced dementia develop a superimposed acute illness—*e.g.*, hip fracture or pneumonia—they face a very poor prognosis with survival being limited and suggesting palliative or comfort care should be the preferred treatment in these cases).

154 Peter Whoriskey & Catherine Skipp, *3 Arrested in New Orleans Hospital Deaths*, WASH. POST, Jul. 19, 2006, at A3. *See* Fredericka K. Shea, *Hurricane Katrina and the Legal and Bioethical Implications of Involuntary Euthanasia as a Component of Disaster Management in Extreme Emergency Situations*, 19 ANNALS HEALTH L. 133 (2010).

155 Tyler J. Curiel, *Murder or Mercy: Hurricane Katrina and The Need for Disaster Training*, 355 N. ENGL. J. MED. 2067 (Nov. 16, 2006).

156 *Ibid.* at 2068.

157 George P. Smith, II, *Triage: Endgame Realities*, 1 J. CONTEMP. HEALTH L. & POL'Y 143 (1985).

158 Whoriskey & Skipp, *supra* note 154.

159 Gavin Filosa, *No Charges Filed against Doctor in Memorial Case*, THE TIMES PICAYUNE, Jul. 24, 2007, at 1. *See* Shea, *supra* note 154.

160 Sylvia Moreno, *Case Puts Texas Futile-Treatment Law Under a Microscope*, WASH. POST, Apr. 11, 2007, at A3.

161 TEX. CODE ANN., Health & Safety, § 166.046 (Vernon's 2010).

162 COLO. REV. STAT., §15–18–113(5) (2010), Colorado Medical Treatment Decision Act, as repealed and re-enacted.

163 FLA. STAT. ANN. §765.1105 (2010).

164 VA. CODE ANN. § 54.1–2987 (2009).

165 TEX. CODE ANN., *supra* note 161.

166 COLO. REV. STAT., *supra* note 162.

167 FLA. STAT. ANN., *supra* note 163.

168 VA. CODE ANN., *supra* note 164.

169 Moreno, *supra* note 160. An updated list of the states within these classifications is to be found at www.nrlc.org/euthanasia/AdvancedDirectives/ReportRevised2007 (accessed May 24, 2010).

170 *Ibid. See* Emily Ramshaw, *Bills Challenge Care Limits for Terminal Patients*, DALLAS MORNING NEWS, Feb. 15, 2007, at A1 (providing statistics which set the costs for providing life-sustaining treatment to individuals in a vegetative state at between $60,000.00 and $80,000.00 and observing in most cases of this nature, a private insurer or the government handles them as charities).

    Medicare expenditures are significant for end-of-life care for chronic diseases (diabetes, cancer, and heart disease) ranging from $28,763.00 to $52,911.00—with most of this care being given in hospital. Robert Pear, *Researches Find Huge Variations in End-of-Life Treatment*, N.Y. TIMES, Apr. 7, 2008, at A17.

171 Emily Ramshaw, *Senate OKs Longer End-of-Life Care*, DALLAS MORNING NEWS, May 15, 2007, at A4.

172 *Ibid.*

173 Todd Ackerman, *Futile Care Bill Dead*, HOUSTON CHRONICLE, May 30, 2007, at A1.

174 Michael Grabell, *Boy Dies After Dispute*, DALLAS MORNING NEWS, May 31, 2007, at B1.

175 SHERWIN B. NULAND, HOW WE DIE: REFLECTIONS ON LIFE'S FINAL CHAPTER at 142 (1994).

176 *Ibid.* at 255.

177 *Ibid.* at 242.

178 *See generally* Smith, *supra* note 157.

179 Pellegrino, *supra* note 25 at 227.

180 *Ibid.* at 240.

181 *Ibid.* at 235.

    But see Pam Belluck, *Even as Doctors Say Enough, Families Fight to Prolong Life*, N.Y. TIMES, Mar. 27, 2005, at A1.

182 Pellegrino, *supra* note 25 at 223.

183 George P. Smith, II, *All's Well That Ends Well: Toward a Policy of Assisted Rational Suicide or Merely Enlightened Self-Determination*, 22 U.C. DAVIS L. REV. 275, 415 (1989); Smith, *supra* note 67.

184 Marcia Angell, *After Quinlan: The Dilemma of the Persistent Vegetative State*, 330 N. ENGL. J. MED. 1534, 1535 (1994).

185 Nancy S. Jecker & Lawrence J. Schneiderman, *Is Dying Young Worse Than Dying Old?*, 34 THE GERONTOLOGIST 66, 71 (1994). *See* Beat Sitter-Liver, *Finitude—A Neglected Perspective in Bioethics* in *BIOETHICS – CULTURAL CONTEXTS* at ch. 3 (Christoph Rehmann-Sutter, *et al.*, eds. 2006).

186 Alan Meisel, *Physician-Assisted Suicide: Shifting the Focus From Means to Ends*, at 283, 297 in PHYSICIAN-ASSISTED DYING: THE CASE FOR PALLIATIVE CARE AND PATIENT CHOICE (Timothy E. Quill & Margaret P. Battin, eds. 2004).

187 W. Clay Jackson, *Palliative Sedation vs. Terminal Sedation: What's in a Name?*, 19 AM. J. HOSPICE & PALLIATIVE CARE 81 (Mar./Apr. 2002). *See generally* George P. Smith, II, *Euphemistic Codes and Tell-Tale Hearts: Humane Assistance in End-of-Life Cases*, 10 HEALTH MATRIX J. LAW-MED. 175 (2000).

188 Nicholas Dixon, *On the Difference between Physician-Assistance Suicide and Active Euthanasia*, 28 HASTINGS CENTER RPT. 25 (1998). *See also* Smith, *supra* note 183. *See generally* ROGER S. MAGNUSSON, ANGELS OF DEATH: EXPLAINING THE EUTHANASIA UNDERGROUND (2002).

189 McStay, *supra* note 74 at 52.

190 *Ibid.* at 55 *passim*.

191 Lo & Rubenfeld, *supra* note 82 at 1813.

192 *See* Fletcher *supra* notes 145–47; BATTIN, *supra* note 18.

193 THOMASMA & GRABER, *supra* note 19.

194 Lo & Rubenfeld, *supra* note 82 at 1813.

195 *Ibid.*

196 *See* Alexander McCall Smith, *Euthanasia: The Strengths of The Middle Ground*, 7 MED. L. REV. 195, 206–7 (1999). *See also supra* notes 86–105 and accompanying text.

197 Lo & Rubenfeld, *supra* note 82 at 1812.

198 *Ibid.* at 1813. *See generally* Timothy E. Quill & Ira R. Byock, *Responding to Intractable Suffering*, 132 ANNALS INTERNAL MED. 408 (2000).

199 Lo & Rubenfeld, *supra* note 82 at 1815.

200 *Ibid.* at 1814, 1815.

201 *See* George P. Smith, II, *Terminal Sedation as Palliative Care: Revalidating a Right to a Good Death*, 7 CAMB. Q. HEALTHCARE ETHICS 382 (1998).

Appendix: Bibliography of the writings of George P. Smith, II, bioethics and health law

Books, chapters within books, and monographs

Books

DISTRIBUTIVE JUSTICE AND THE NEW MEDICINE (2008), Elgar Press, Boston and London, England.

THE CHRISTIAN RELIGION AND BIOTECHNOLOGY: A SEARCH FOR PRINCIPLED DECISION-MAKING (2005), Springer, Dordrecht, the Netherlands.

HUMAN RIGHTS AND BIOMEDICINE (2000), Kluwer International, The Hague, the Netherlands.

FAMILY VALUES AND THE NEW SOCIETY: DILEMMAS OF THE 21ST CENTURY (1998), Praeger Publishers, Westport, Connecticut, and London, England.

LEGAL AND HEALTHCARE ETHICS FOR THE ELDERLY (1996), Taylor & Francis, Washington, D.C., and London, England.

BIOETHICS AND THE LAW: MEDICAL, SOCIO-LEGAL AND PHILOSOPHICAL DIRECTIONS FOR A BRAVE NEW WORLD (1993), Rowman and Littlefield, Lanham, Maryland.

THE NEW BIOLOGY: LAW, ETHICS AND BIOTECHNOLOGY (1989), Plenum Press, New York, New York.

FINAL CHOICES: AUTONOMY IN HEALTH CARE DECISIONS (1989), Charles C. Thomas Publishers, Springfield, Illinois.

MEDICAL-LEGAL ASPECTS OF CRYONICS: PROSPECTS FOR IMMORTALITY (1983), Associated Faculty Press, Port Washington, New York.

ETHICAL, LEGAL AND SOCIAL CHALLENGES TO A BRAVE NEW WORLD (1982), Associated Faculty Press, Port Washington, New York. (Two edited volumes.)

GENETICS, ETHICS AND THE LAW (1981), (Second printing, 1982), Associated Faculty Press, Port Washington, New York.

Chapters

Access to Health Care: Economic, Medical, Ethical and Socio-Legal Challenges, in HUMAN RIGHTS AND HEALTH CARE, ch. 20 (D.N. Weisstub & G.D. Pinto eds.), Kluwer (2008).

Chapter 6, *Managing Death: End of Life Charades and Decisions*, in AGING: DECISIONS AT THE END OF LIFE (D. N. Weisstub, D.C. Thomasma, S. Gauthier & G.F. Tomossy eds.), International Library of Law, Ethics and The New Medicine, Kluwer Academic Press (2001).

The Baby M Decision: Love's Labor Lost, in SURROGATE MOTHERHOOD: POLITICS AND PRIVACY 233 (L. Gostin, ed.), Indiana University Press (1990).

Religion, Law and Conscience in A Brave New World, in THEOLOGICAL AWARENESS AND TEMPORAL RESPONSIBILITIES 65 (Serra Foundation, ed.), Catholic University of America Press (1985).

Chapter 8, *Long Days Journeys Into Night: The Tragedy of The Handicapped At Risk Infants*, in MORAL ISSUES IN MENTAL RETARDATION (Laura & A. Ashman eds.) Croom Helm Publishing House (1985).

Monographs (Limited printing by author)

GOD, CAESAR, AND DARWIN: PARAMETERS AND PERIMETERS OF THE TOWN SQUARE (2007). McGill University, Canada.

INTRACTABLE PAIN, PALLIATIVE MANAGEMENT AND THE PRINCIPLE OF MEDICAL FUTILITY (2007). Congress of The International Academy of Law and Mental Health, Padua, Italy.

WHEN MERCY SEASONS JUSTICE (2007). University of St. Andrews, Scotland.

OF PANJANDRUMS, POOH-BAHS, PARVENUS, AND PROPHETS: LAW, RELIGION, AND MEDICAL SCIENCE (2005). Macquarie University, Division of Law, Sydney, Australia.

UNIVERSAL HUMAN RIGHTS AND BIOMEDICINE (2001). Faculty of Law, University of New South Wales, Sydney, Australia.

LAW, SCIENCE, AND RELIGION IN A CHANGING WORLD ORDER: DESIGNING A TEMPLATE FOR THE AGE OF BIOTECHNOLOGY (2001). Cambridge University, Cambridge, England.

COMPLEXITIES IN END-OF-LIFE MEDICAL TREATMENT (2000). The Mind/Body Medical Institute, Harvard University Medical School, Cambridge, Massachusetts.

THE ELDERLY AND HEALTH CARE RATIONING (2000). The Poynter Center for The Study of Ethics and American Institutions, Indiana University, Bloomington, Indiana.

THE LAST RIGHT: EUTHANASIA, SUICIDE OR SELF-DETERMINATION—ETHICAL, LEGAL, AND PHILOSOPHICAL CONCERNS (1999). Cambridge University, Cambridge, England.

GENETIC ENHANCEMENT OR EUGENIC IMPROVEMENT: CONTROLLING THE BRAVE NEW WORLD (1999). University of Victoria, British Columbia, Canada.

THE PLIGHT OF THE DEVELOPMENTALLY DISABLED (1999). Fordham University School of Law, New York, New York.

BIOETHICS AND THE ADMINISTRATION OF JUSTICE (1998). The University of Sydney, Faculty of Law, Sydney, Australia.

PROCREATIVE LIBERTY OR PROCREATIVE RESPONSIBILITY (1998). The Center for Clinical Bioethics, Georgetown University, Washington, D.C.

DEVELOPING A STANDARD FOR ADVANCING GENETIC HEALTH AND SCIENTIFIC INVESTIGATIONS (1997). The Hoover Institution, Stanford University, Palo Alto, California.

FINAL EXITS: SAFEGUARDING SELF-DETERMINATION AND THE RIGHT TO BE FREE FROM CRUEL AND UNUSUAL PUNISHMENT (1997). Northwestern University, Medical School, Chicago, Illinois.

ETHICAL IMPERATIVES IN LAW AND MEDICINE (1997). University of Texas Health Care Center, Tyler, Texas.

CHALLENGING FAMILY VALUES IN THE NEW SOCIETY (1996). Indiana University School of Law, Bloomington, Indiana.

Articles

Bioethics and Human Rights: Toward a New Constitutionalism, 13 CONSTITUTIONAL LAW & POLICY REVIEW 68 (2011), Australia.

Refractory Pain, Existential Suffering and Palliative Care: Releasing the Unbearable Lightness of Being, 20 CORNELL JOURNAL OF LAW & PUBLIC POLICY 469 (2010–11).

Regulating Morality through the Common Law and Exclusionary Zoning, 60 CATHOLIC UNIVERSITY LAW REVIEW 403 (2011).

Social Justice and Health Care Management: An Elusive Quest, 9 HOUSTON JOURNAL OF HEALTH LAW & POLICY 1 (2009).

Variables in Health Care Policymaking: Resolving a Quandry?, 16 JOURNAL OF LAW & MEDICINE 1 (2009), Australia.

Re-shaping the Common Good in Times of Public Health Emergencies: Validating Medical Triage, 17 ANNALS OF HEALTH LAW 1 (2009).

Policy Making and The New Medicine: Managing a Magnificent Obsession, 3 JOURNAL OF HEALTH & BIOMEDICAL LAW 303 (2008).

Cigarette Smoking as a Public Health Hazard: Crafting Common Law and Legislative Strategies for Abatement, 11 MICHIGAN STATE JOURNAL OF MEDICINE & LAW 251 (2007).

Law, Religion, and Medical Science: Conjunctive or Disjunctive?, MACQUARIE LAW SYMPOSIUM JOURNAL 9 (2006), Australia.

Human Rights and Bioethics: Formulating a Universal Right to Health, Health Care, or Health Protection?, 38 VANDERBILT JOURNAL OF TRANSNATIONAL LAW 1294 (2005).

Law, Medicine, and Religion: Towards a Dialogue and a Partnership in Biomedical Technology and Decisionmaking, 21 JOURNAL OF CONTEMPORARY HEALTH LAW & POLICY 169 (2005).

The Vagaries of Informed Consent, 1 INDIANA HEALTH LAW REVIEW 111 (2004).

Just Say No!—The Right to Refuse Psychotropic Medication in Long-Term Care Facilities, 13 ANNALS OF HEALTH LAW 1 (2004).

Distributive Justice and Health Care, 18 JOURNAL OF CONTEMPORARY HEALTH LAW & POLICY 421 (2002).

Re-evaluating The Freedom of Scientific Inquiry through Biotechnology and Human Rights, 98 PROCEEDINGS OF THE AMERICAN SOCIETY OF INTERNATIONAL LAW 115 (2002).

Allocating Health Care Resources to The Elderly, 1 ELDER LAW REVIEW (2002), an electronic journal published by The University of Western Sydney, Australia (www.uws.edu.au/law/elderlaw/issueone.html).

Setting Limits: Medical Technology and The Law 23 SYDNEY LAW REVIEW 283 (2001), Australia.

Genetic Enhancement Technologies and The New Society, 4 MEDICAL LAW INTERNATIONAL 85 (2000), England.

Euphemistic Codes and Tell-Tale Hearts: Humane Assistance in End-of-Life Cases, 10 HEALTH MATRIX, JOURNAL OF LAW MEDICINE 175 (2000).

The Elderly and Patient Dumping, 73 FLORIDA BAR JOURNAL 85 (1999).

Judicial Decisionmaking in the Age of Biotechnology, 13 NOTRE DAME JOURNAL OF LAW, ETHICS & PUBLIC POLICY 93 (1999).

Patient Dumping: Implications for the Elderly, 6 ELDER LAW JOURNAL 165 (1998).

Terminal Sedation as Palliative Care: Revalidating a Right To a Good Death, 7 CAMBRIDGE QUARTERLY OF HEALTHCARE ETHICS 382 (1998).

Harnessing The Human Genome through Legislative Constraint, 5 EUROPEAN JOURNAL OF HEALTH LAW 53 (1998), the Netherlands.

Complexities in Biomedical Decisionmaking, 1 PERSPECTIVES ON LAW & THE PUBLIC INTEREST (1997), an electronic journal published by The University of Richmond Law School, renamed THE JOURNAL OF LAW & PUBLIC INTEREST, http://law.richmond. edu/rjolpi/IssuesArchived/1998_Fall_Biomedicine_Ethics/Smith_Fin.html. Subsidiary citation: http://law.richmond.edu/rjolpi.

Our Hearts Were Once Young and Gay: Health Care Rationing and The Elderly, 8 FLORIDA JOURNAL OF LAW & POLICY 1 (1996).

Utility and The Principle of Medical Futility: Safeguarding Autonomy and The Prohibition Against Cruel and Unusual Punishment, 12 JOURNAL OF CONTEMPORARY HEALTH LAW & POLICY 1 (1996).

Pathways to Immortality in the New Millennium: Human Responsibility, Theological Direction or Legal Mandate, 15 ST. LOUIS UNIVERSITY PUBLIC LAW REVIEW 557 (1996).

Genetic Determinism or Genetic Discrimination? 11 JOURNAL OF CONTEMPORARY HEALTH LAW & POLICY 23 (1995) (with Thaddeus J. Burns).

Accessing Genomic Information or Safeguarding Genetic Privacy, 9 JOURNAL OF LAW & HEALTH 121 (1995).

Restructuring The Principle of Medical Futility, 11 JOURNAL OF PALLIATIVE CARE 9 (1995), McGill University, Canada.

Biological Determinism or Genetic Discrimination, 3 PROCEEDINGS, 10TH WORLD CONGRESS ON MEDICAL LAW 164 (1994), Israel.

Biomedicine and Biomedical Ethics: De Lege Lata, De Lege Ferenda, 9 JOURNAL OF CONTEMPORARY HEALTH LAW & POLICY 233 (1993).

Reviving the Swan, Extending the Curse of Methuselah or Adhering to the Kevorkian Ethic? 2 CAMBRIDGE QUARTERLY OF HEALTHCARE ETHICS 49 (1993).

Market and Non Market Mechanisms for Procuring Human and Cadaveric Organs: When the Price is Right, 1 MEDICAL LAW INTERNATIONAL 17 (1993), England.

Toward an International Standard of Scientific Inquiry, 2 HEALTH MATRIX, JOURNAL OF LAW-MEDICINE 167 (1992).

Murder She Wrote, or Was It Merely Selective Non-Treatment? 8 JOURNAL OF CONTEMPORARY HEALTH LAW & POLICY 49 (1992).

Incest and Intrafamilial Child Abuse: Fatal Attractions or Forced and Dangerous Liaisons? 29 JOURNAL OF FAMILY LAW 833 (1991).

The Ethics of Ethics Committees, 6 JOURNAL OF CONTEMPORARY HEALTH LAW & POLICY 157 (1990).

Re-thinking Euthanasia and Death with Dignity: A Transnational Challenge, 12 ADELAIDE LAW JOURNAL 480 (1990), Australia.

Stop, in the Name of Love! 19 ANGLO-AMERICAN LAW REVIEW 55 (1990), University of Bristol Law Faculty, England.

Assisted Noncoital Reproduction: A Comparative Analysis, 8 BOSTON UNIVERSITY INTERNATIONAL LAW JOURNAL 21 (1990).

Recognizing Personhood and The Right to Die with Dignity, 6 JOURNAL OF PALLIATIVE CARE 24 (1990), McGill University, Canada.

The Frankenstein Myth and Contemporary Human Experimentation: Spectre, Legacy, Curse or Imperative, 2 BIOLAW S463 (1990).

The Baby M Decision: Love's Labor Lost, 16 LAW, MEDICINE & HEALTH CARE 121 (1990).

Fetal Abuse: Culpable Behavior by Pregnant Women or Parental Immunity? 3 JOURNAL OF LAW & HEALTH 23 (1989).

All's Well That Ends Well: Toward a Policy of Assisted Rational Suicide or Merely Enlightened Self-Determination? 22 UNIVERSITY OF CALIFORNIA-DAVIS LAW REVIEW 275 (1989).

Biotechnology and The Law: Social Responsibility v. Freedom of Scientific Inquiry, 39 MERCER LAW REVIEW 437 (1988).

Limitations on Reproductive Autonomy for the Mentally Handicapped, 4 JOURNAL OF CONTEMPORARY HEALTH LAW & POLICY 71 (1988).

Nudity, Obscenity and Pornography: The Streetcars Named Lust and Desire, 4 JOURNAL OF CONTEMPORARY HEALTH LAW & POLICY 155 (1988).

Medico-Legal Challenges Into The 21st Century, REPORTS OF THE MEDICO-LEGAL SOCIETY OF SINGAPORE 22 (1988).

The Province and Function of Law, Science and Medicine: Leeways of Choice, Patterns of Discourse, 10 UNIVERSITY OF NEW SOUTH WALES LAW JOURNAL 103 (1987).

Death Be Not Proud: Medical, Ethical and Legal Dilemmas in Resource Allocation, 3 JOURNAL OF CONTEMPORARY HEALTH LAW & POLICY 47 (1987).

Cryonic Suspension and The Law, 17 OMEGA—THE JOURNAL OF DEATH & DYING 1 (1986–87), Arizona State University.

Procreational Autonomy v. State Intervention: Opportunity or Crisis for a Brave New World? 2 NOTRE DAME JOURNAL OF LAW, ETHICS & PUBLIC POLICY 635 (1986).

Intimations of Life: Extracorporeality and The Law, 21 GONZAGA LAW REVIEW 395 (1986).

Genetics, Eugenics and Public Policy, SOUTHERN ILLINOIS LAW REVIEW 435 (1985).

Lost Horizons, Captains Courageous and Disabled Newborns: Raging Against The Dying Light, 1 REPORTS OF THE SEVENTH WORLD CONGRESS ON MEDICAL LAW 75, Belgium (1985).

Triage: Endgame Realities, 1 JOURNAL OF CONTEMPORARY HEALTH LAW & POLICY 143 (1985).

Australia's Frozen 'Orphan' Embryos: A Medical, Legal and Ethical Dilemma, 24 JOURNAL OF FAMILY LAW 27 (1985).

Defective Newborns and Government Intermeddling, 25 MEDICINE, SCIENCE & THE LAW 44 (1985), British Academy of Forensic Science, London.

Sexual Autonomy or Government Intervention: Artificial Fathers and Surrogate Mothers, REPORTS OF THE WORLD CONGRESS ON LAW & MEDICINE 24, India (1985).

Life or Death—Who Decides? 7 PROCEEDINGS OF THE MEDICAL LEGAL SOCIETY OF NEW SOUTH WALES, AUSTRALIA, 190 (1985).

Sexuality, Privacy and The New Biology, 67 MARQUETTE LAW REVIEW 263 (1984) (with Roberto Iraola).

Quality of Life, Sanctity of Creation: Palliative or Apotheosis? 63 NEBRASKA LAW REVIEW 709 (1984).

Eugenics and The Family: Exploring the Yin and the Yang, 8 UNIVERSITY OF TASMANIA LAW REVIEW 4 (1984), Australia.

The Plight of The Genetically Handicapped Newborn: A Comparative Analysis, 9 HOLDSWORTH LAW REVIEW 164 (1984), University of Birmingham Law Faculty, England.

Handicapped Babies and The Law: The United States Position, THE INTERNATIONAL LEGAL PRACTITIONER 86 (September, 1984).

Intimations of Immortality: Clones, Cryons and The Law, 6 UNIVERSITY OF NEW SOUTH WALES LAW JOURNAL 119 (1983), Australia.

The Iceperson Cometh: Cryonics and The Law, 1 THE JOURNAL OF CONTEMPORARY HEALTH ISSUES 23 (1983), Case-Western Reserve University Medical School.

Cryonic Suspension—A Prospect for Immortality (for the United States House of Representatives Committee on Science and Technology), 129 CONGRESSIONAL RECORD E5784 (Nov. 18, 1983).

The Razor's Edge of Human Bonding: Artificial Fathers and Surrogate Mothers, 5 WESTERN NEW ENGLAND LAW REVIEW 639 (1983).

The Promise of Abundant Life: Patenting a Magnificent Obsession, 8 UTAH JOURNAL OF CONTEMPORARY LAW 85 (1982).

The Perils and Peregrinations of Surrogate Mothers, 1 INTERNATIONAL JOURNAL OF MEDICINE & LAW 325 (1982), University of Haifa, Israel.

Intrusions of a Parvenu: Science, Religion and The New Biology, 3 PACE UNIVERSITY LAW REVIEW 63 (1982).

Beyond the Land of Oz: Clones, Cyborgs and Chimeras, 2 REPORTS OF THE SIXTH WORLD CONGRESS ON MEDICAL LAW 15 (1982); JUS MEDICUM 35 (1984).

Artificial Insemination Redivivus: Permutations within a Penumbra, 2 THE JOURNAL OF LEGAL MEDICINE 113 (1981).

Medicine, Law and Morality: The Szaszian Imperative, 1 PROCEEDINGS, ASCLEPIUS AT SYRACUSE: THOMAS SZASZ, LIBERTARIAN HUMANIST, 65 (M.E. Grenander ed. 1981).

Great Expectations or Convoluted Realities: Artificial Insemination in Flux, 3 FAMILY LAW REVIEW 37 (1980), Canada.

A Close Encounter of the First Kind: Artificial Insemination and an Enlightened Judiciary, 17 JOURNAL OF FAMILY LAW 41 (1978).

Uncertainties on the Spiral Staircase: Metaethics and The New Biology, 41 THE PHAROS MEDICAL JOURNAL 10 (1978), Stanford University Medical School.

The Medico-Legal Challenges of Preparing for a Brave Yet Somewhat Frightening New World, 5 JOURNAL OF LEGAL MEDICINE 9 (GMT Medical Systems Division, 1st Series) (April, 1977).

Manipulating the Genetic Code: Jurisprudential Conundrums, 64 GEORGETOWN UNIVERSITY LAW JOURNAL 697 (1976).

For Unto Us A Child is Born—Legally, 56 AMERICAN BAR ASSOCIATION JOURNAL 143 (1970).

Artificial Insemination—No Longer a Quagmire, 3 FAMILY LAW QUARTERLY 1 (1969).

Through A Test Tube Darkly: Artificial Insemination and The Law, 67 MICHIGAN LAW REVIEW 127 (1968).

Reviews and review essays

Review Symposium, *The Ethical Canary*, 9 INDIANA JOURNAL OF GLOBAL STUDIES 555 at 584 (2002) (reviewing MARGARET SOMERVILLE, THE ETHICAL CANARY: SCIENCE, SOCIETY AND THE HUMAN SPIRIT (2001)).

Review Essay, *Biology, Bioethics, and The New Society*, 14 JOURNAL OF CONTEMPORARY HEALTH LAW & POLICY 531 (1998) (reviewing JAMES F. CHILDRESS, PRACTICAL REASONING IN BIOETHICS (1997); THOMAS F. MURRAY, MARK A. ROTHSTEIN & ROBERT F. MURRAY, JR., THE HUMAN GENOME AND THE FUTURE OF HEALTHCARE (1996)).

Review Essay, *Civil Liberties, Sexuality and The Law*, 23 NEW YORK UNIVERSITY REVIEW OF LAW & SOCIAL CHANGE, 333 (1998) (reviewing DONALD G. CASSWELL, LESBIANS, GAY MEN AND CANADIAN LAW (1996)).

Review Essay, 35 JURIMETRICS 115 (1995) (reviewing JOHN A. ROBERTSON, CHILDREN OF CHOICE (1994)).

Review Essay, 7 JOURNAL OF CONTEMPORARY HEALTH LAW & POLICY 443 (1991) (reviewing IAN KENNEDY & ANDREW GRUBB, MEDICAL LAW: TEXT AND MATERIALS (1989)).

Review Essay, 6 JOURNAL OF CONTEMPORARY HEALTH LAW & POLICY 437 (1990) (reviewing DIETER GIESEN, INTERNATIONAL MALPRACTICE LAW (1988)).

Review Essay, 25 JOURNAL OF FAMILY LAW, 773 (1987) (reviewing JOHN H. BECKSTROM, SOCIOBIOLOGY AND THE LAW (1985)).

Review Essay, 30 AMERICAN JOURNAL OF JURISPRUDENCE 231 (1985) (reviewing LEGAL CHANGE: ESSAYS IN HONOR OF JULIUS STONE (A. R. Blackshield ed. 1983)).

Review Essay, 42 THE JURIST OF CATHOLIC UNIVERSITY 569 (1982) (reviewing HAROLD A. BUETOW, THE SCABBARDLESS SWORD: CRIMINAL JUSTICE AND THE QUALITY OF MERCY (1982)).

Review Essay, 40 THE JURIST OF CATHOLIC UNIVERSITY 208 (1980) (reviewing JOHN P. BOYLE, THE STERILIZATION CONTROVERSY: A NEW CRISIS FOR THE CATHOLIC HOSPITAL? (1977) and SUSAN T. NICHOLSON, ABORTION AND THE ROMAN CATHOLIC CHURCH (1978)).

Review Essay, 38 THE JURIST OF CATHOLIC UNIVERSITY 459 (1978) (reviewing PHILIP REILLY, GENETICS, ETHICS AND SOCIAL POLICY (1977)).

Review Essay, 23 ARKANSAS LAW REVIEW 557 (1969) (reviewing LAW IN A CHANGING AMERICA, Geoffrey C. Hazard, Jr., ed. 1968).

Major invited papers presented

"Managing End-of-Life Care: Medico-Legal, Social, and Ethical Challenges," University Memorial Lecture honoring Myles N. Brand, President Emeritus, Indiana University, Bloomington, Indiana, November, 2011.

"Bioethics and Human Rights: Toward a New Constitutionalism," A George G. Winterton Memorial Lecture, University of Sydney Faculty of Law, Australia, August, 2010.

"Stewardship, The Common Good and Resource Management: Socio-Economic, Legal, and Philosophical Challenges," Center for Ethics and Culture, University of Notre Dame, Indiana, November, 2009.

"Toward a Universal Right to Health, Health Care, or Health Protection?", Centre for Health Governance, Law and Ethics, University of Sydney Faculty of Law, Australia, August, 2008.

"God, Caesar, and Darwin: Re-defining the Boundaries of The Town Square through Law, Religion, and Biotechnology," McGill University, Canada, Conference on Pluralism, Politics, and God?: Considering Rational Theism in the Public Square, September, 2007.

"Pain Management, Palliative Care and Self-Determination," Thirtieth Congress, International Academy of Law and Mental Health, Padova, Italy, June, 2007.

"The Quality of Mercy and Common Dignity: Safeguarding The Last Right," University Lecture in Religion and Politics, University of St. Andrews, Scotland, March, 2007.

"Biotechnology, Spirituality, Modern Science, and Law: Shaping or Testing the New Modernity? (or, The Curse of Itching Ears)." Notre Dame Center for Ethics and Culture, South Bend, Indiana, December, 2006. Accessed at: http://ethicscenter.nd.edu/events/fallconfs/mod.shtml.

"Finding a Point of Equilibrium—Law, Religion, and Medical Biotechnology," The Institute of Ethics, American Medical Association, Chicago, Illinois, March, 2006.

"'In God We Trust?': Continuities and Discontinuities in Law, Science, and Medicine," Centre for the Study of Religion and Politics, University of St. Andrews, Scotland, April, 2006.

"Normative Standards and Health Care Resource Management," The Rothermere American Institute, Oxford University, England, June, 2006.

"Of Panjandrums, Pooh-Bahs, Parvenus, and Prophets: Law, Religion, and Medical Science," A Dedicatory Lecture honoring Justice Michael D. Kirby, The High Court of Australia, at The Macquarie University Division of Law, Sydney, Australia, July, 2005.

"*Parens Patriae*, Paternalism, Autonomy and The Ulysses Contract: Pre Commitment Ambiguities and The Right to Refuse Treatment," Twenty-ninth Congress, International Academy of Law and Mental Health, Paris, France, July, 2005.

"Contemporary Issues in Law, Science and Medicine: Charting New Frontiers in Bioethics and Health Law," United States Department of Commerce, The Office of The Under Secretary for Technology, Program in Science and Technology, Washington, D.C., January, 2002.

"Economic Efficiency, Justice, and Health Care Delivery," Twenty-seventh Congress, International Academy of Law and Mental Health, Amsterdam, the Netherlands, July, 2002.

"Managing Death: End of Life Charades and Decisions," Twenty-fifth Congress, International Academy of Law and Mental Health, Siena, Italy, July, 2000.

"Ethical Challenges in Managed Care," The University of Sydney, Faculty of Law, Sydney, Australia, July, 1998.

"Bioethical and Health Care Delivery Problems: Challenges to the Administration of Justice," The University of Sydney, Faculty of Law, Sydney, Australia, July, 1998.

"Bioethics and The Judiciary," Federal Judicial Conference of The Tenth Circuit, United States Court of Appeals, Denver, Colorado, June, 1998.

"Genetic Enhancement Technologies: Programming a Brave or a Confused New World," Fourth World Congress of Bioethics, Nihon University, Tokyo, Japan, November, 1998.

"Bioethical Challenges in the New Millennium," University of Washington School of Medicine, Seattle, Washington, December, 1997.

"The Challenges of Ethics, Law, and Medicine," University of Texas Health Care Center at Tyler, Texas, November, 1996.

"Murphy Brown, Ozzie and Harriett, or Ludwig Wittgenstein: Pratterian Conflicts in Family Values for the New Society," The Harry Pratter Dedicatory Lecture, Indiana University Law School, Bloomington, Indiana, April, 1996.

"Genetic Privacy and The Human Genome Project: Restraining the Jabberwock and the Jubjub Bird." The Wells Scholars Program, Indiana University, Bloomington, Indiana, April, 1996.

"Challenging Family Values: All in the Name of Love and Self-Determination," The Honeywell Foundation – Indiana University Foundation Lecture honoring Martha Biggerstaff Jones, Wabash, Indiana, April, 1996.

"Biological Determinism or Genetic Discrimination," Tenth World Congress on Medical Law, Jerusalem, Israel, August, 1994, awarded the Gitzelter Prize for original scholarship.

"Biomedical Conflicts for the New Millennium," University of Auckland Law Faculty, New Zealand, July, 1994.

"Genetic Improvement, Biological Diversity and Death with Dignity: Dilemmas of the 21st Century," University of Otago Law Faculty, Dunedin, New Zealand, July, 1994.

"Medical Futility: Safeguarding the Constitutional Protection Against Cruel and Unusual Punishment," Center for The Study of Aging and Human Development, Duke University Medical Center, Durham, North Carolina, May, 1994.

"Medical Futility or Human Compassion: Some 'Indecent' Proposals," Center for The Study of Society and Medicine, Columbia University College of Physicians and Surgeons, New York, New York, December, 1993.

"Quiet Desperation or Heightened Living: The Plight of the Elderly," University of Victoria Faculty of Law, British Columbia, February, 1992.

"Health Care Delivery for the Elderly," University of Auckland Faculty of Law, New Zealand, July, 1991.

"Human Experimentation or Human Advancement?" Monash University, Melbourne, Australia, August, 1990.

"Stop, in the Name of Love!" The International Meeting of The American Society of Law and Medicine, London, England, July, 1989.

Murder She Wrote, or Was It Merely Selective Non-Treatment? Hughes Hall, Cambridge University, England, May, 1989.

Tender is the Night and Gentle the Dawn, The Centenary Congress of the Australian and New Zealand Association for the Advancement of Science, Sydney, Australia, May, 1988.

Opportunities for The New Biology: Perplexities in The Yin and The Yang, The National University of Singapore, July, 1987.

Medico-Legal Challenges of The 21st Century, Medico-Legal Society of Singapore, July, 1987.

The Province and Function of Law, Science and Medicine: Leeways of Choice, Patterns of Discourse, The Julius Stone Memorial Lecture, University of New South Wales, Sydney, Australia, August, 1987.

Partings and Sweet Sorrows, The American Bar Foundation, Chicago, Illinois, May, 1987.

Legal Aspects of Selective Non-Treatment of Patients, University of Texas Medical School, Houston, Texas, January, 1987.

Self Determination v. Rational Suicide, The International Meeting of The American Society of Law and Medicine, Sydney, Australia, August, 1986.

The Right to Property in American Constitutional Law, The Konrad Adenauer Foundation, Notre Dame University, April, 1986.

Beginnings and Endings in Life: Medical and Legal Conundrums, The University of Texas Medical School, Houston, Texas, March, 1986.

Medical, Legal and Religious Challenges to the New Biology and The Quandary of In Vitro Fertilization or, Procreational Autonomy: Possessory Interest or Vested Right? The Thomas J. White Lecture, Notre Dame University Law School, February, 1986.

Death Be Not Proud: Medical, Ethical and Legal Dilemmas, The Rosemary Donley Lecture, The Catholic University of America School of Nursing, Washington, D.C., March, 1986.

Lost Horizons, Captains Courageous and Handicapped Newborns: Raging Against the Dying Light, Seventh World Congress on Medical Law, University of Gent, Belgium, August, 1985.

To Be or Not To Be: Self-Deliverance v. Parens Patriae, Indiana University, Institute of Advanced Study, Bloomington, Indiana, July, 1985.

Sexual Autonomy or Government Intervention: Artificial Fathers and Surrogate Mothers, World Congress on Law and Medicine, New Delhi, India, February, 1985.

The Extent of Government Intervention with Handicapped At Risk Newborns, University of Texas Medical School, Houston, February, 1985.

"Religion, Law and Conscience in a Brave New World," Serra International Foundation, Washington, D.C., January, 1985.

Parens Patriae, Familial Autonomy and Orwellian Spectres: Look Back in Anger? Twentieth Biennial Meeting of The International Bar Association, Vienna, Austria, September, 1984.

1984: A Brave or a Confused New World? The 1984 Fulbright Lectures, Australia, March-August, 1984.

- *Procreational Autonomy: Values Gone Awry?*
- *The Handicapped Newborn: Blessing or Burden?*
- *Eugenics and Family Planning: Exploring the Yin and the Yang.*
- *Surrogate Mothers of the World Unite!*
- *El Dorado and The Promise of Cryonic Suspension.*
- *Questions Surrounding the Formation of Life Saving Strategies for Neonates: Triage and the Allocation of Scarce Resources.*
- *Strangled Cries in the Maternity Ward: The Plight of The Handicapped Newborn and The Orwellian Spectre of Big Brother* (presented to the Medico-Legal Society of New South Wales).

Quality of Life v. Sanctity of Creation, Cambridge University Medical School, February, 1984.

Transnational Problems of The Environment, Cambridge University Law School, March, 1984.

Beyond the Land of Oz: Clones, Cyborgs and Chimeras, Sixth World Congress on Medical Law, Gent, Belgium, August, 1982.

Medicine, Law and Morality: The Szaszian Imperative, Asclepius at Syracuse: Thomas Szasz, Libertarian Humanist, State University of New York at Albany (The Institute for Humanistic Studies), April, 1980.

Cryonics and the Law, Rockefeller Foundation, Bellagio, Italy, December, 1980.

Cryo-banking and the Law: Perspectives in Family Planning, American Association for the Advancement of Science, Houston, Texas, January, 1979.

Law, Science and Medicine: The Challenges of the 21st Century, Judge Advocate General's School, Quantico, Virginia, July, 1979.

Pro Bono

Brief Amicus Curiae, Margaret Heckler (Otis Bowen) Secretary of the United States Department of Health and Human Services v. American Hospital Association, *et al*. (In the United States Supreme Court, Washington, D.C., September, 1985), 476 U.S. 610 (1986).

Submissions to the United States Senate Labor Subcommittee on Public Health and Safety, Hearing on Cloning, March, 1997.

Submissions to the Subcommittee on The Constitution of the United States House of Representatives Committee on the Judiciary, Oversight Hearing on Assisted Suicide in the United States, April, 1996.

Statement to the United States Senate Finance Committee. Hearings on The Patient Self-Determination Act, July, 1990.

Testimony before the United States Commission on Civil Rights on The Protection of Handicapped Newborns, June, 1985, July, 1986.

Statement to the Investigations and Oversight Sub Committee of Science and Technology Committee, United States House of Representatives. Hearings on Human Embryo Transfer, August, 1984.

Testimony before the Common Council, District of Columbia, regarding The Natural Death Act of 1981 and The Determination of Death Act of 1981, May, 1981.

Retrospectives

Edmund D. Pellegrino, M.D., *"Twenty-fifth Anniversary Dedication,"* 25 JOURNAL OF CONTEMPORARY HEALTH LAW AND POLICY i (2009).

Justice Michael D. Kirby, *"Human Rights and Bioethics,"* 25 JOURNAL OF CONTEMPORARY HEALTH LAW AND POLICY 309 (2009).

George P. Smith, II, *"Twenty-fifth Anniversary Bibliographic Listing,"* 25 JOURNAL OF CONTEMPORARY HEALTH LAW AND POLICY 462 (2009).

Rosalind F. Croucher & Cameron Stewart, *"Conversations in Law, Religion, and Medical Science,"* 1 MACQUARIE LAW SYMPOSIUM JOURNAL 1 (2006), Australia.

Justice Michael D. Kirby, High Court of Australia, *"The New Biology and International Sharing—Lessons from The Life and Works of George P. Smith, II,"* 7 INDIANA JOURNAL OF GLOBAL STUDIES 425 (2000).

Raymond C. O'Brien, *"The World of Law, Science, and Medicine According to George P. Smith, II,"* 8 JOURNAL OF CONTEMPORARY HEALTH LAW AND POLICY 163 (1992).

A Twenty-Fifth Anniversary of Professional Service Tribute, 135 CONGRESSIONAL RECORD E3418 (October 13, 1989); *A Bibliographic Tribute,* 6 JOURNAL OF CONTEMPORARY HEALTH LAW AND POLICY 483 (1990).

Dedicatory Issue of 2 JOURNAL OF CONTEMPORARY HEALTH LAW AND POLICY 1 (1986) in honor of professional contributions in Law, Science and Medicine. *See* 132 CONGRESSIONAL RECORD E1938 (June 4, 1986).

Select bibliography

George J. Annas, WORST CASE BIOETHICS: DEATH, DISASTER, AND PUBLIC HEALTH (2010).

AMERICAN BIOETHICS AFTER NUREMBERG: PRAGMATISM, POLITICS, AND HUMAN RIGHTS (2005).

THE RIGHTS OF PATIENTS (3rd ed. 2004).

SOME CHOICES: LAW, MEDICINE AND THE MARKET (1998).

STANDARD OF CARE: THE LAW OF AMERICAN BIOETHICS (1993).

Margaret P. Battin, ENDING LIFE: ETHICS AND THE WAY WE DIE (2005).

Tom W. Beauchamp and James P. Childress, PRINCIPLES OF BIOMEDICAL ETHICS (6th ed. 2009).

Belinda J. Bennett, HEALTH LAW'S KALEIDOSCOPE (2008).

Daniel Callahan, WHAT PRICE BETTER HEALTH (2003).

SETTING LIMITS: MEDICAL GOALS IN AN AGING SOCIETY (1987).

Arthur R. Caplan, AM I MY BROTHER'S KEEPER? (1997).

James F. Childress, PRACTICAL REASONING IN BIOETHICS (1997).

WHO SHOULD DECIDE? PATERNALISM IN HEALTH CARE (1982).

Janet L. Dolgin & Lois L. Shepherd, BIOETHICS AND THE LAW (2005).

Roger W. Dworkin, LIMITS: THE ROLE OF LAW IN BIOETHICAL DECISION MAKING (1997).

Richard A. Epstein, PRINCIPLES FOR A FREE SOCIETY: RECONCILING INDIVIDUAL LIBERTY WITH THE COMMON GOOD (1998).

Joseph J. Fins, A PALLIATIVE ETHIC OF CARE (2006).

Joseph Fletcher, MORAL RESPONSIBILITY: SITUATION ETHICS AT WORK (1967).

MEDICINE AND MORALS (1954).

Barry R. Furrow, et al., BIOETHICS: HEALTH CARE AND ETHICS (6th ed. 2008).

Lawrence O. Gostin, PUBLIC HEALTH LAW AND ETHICS (2002).

Jonathan Herring, OLDER PEOPLE IN LAW AND SOCIETY (2009).

MEDICAL LAW AND ETHICS (2006).

Albert R. Jonsen, THE BIRTH OF BIOETHICS (1992).

THE NEW MEDICINE AND THE OLD ETHICS (1990).

Leon R. Kass, LIFE, LIBERTY AND THE DEFENSE OF DIGNITY: THE CHALLENGE OF BIOETHICS (2002).

Jay Katz, THE SILENT WORLD OF DOCTOR AND PATIENT (1986).

EXPERIMENTATION WITH HUMAN BEINGS (1972).

Ian Kerridge et al., ETHICS AND LAW FOR THE HEALTH PROFESSIONS (3rd ed. 2009).

John F. Kilner, WHO LIVES? WHO DIES? ETHICAL CRITERIA IN PATIENT SELECTION (1990).

Michael D. Kirby, JUDICIAL ACTIVISM: AUTHORITY, PRINCIPLE AND POLICY IN THE JUDICIAL METHOD (2004).

Helga Kuhse, THE SANCTITY-OF-LIFE DOCTRINE IN MEDICINE (1987).

Joanne Lynn, SICK TO DEATH—AND NOT GOING TO TAKE IT ANYMORE (2004).

Roger S. Magnusson, ANGELS OF DEATH: EXPLAINING THE EUTHANASIA UNDERGROUND (2002).

Richard A. McCormick, THE CRITICAL CALLING (1988).

HOW BRAVE A NEW WORLD (1981).

Sheila A. M. McLean, ASSISTED DYING: REFLECTIONS ON THE NEED FOR LAW REFORM (2009).

AUTONOMY, CONSENT AND THE LAW (2009).

MODERN DILEMMAS: CHOOSING CHILDREN (2006).

OLD LAW AND NEW MEDICINE (1998).

Sherwin B. Nuland, HOW WE DIE: REFLECTIONS ON LIFE'S FINAL CHAPTER (1994).

James L. Orlowski, ETHICS IN CRITICAL CARE MEDICINE (1999).

Edmund D. Pellegrino and David C. Thomasma, FOR THE PATIENT'S GOOD: THE RESTORATION OF BENEFICENCE IN HEALTH CARE (1988).

A PHILOSOPHICAL BASIS OF MEDICAL PRACTICE: TOWARD A PHILOSOPHY AND ETHIC OF THE HEALING PROFESSION (1981).

John C. Polkinghorne, EXPLORING REALITY: THE INTERVENING OF SCIENCE AND RELIGION (2005).

Richard A. Posner, NOT A SUICIDE PACT: THE CONSTITUTION IN TIME OF NATIONAL EMERGENCY (2006).

CATASTROPHE: RISK AND RESPONSE (2004).

LAW, PRAGMATISM AND DEMOCRACY (2003).

Timothy E. Quill and Margaret P. Battin, eds., PHYSICIAN ASSISTED DEATH: THE CASE FOR PALLIATIVE CARE AND PATIENT CHOICE (2004).

Fiona Randall and Robin S. Downie, PALLIATIVE CARE ETHICS: A GOOD COMPANION (1996).

Carl E. Schneider, THE PRACTICE OF AUTONOMY, PATIENTS, DOCTORS AND MEDICAL DECISIONS (1998).

Lois L. Shepherd, IF THAT EVER HAPPENS TO ME: MAKING LIFE AND DEATH DECISIONS AFTER TERRY SCHIAVO (2009).

David C. Thomasma and Glen Graber, HUMAN LIFE IN THE BALANCE (1998).

David C. Thomasma and Judith L. Kissell, THE HEALTH CARE PROFESSIONAL AS FRIEND AND HEALER: BUILDING ON THE WORK OF EDMUND D. PELLEGRINO (2000).

Griffin Trotter, THE ETHICS OF COERCION IN MASS CASUALTY AND MEDICINE (2007).

Kenneth Wing *et al.*, PUBLIC HEALTH LAW (2008).

Index

Taylor & Francis ——————————————

eBooks

FOR LIBRARIES

ORDER YOUR
FREE 30 DAY
INSTITUTIONAL
TRIAL TODAY!

Over 23,000 eBook titles in the Humanities,
Social Sciences, STM and Law from some of the
world's leading imprints.

Choose from a range of subject packages or create your own!

Benefits for
you

▶ Free MARC records
▶ COUNTER-compliant usage statistics
▶ Flexible purchase and pricing options

Benefits
for your
user

▶ Off-site, anytime access via Athens or referring URL
▶ Print or copy pages or chapters
▶ Full content search
▶ Bookmark, highlight and annotate text
▶ Access to thousands of pages of quality research
 at the click of a button

For more information, pricing enquiries or to order
a free trial, contact your local online sales team.

UK and Rest of World: **online.sales@tandf.co.uk**

US, Canada and Latin America:
e-reference@taylorandfrancis.com

www.ebooksubscriptions.com

Taylor & Francis eBooks
Taylor & Francis Group

A flexible and dynamic resource for teaching, learning and research.